Alexander of Aphrodisias

On Aristotle Topics 2

Ancient Commentators on Aristotle

GENERAL EDITORS: Richard Sorabji, Honorary Fellow, Wolfson College, University of Oxford, and Emeritus Professor, King's College London, UK; and Michael Griffin, Assistant Professor, Departments of Philosophy and Classics, University of British Columbia, Canada.

This prestigious series translates the extant ancient Greek philosophical commentaries on Aristotle. Written mostly between 200 and 600 AD, the works represent the classroom teaching of the Aristotelian and Neoplatonic schools in a crucial period during which pagan and Christian thought were reacting to each other. The translation in each volume is accompanied by an introduction, comprehensive commentary notes, bibliography, glossary of translated terms and a subject index. Making these key philosophical works accessible to the modern scholar, this series fills an important gap in the history of European thought.

A webpage for the Ancient Commentators Project is maintained at ancientcommentators.org.uk and readers are encouraged to consult the site for details about the series as well as for addenda and corrigenda to published volumes.

Alexander of Aphrodisias

On Aristotle Topics 2

Translated by
Laura M. Castelli

BLOOMSBURY ACADEMIC
LONDON • NEW YORK • OXFORD • NEW DELHI • SYDNEY

BLOOMSBURY ACADEMIC
Bloomsbury Publishing Plc
50 Bedford Square, London, WC1B 3DP, UK
1385 Broadway, New York, NY 10018, USA
29 Earlsfort Terrace, Dublin 2, Ireland

BLOOMSBURY, BLOOMSBURY ACADEMIC and the Diana logo are trademarks of Bloomsbury Publishing Plc

First published in Great Britain 2020
This paperback edition published in 2022

Copyright © Laura M. Castelli 2020

Laura M. Castelli has asserted her right under the Copyright, Designs and Patents Act, 1988, to be identified as Author of this work.

For legal purposes the Acknowledgements below constitute an extension of this copyright page.

A catalogue record for this book is available from the British Library.

Library of Congress Cataloging-in-Publication Data
Names: Alexander, of Aphrodisias. | Castelli, Laura Maria, translator, editor.
Title: On Aristotle, Topics 2 / Alexander of Aphrodisias ; translated by Laura M. Castelli.
Other titles: Commentaria in Topica Aristotelis. 2. English | Alexander of Aphrodisias, on Aristotle, Topics 2
Description: London ; New York : Bloomsbury Academic, 2020. | Series: Ancient commentators on Aristotle | Includes bibliographical references and indexes. | English translation from ancient Greek of Alexander's commentary on Book 2 of Aristotle's Topics; includes a glossary in English and Greek. | Summary: "Aristotle's Topics is a handbook for dialectic, which can be understood as a philosophical debate between a questioner and a respondent. In book 2, Aristotle mainly develops strategies for making deductions about 'accidents', which are properties that might or might not belong to a subject (for instance, Socrates has five fingers, but might have had six), and about properties that simply belong to a subject without further specification. In the present commentary, here translated into English for the first time, Alexander develops a careful study of Aristotle's text. He preserves objections and replies from other philosophers whose work is now lost, such as the Stoics. He also offers an invaluable picture of the tradition of Aristotelian logic down to his time, including innovative attempts to unify Aristotle's guidance for dialectic with his general theory of deductive argument (the syllogism), found in the Analytics. The work will be of interest not only for its perspective on ancient logic, rhetoric, and debate, but also for its continuing influence on argument in the Middle Ages and later"– Provided by publisher.
Identifiers: LCCN 2020018997 (print) | LCCN 2020018998 (ebook) | ISBN 9781350151284 (hb) | ISBN 9781350151291 (ePDF) | ISBN 9781350151307 (epub)
Subjects: LCSH: Aristotle. Topics. Book 2. | Rhetoric–Early works to 1800. | Logic–Early works to 1800. | Dialectic–Early works to 1800. | Topic (Philosophy) | Alexander, of Aphrodisias–Criticism and interpretation. Classification: LCC B442 .A95213 2020 (print) | LCC B442 (ebook) | DDC 160–dc23
LC record available at https://lccn.loc.gov/2020018997
LC ebook record available at https://lccn.loc.gov/2020018998

ISBN: HB: 978-1-3501-5128-4
         PB: 978-1-3501-9502-8
         EPUB: 978-1-3501-5130-7
         ePDF: 978-1-3501-5129-1

Series: Ancient Commentators on Aristotle

Typeset by RefineCatch Limited, Bungay, Suffolk

To find out more about our authors and books visit www.bloomsbury.com and sign up for our newsletters.

Acknowledgements

The present translations have been made possible by generous and imaginative funding from the following sources: the National Endowment for the Humanities, Divison of Research Programs, an independent federal agency of the USA; the Leverhulme Trust; the British Academy; the Jowett Copyright Trustees; the Royal Society (UK); Centro Internazionale A. Beltrame di Storia dello Spazio e del Tempo (Padua); Mario Mignucci; Liverpool University; the Leventis Foundation; the Arts and Humanities Research Council; Gresham College; the Esmée Fairbairn Charitable Trust; the Henry Brown Trust; Mr and Mrs N. Egon; the Netherlands Organisation for Scientific Research (NOW/GW); the Ashdown Trust; the Lorne Thyssen Research Fund for Ancient World Topics at Wolfson College, Oxford; Dr Victoria Solomonides, the Cultural Attaché of the Greek Embassy in London; and the Social Sciences and Humanities Research Council of Canada. The editors wish to thank Jakob Fink, Katerina Ierodiakonou, Mirjam Kotwick, and Chiara Militello for their comments; Marilù Papandreou for preparing the volume for press; and Georgina Leighton, acting Commisioning Editor for Classics with Bloomsbury Academic, for her diligence in seeing this volume of the series to press.

Contents

Conventions

[...]   Square brackets enclose words or phrases that have been added to the translation for purposes of clarity.

<...>   Angle brackets enclose conjectures relating to the Greek text, i.e. additions to the transmitted text deriving from parallel sources and editorial conjecture, and transposition of words or phrases. Accompanying notes provide further details.

(...)   Round brackets, besides being used for ordinary parentheses, contain transliterated Greek words.

Abbreviations

Adv. Math.	*Adversus Mathematicos*
An. Post.	*Analytica Posteriora*
An. Pr.	*Analytica Priora*
Ath. Resp.	*Atheniensium Respublica*
Cael.	*de Caelo*
CAG	Commentaria in Aristotelem Graeca, 23 vols (Berlin: Reimer, 1882–1909)
Cat.	*Categoriae*
Crat.	*Cratylus*
DA	*de Anima*
De Top. Diff.	*de Topicis Differentiis*
EN	*Ethica Nicomachea*
Gorg.	*Gorgias*
Hist.	*Historiae*
Hp. Ma.	*Hippias Major*
Insom.	*de Insomniis*
Inst. Log.	*Institutio Logica*
Int.	*de Interpretatione*
LSJ	H.G. Liddell, R. Scott, and H. Jones, *A Greek-English Lexicon* (Oxford: Clarendon Press, 1996)
Metaph.	*Metaphysica*
PA	*de Partibus Animalium*
Parm.	*Parmenides*
Phaedr.	*Phaedrus*
Phys.	*Physica*
Prot.	*Protagoras*
Pyrr. Hyp.	*Pyrrhonei Hypotyposes*
Resp.	*Res Publica*
Rhet.	*Rhetorica*
SE	*de Sophisticis Elenchis*
Sol.	*Solon*
SVF	von Arnim, *Stoicorum Veterum Fragmenta*, 4 vols (Leipzig: Teubner, 1903–24)
Top.	*Topica*

Introduction

Alexander, Aristotle's *Topics* and Peripatetic Logic

1. Preliminary remarks

The *Topics* is presented by Aristotle himself as an investigation aiming at putting us in the condition of being able to argue for or to defend any claim without falling into contradiction and to do this by assuming premises which are reputable (*endoxa*) (*Top.* 1.1, 100a18–21). The practice of arguing in support of or of defending a certain claim is described with reference to a dialogical practice with two fixed roles: the role of the questioner and the role of the answerer. Somewhat simplifying, the questioner starts by asking the answerer whether a certain claim P (or its contradictory) is the case. If the answerer replies that P is the case, the questioner will try to obtain from the answerer the premises of an argument leading to the contradictory of P as its conclusion; if the answerer replies that P is not the case, the questioner will try to obtain the premises for an argument leading to P as its conclusion. Either way, the questioner's task consists in revealing that the answerer is committed to some contradiction and, in this sense, endorses a set of inconsistent claims. The answerer's task, on the other hand, consists in avoiding commitment to a contradiction and, more generally, in making it evident that she does not 'suffer' under the attack of the questioner, i.e. that she is all the time aware of the consequences of the claims that she concedes or rejects, without falling victim to the dialectical skills of the interlocutor.[1] The exchange between questioner and answerer responds to some general rules and formal constraints, which are described and codified by Aristotle in the *Topics*. In particular, *Top.* 1 and 8 provide the general framework for this sort of dialogical practice by spelling out, e.g., what this sort of argumentative practice is useful for; how the arguments carried out in this way can be classified based on the type of predication expressed in their premises and in the conclusion[2] and based on their general contents;[3] what are the general tools the dialectician can resort to in order to find the appropriate premises for the conclusion she is supposed to establish; what sort of claims can be regarded as reputable and are therefore suitable premises for dialectical arguments; how the questioner and the answerer are supposed to fulfill their respective tasks successfully, etc. *Top.* 2–7 are more technical in character in that they provide lists of *topoi*, i.e. argumentative patterns and strategies that can be used in order to find the appropriate (type of) premises for a given (type of) conclusion.

Two correlated aspects are particularly puzzling for the contemporary interpreters of Aristotle's *Topics*. Firstly, in *Top.* 1.1, 100a25–7 Aristotle provides an account of *sullogismos* ('deduction' or 'deductive argument' or more technically 'syllogism')[4] which is clearly supposed to apply to the arguments he is going to present in the course of the discussion of dialectical argumentative practice; in fact, this account is never called into question in the course of the *Topics*. This account is virtually identical to the account of *sullogismos* which Aristotle gives elsewhere and, in particular, in *An. Pr.* 1.1, 24b18–20, where it immediately precedes the technical analysis of figure syllogisms. The problem is that the vastest majority of deductive arguments Aristotle seems to have in mind in *Top.* 2 ff. looks rather different from the standard figure *sullogismoi* familiar from the *Analytics*. The latter are deductive arguments with exactly two premises and one conclusion, in which both premises and the conclusion are in predicative form (S is P); three terms appear each twice in the argument: one term (the middle term) is in common between the two premises but does not appear in the conclusion, whereas each of the two terms of the conclusion appears in exactly one of the two premises. Although one can find in the *Topics* examples of arguments with this structure (or, rather, with a structure easily reducible to this one), such cases are by no means the rule. In fact, it is hard to tell whether the majority of the arguments discussed in the *Topics* have anything to do with the standard figure syllogisms of the *Analytics*. Second, the arguments of the *Topics* are typically built on *topoi* (literally: 'places').[5] The only account of *topos* in Aristotle can be found in *Rhet.* 2.26, 1403a17–28: 'I call "element" and "*topos*" the same thing: for an element and a *topos* is that under which several enthymemes fall'. This account only tells us that a *topos* is something under which many deductive arguments[6] fall. Furthermore, from the lists of *topoi* in *Top.* 2–7 and other passages (e.g. *Top.* 7.5, 155a37–8) we gather that *topoi* are something we can use in order to find the appropriate premises for a given conclusion, i.e. that *topoi* have some sort of heuristic function. However, these pieces of evidence leave a number of questions open: is a *topos* merely a heuristic device or does it play a structural role in the construction of an argument? If so, are *topoi* supposed to be anything like schemes or general premises of deductive arguments? And what is the relation (if any) between *topoi* and the theory of syllogism developed in the *Analytics*?

For most modern interpreters the difficulties about the relations between *Topics* and *Analytics* are not necessarily supposed to be solved within a unified account in which both the syllogistic theory of the *Analytics* and the topical approach to deductive arguments of the *Topics* find a well-defined place. Rather, difficulties are often bypassed by resorting to assumptions about the chronological order in which Aristotle's writings were composed and the different stages in the development of Aristotle's philosophical views they reflect. In the case of *Topics* and *Analytics*, the main idea is that the *Topics* (Aristotle's treatise on dialectical *sullogismoi* stemming from the codification of the Academic practice of dialogical argumentative exercises)[7] represents an early stage of Aristotle's approach to logic. Such a stage would then be superseded by and abandoned in favour of the theory of syllogism of the *Analytics* (and, in particular, of the *Prior Analytics*).[8] More recent studies have questioned the basic assumption of a radical break between the *Topics* and the *Prior Analytics*,[9] but, despite important attempts at bringing the *Topics* and *Analytics* closer to each other, whether and how the views about deductive arguments in these writings can be fully reconciled remains, even in the best scenarios, a matter of controversy. More generally, awareness of the complex story of the assemblage of the Aristotelian *corpus* is an irreversible achievement of modern Aristotelian scholarship. Even if the extreme developmentalism of Jaeger and his pupils has been superseded, it is unavoidable (and rightly so) for the modern scholar to use some caution in reconstructing Aristotle's systematic views across different parts of his writings.

In this respect, Alexander's approach to the relation between *Topics* and *Analytics* and his corresponding analysis of the sample arguments in the *Topics* reflect a distinctive and rather different perspective. For the idea of resorting to the philosophical development of the author as a way to explain away more or less evident divergences in Aristotle's writings is pretty much foreign to Alexander (as well as to late antique and medieval commentators more generally). Alexander is in a way forced to develop a compatibilist reading of *Topics* and *Analytics* as parts of a unified system of Peripatetic logic. For this reason, Alexander's approach is valuable both as a piece of exegesis and as a piece of history and philosophy of logic. The reasons why Alexander can endorse a compatibilist approach to *Topics* and *Analytics* are for the most part not (or, at least, not without qualification) viable options for the contemporary reader of Aristotle's works since for Alexander the developments of Peripatetic logic after Aristotle, especially those due to his immediate followers and contemporaries Theophrastus and Eudemus, are complementary and, in some cases, even explanatory of what Aristotle never did but meant to do. For example, Alexander relies without hesitation on a (post-Aristotelian) theory of so-called hypothetical syllogisms in order to explain how some topical arguments work. This sort of assumption about the existence of a system of Peripatetic logic which somehow remained faithful to Aristotle's alleged intentions and can therefore be brought in in order to read Aristotle's text is, from the point of view of modern scholarship, highly questionable. However, the general picture of how Peripatetic philosophy as a whole can encompass a system of logic, of which both *Topics* and *Analytics* are parts, is a complex and interesting one in its own right. Some familiarity with this general picture is necessary in order to appreciate Alexander's analysis of sample arguments in his commentary on *Top.* 2. Accordingly, this introduction aims at sketching this general picture as the backdrop against which more specific points in Alexander's text can be read and analysed.

Although I believe that such a picture can be drawn based on the evidence at our disposal, Alexander does not expose the whole of it systematically. Rather, the pieces of the puzzle have to be found in his commentaries on *Topics* 1–4[10] and on *Prior Analytics* 1. I have organized scattered evidence around two main problems arising within Alexander's systematic approach: first, what is the relation between the deductive arguments Aristotle discusses in the *Topics* and the general syllogistic presented in the *Prior Analytics*; and, second, what sort of *arkhai* ('principles') of deductive arguments *topoi* are supposed to be. In section 2 I outline Alexander's general views about Peripatetic logic and the structure of the *Organon*. In section 3 I take a closer look at some examples which illustrate how Alexander's general views about the relation between *Topics* and *Analytics* impact on his analysis of specific points in Aristotle's text. Further examples can be found in the text of the commentary. Finally, in section 4, I discuss Alexander's account of *topoi* as *arkhai*.

2. The general view: The *Topics*, the *Organon*, and Peripatetic logic

Evidence about Alexander's programmatic views concerning the relation between Aristotle's logical writings can be found in both commentaries on the first book of the *Prior Analytics* and on books 1–4 of the *Topics*.[11] The general idea is that *An. Pr.* provides a general theory of *sullogismos*, while *An. Post.*, *Top.* and *SE* deal each with a species of *sullogismoi* – respectively: demonstrative, dialectical and sophistical (Alex., *in Top.* 2,2–15).[12] This very general and rather unspectacular picture, however, needs refining on a number of points in order to do full justice to Alexander's views. To start with, although Alexander regards the theory of figure syllogisms as the core part of Peripatetic logic, he also thinks that Peripatetic logic encompasses significantly more than what is included in *An. Pr.* In particular, he picks up on Aristotle's hints about a due account of the different kinds of *sullogismoi* from a hypothesis (Arist., *An. Pr.* 1.44, 50a39 ff.)[13] – an account which, as Alexander points out, cannot be found in Aristotle. He refers to Theophrastus, Eudemus and other Peripatetics as those who have expanded on Aristotle's allusion (Alex., *in An. Pr.* 390,1–3; cf. 263,14)[14] and he includes in his commentary a good deal of information about the Peripatetic stance on such arguments. Alexander seems to distinguish four main types of *sullogismoi* from a hypothesis: (1) *sullogismoi* from a hypothesis in which the hypothesis is the opposite of what has to be argued for (e.g. *reductio ad absurdum*); (2) arguments in which the hypothesis is something assumed merely on the basis of an explicit agreement (*ex homologias*); (3) mixed *sullogismoi*[15] from a hypothetical premise (the tropic premise of Stoic syllogistic: a conditional, a disjunction or the negation of a conjunction) and a categorical premise labeled 're-assumption' (*to metalambanomenon*: literally, 'what is replaced') or 'co-assumption' (*to proslambanomenon*, 'what is taken in addition').[16] Arguments from the more, the similar and the less, which according to Alexander are *sullogismoi* from a hypothesis based on quality (Alex., *in An. Pr.* 324,18–325,24; cf. Arist., *An. Pr.* 1.29, 45b17), are a particular class within type (3). To these three types Alexander adds (4) wholly hypothetical *sullogismoi*, which are, in important respects, a completely different class of deductive arguments.[17]

In Alexander's standard account of *sullogismoi* from a hypothesis, (1)–(3) are complex deductive arguments including a standard categorical syllogism which is used to establish a predicative proposition (the co-assumption or re-assumption), which is functional to establish the desired conclusion. The latter is then reached through the hypothesis and not as the conclusion of a categorical syllogism. For example, the following argument is a syllogism from a hypothesis:

[1]
[P1] If virtue is knowledge, virtue is teachable.
    [P*1] That through the presence of which one knows is knowledge.
    [P*2] We know what things are right through the presence of virtue.
Therefore:

[P2] Virtue is knowledge.

Therefore: [C] Virtue is teachable.

In this argument the co-assumption [P2] is the conclusion of a categorical syllogism having [P*1] and [P*2] as its premises. Once [P2] has been established, we can derive the desired conclusion [C] by resorting to [P1]. Alexander thinks that this whole complex argument is a *sullogismos* from a hypothesis and thinks that all of (1)–(3) work, despite differences, in the same way. Alexander's reading of Stoic *sullogismoi* under the rubric of Aristotle's *sullogismoi* from a hypothesis of type (3) automatically brings in a crucial assumption about the overall structure of these arguments which is certainly not part of the Stoic conception of *sullogismos*: all *sullogismoi* from a hypothesis include, for Alexander, a categorical syllogism, i.e. the syllogism which is used to establish the co-assumption.[18] As far as we know, however, Stoic *sullogismoi* are rather arguments like this:

[2]

[P1] If virtue is knowledge, virtue is teachable.

[P2] Virtue is knowledge.

[C] Therefore: Virtue is teachable.

While for the Stoics arguments like [2], rather than Aristotle's figure syllogisms, are *sullogismoi*, Alexander states explicitly that for Aristotle arguments like [2] are arguments that reach their conclusion (*perainontai*), i.e. are valid arguments, but are not *sullogismoi*. In this respect, Alexander adds, Aristotle's views are exactly the opposite of those of the Stoics (Alex., *in An. Pr.* 390,9–18). In order to avoid ambiguity, I shall follow Alexander's fashion in this passage and label arguments like [2] 'hypothetical *logoi*'.

    If we only focus on Alexander's commentary on *An. Pr.*, including his assessment of Aristotle's views about hypothetical *logoi* as opposed to *sullogismoi*, we can get the impression that the development of a theory of hypothetical *logoi* and, correspondingly, of the non-categorical component of hypothetical *sullogismoi*, while important for the sake of completeness of Peripatetic logic, expands on a somewhat marginal aspect of Aristotle's logical theory. If we consider Alexander's commentary on the *Topics*, however, we get a rather different picture: for from the commentary on the *Topics* it becomes fairly clear that, for Alexander, Aristotle himself had some theory and made use (also in his scientific writings) of various types of arguments from a hypothesis.[19] This situation might give us part of the reason why Alexander at more than one place is less straightforward about the nature of the hypothetical component in [1] (and, as a consequence, on the assessment of hypothetical *logoi* like [2]) than his uncontroversial identification of Aristotle's views about conclusive arguments that are not *sullogismoi* might suggest.[20] For while the primacy of categorical syllogisms is never questioned, the commentaries on *An. Pr.* and *Top.* do not convey a clear-cut (and perhaps not even a well thought-through) stance about the status of hypothetical *logoi*. It is important to stress that what is at stake is not a merely terminological issue (about what types of deductive arguments should be called *sullogismoi*): from Alexander's point of view, the domain of *sullogismoi* and of their study coincides with the territory of logical investigations which are a legitimate part of philosophy (rather than idle and useless speculation). The boundaries of that territory are marked by what can be used in doing science and philosophy. As we shall see, it is not completely obvious that whether an argument belongs in this territory is a merely definitional question about whether an argument responds to the definition of *sullogismos* given in *An. Pr.* 1.1 and *Top.* 1.1.

To start with, Alexander spells out the relations between *An. Pr.* and *An. Post.*, *Top*, and *SE* by saying that, according to Peripatetic philosophers, *sullogismoi* qua *sullogismoi* do not differ from each other.[21] *Sullogismoi*, however, differ from each other in three respects (*in Top.* 1,19–3,24; cf. *in Top.* 16,25–31; 22,7–8; *in An. Pr.* 292,21–293,10): (a) with respect to the form (*eidos*) of their premises; (b) with respect to their modes (*tropoi*) and figures (*skhêmata*); (c) with respect to their matter (*hulê*). With respect to (a), we can distinguish between categorical and hypothetical *sullogismoi*; with respect to (b), we can distinguish *sullogismoi* cast in the different figures and modes of categorical syllogism (and, perhaps, different types of hypothetical arguments – but Alexander is not explicit on this point); with respect to (c), i.e. with reference to the matter of the premises, we can distinguish between demonstrative, dialectical and sophistical *sullogismoi*. These are the objects of the three specific treatises: *An. Post.*, *Top.*, and *SE* respectively. (a) and (c) are particularly important in order to spell out Alexander's views not only about the relations between the different writings of the *Organon*, but also about Peripatetic logic more generally.

With respect to the form of their premises, *sullogismoi* can be either categorical or hypothetical. This point, in addition to Alexander's explicit specification (*in Top.* 2,2–3) that for the Peripatetics no *sullogismos* differs from another with respect to being a *sullogismos*, has some important consequences. For there is a question as to the likelihood of a debate among ancient logicians about whether categorical or hypothetical *sullogismos* have priority. It seems doubtful that such a debate could have arisen between Stoic and Peripatetic logicians in the first place, given that we have evidence to the effect that what the Peripatetics regarded as *sullogismoi* were not regarded as *sullogismoi* by the Stoics and vice versa.[22] In this respect, Alexander offers an interesting case. For, on the one hand, he clearly regards Aristotle's views about what arguments are *sullogismoi* as opposite to the Stoic views on the same matter; on the other hand, he himself seems to make room for a reading of the definition of *sullogismos* broad enough to accommodate questions of priority and the way in which he does this seems to leave room for the possibility that not only what he regards as hypothetical *sullogismoi* strictly speaking, but also hypothetical *logoi* may comply with the definition of *sullogismos*.

Before taking a closer look at how Alexander does this, let me briefly address a text which might be taken as evidence for the existence of a debate about whether the categorical or the hypothetical *sullogismos* has priority. In his commentary on the *Topics* Alexander gives as an example of a comparative logical problem: 'What sort of *sullogismos* is first, the categorical or the hypothetical one' (Alex., *in Top.* 218,5).[23] The question makes sense in light of Alexander's claims mentioned above that *sullogismoi* differ with respect to the form of their premises in that they are categorical or hypothetical, but *sullogismoi* do not differ from each other in that they are *sullogismoi*. The problem that Alexander mentions, however, need not tell us anything about a debate between schools, since it can be taken as a problem within Peripatetic logic. Alexander's problem can be taken as a question about what he, from a Peripatetic perspective, calls, respectively, 'categorical' and 'hypothetical' *sullogismos*; the latter, as we have seen, are arguments which include a categorical syllogism in addition to a non-syllogistic inference. With respect to these arguments, the question of priority of categorical *sullogismoi* over hypothetical *sullogismoi* can be asked and answered: categorical *sullogismoi* are *sullogismoi* strictly speaking and without qualification, whereas hypothetical *sullogismoi* are *sullogismoi* with qualification or 'by addition'[24] (where the qualification may have to do with the fact that standard hypothetical *sullogismoi* are made of a categorical *sullogismos* and a non-syllogistic inference based on the hypothesis). However, it seems hard to see how the relations of priority between categorical and standard hypothetical *sullogismoi* so understood might end up being the object of a question (let alone of a controversy) which is meant to be not fully trivial: in the technical understanding of categorical and hypothetical *sullogismoi* it seems evident that categorical *sullogismoi* enjoy priority in that they are a constitutive part of the others. An alternative reading of the question can be given based on some evidence we find in Galen. According to Galen, Boethus ascribed priority to hypothetical *sullogismoi* (Gal., *Inst. Log.* Kalbfleisch, VII 2). In this text Galen clearly refers to the Peripatetic Boethus of Sidon (and not to his Stoic namesake). Again, if we give credit to this evidence, this passage only provides evidence for an intra-Peripatetic debate (rather than for a debate between the Stoic and the Peripatetic school). On this second reading, one may wonder whether the arguments to which Boethus ascribed priority were (in the terminology introduced earlier) hypothetical *sullogismoi* or rather hypothetical *logoi*. Again, if the claim that Galen ascribes to Boethus were that arguments like [1] have priority over categorical syllogisms, it would be difficult to think of a plausible reason for endorsing such a claim given that categorical syllogisms are an essential and constitutive part of arguments like [1], i.e. what Alexander would regard as standard hypothetical *sullogismoi*. One might therefore wonder whether Boethus's claim may have been indeed that arguments like [3], i.e. what I labeled 'hypothetical *logoi*', enjoy some sort of priority over categorical syllogisms. In what follows I shall discuss some evidence within Alexander's commentaries suggesting that it is far from obvious that even within the Peripatetic tradition what I labelled hypothetical *logoi* could not be called *sullogismoi* in the first place and have a claim to inclusion within Peripatetic logic.

In fact, one may wonder whether Alexander resorts consistently throughout his logical commentaries to the distinction between 'standard' hypothetical *sullogismoi* (with a categorical component) and Stoic syllogisms, i.e. what he calls hypothetical *logoi* in reporting Aristotle's views in his commentary *in An. Pr.* 390,9–18. Furthermore, one may wonder whether Alexander himself consistently endorses the view that hypothetical *logoi* are not *sullogismoi* (which he, again, distinctively and explicitly ascribes to Aristotle) and, more particularly, whether he thinks that this is so because the definition of *sullogismos* does not apply to them in the first place. In this respect, it is not completely evident that Alexander would deny that at least some hypothetical *logoi* fall under the definition of *sullogismos* which we find in *An. Pr.* 1.1 and in *Top.* 1.1. Both Alexander's analysis of the definition of *sullogismos* in the two commentaries and a puzzling discussion about whether a certain type of argument complies with a certain requirement in the definition seem to make room for the possibility that the definition of *sullogismos* applies to (at least some) hypothetical *logoi*.

Alexander comments on the definition of *sullogismos* in *An. Pr.* 1.1, 24b18 (Alex., *in An. Pr.* 16,21–23,13) and in *Top.* 1.1, 100a25 (Alex., *in Top.* 7,10–15,14). The definition of *sullogismos* in Aristotle's *An. Pr.* 1.1 runs as follows:

[T 2.1] Arist., *An. Pr.* 1.1, 24b18–20

A *syllogism* is an argument in which, certain things being posited, something other than those that are laid down comes about from necessity because these things are so.[25]

The first interesting points can be found in Alexander's comments on the clause that 'some things being posited' something else follows from necessity.

[T 2.2] Alex., *in An. Pr.* 17,2–9

By 'certain things being posited', he indicates that some propositions must be assumed or conceded by whoever is *syllogizing* – something which is not the case with every utterance. For what is posited in a prayer or a command or a request or an invocation? Some people think that 'posited' does not mean simply 'assumed' but makes clear what sort of thing must be assumed. For that the propositions assumed for a *syllogism* must be predicative is – they say – shown by the word 'posited' (it is these propositions that Aristotle has defined); for he will prove that hypothetical propositions, in and of themselves, do not produce *syllogisms*. This – they say – is why he says 'posited' and not 'assumed'.

(Translation by Barnes et al. 1991; my emphasis)

[T 2.3] Alex., *in Top.* 7,24–8,14

By 'posited', he distinguishes the *syllogism* from other kinds of discourses, such as the narrative one, in which nothing is posited. And 'posited' means for him 'assumed and agreed upon and conceded', conceded either from the interlocutor, if the *syllogism* comes about with respect to someone else, or by oneself, if one *syllogizes* just by showing something to himself. For also the one who argues in this way must assume some things and concede that some things are like this, since it is through these things, taken as agreed upon, that one shows something else. And that he used the word 'posited' well, is clear from the fact that it is not possible to replace it with a more intelligible one. And one does not concede and assume only affirmative [propositions]: for negative propositions, too, are posited and conceded no less than affirmative ones, and it is not at all the case that a *syllogism* requires that all things that are posited are affirmative.

It is possible that 'posited' makes clear that [the assumed proposition is] predicative: for, strictly speaking, these things are posited, i.e. those which are assumed in that they belong or do not belong [or: in that they obtain or do not obtain]. For hypothetical propositions are not posited; rather, they are supposed. And Aristotle thinks that categorical *syllogisms* are *syllogisms* without qualification and strictly speaking, as he says in the *Prior Analytics*; the hypothetical ones, on the other hand, are not *syllogisms* without qualification, but with an additional qualification. On this interpretation he would be giving the account of the *syllogism* said without qualification and strictly speaking.[26]

In both commentaries the first interpretative option consists in taking the clause 'some things being posited' to mark the difference between an argument, in which some things are assumed as premises on the basis of which the conclusion is inferred, and discourses which are not arguments to start with (prayers, tales, etc.). In both commentaries Alexander stresses that the things that are 'posited' are things that have to be assumed or 'agreed upon'. On this reading (which is Alexander's first reading in both commentaries) categorical *sullogismoi*, hypothetical *sullogismoi*, and hypothetical *logoi* all seem to fall under the first part of the definition of *sullogismos*.[27] It is only on the second reading of 'some things being posited' that the clause is taken to exclude hypothetical *sullogismoi* (and not just hypothetical *logoi*!) from the domain of *sullogismoi*.[28] In the commentary on the *Topics* Alexander in any case adds that, while categorical *sullogismoi* are *sullogismoi* 'without qualification and strictly speaking' (*haplôs kai kuriôs*), hypothetical *sullogismoi* are *sullogismoi* 'not without qualification [...] but with addition' (*oukh haplôs [...] alla meta prostheseôs*).[29]

It is not obvious that Alexander discards the first option as a non-starter. The second option seems to infringe the claim to being *sullogismoi* (even if with qualification) not only of hypothetical *logoi*, but also of hypothetical *sullogismoi*. Given Alexander's claim that *sullogismoi* qua *sullogismoi* do not differ from each other, but differ in that they are categorical or hypothetical, the second option would turn out to be in plain contrast with what Alexander seems to introduce in his commentary on the *Topics* as a distinctive Peripatetic view about how *sullogismoi* do or do not differ from each other. If this is correct, then the form or structure of the premises cannot be used as a criterion to eliminate hypothetical *logoi* from the domain of *sullogismoi*.

The second point where we can find some information about Alexander's attitude towards hypothetical *sullogismoi* and *logoi* is in his comments on the clause that 'something different' from the premises follows from necessity from them. That the conclusion differs from the premises is, for Alexander, a distinctive feature of *sullogismoi* in that a *sullogismos* is a tool for progress in knowledge. An inference which does not fulfill this function is just not a *sullogismos*,[30] even if it happens to be (or to have) 'a syllogistic figure' (*skhêma sullogistikon*) and a 'syllogistic pair of premises' (*suzugia sullogistikê*).[31] The cases Alexander has in mind are those that the Stoics call *adiaphorôs perainontes* ('indifferently conclusive') and *diphoroumenoi* (literally: 'that bear double').[32] An example of the first kind is: 'Either it is day or it is light; but it is day; therefore, it is day'.[33] An example of the second kind is: 'If it is day, it is day; but it is day; therefore it is day'.[34] In the commentary on the *Topics* (*in Top.* 10,19–26) Alexander makes it clear that the problem with these arguments is that they lack the appropriate matter in order to be the tools that *sullogismoi* are supposed to be. But no objections are made against the 'form' of these arguments: in fact, in the commentary on *An. Pr.* (*in An. Pr.* 18,18–19) Alexander says explicitly that the figure (*skhêma*) of these arguments may well be syllogistic. The moral to be drawn from these remarks seems to be that, if the matter of these arguments were appropriately differentiated between premises and conclusion, these arguments could be regarded as *sullogismoi*. One might therefore wonder whether these types of arguments are such that one could, in principle, find instances in which the matter is consistent with the requirements for being a syllogism. And at least on one occasion Alexander seems to suggest that this might be the case. For in a rather puzzling discussion which occurs, without major differences, in both commentaries (Alex., *in An. Pr.* 19,3–20,10; *in Top.* 10,30–13,10), Alexander goes through a huge and relatively unfortunate effort to show that disjoint syllogisms from a contradiction do not fail to comply with the definition of the *sullogismos* in the same way in which *adiaphorôs perainontes* and *diphoroumenoi* do. The arguments Alexander has in mind are arguments in which one premise is a disjunction of contradictories, the second premise the negation of one member of the disjunction, and the conclusion the other member of the disjunction. These arguments are *sullogismoi*, Alexander argues, in that they respond to the criterion of the difference of the conclusion from the premises. For example:

[3]
P1: Either it is day or it is not day.
P2: It is day.
C: Therefore, it is day.

Alexander wants to show that this is an instance of the fifth indemonstrable: Either A or B; Not A; Therefore, B. Alexander tries to show that, despite appearances, premise P2 and the conclusion C are different. He tries to do this by introducing a distinction between the *lexis* ('linguistic formulation') and the *dunamis* ('power') of a sentence[35] and arguing that identity in *lexis* is not enough to establish identity in *dunamis*. He further specifies[36] that in order to assess whether two propositions (in this case: the second premise and the conclusion) really seem to be the same, one should check what they signify 'principally' or 'primarily' (*proêgoumenôs*) and what they signify incidentally. Independently of the details of the discussion, all this effort would be completely unintelligible if Alexander simply assumed that hypothetical *logoi* just are not *sullogismoi*.

Furthermore, Alexander's effort would be completely pointless if he had clear thoughts about the idea that all that matters in order to have a hypothetical *sullogismos* is that there be a categorical part in it. I have argued elsewhere[37] that at least part of the reasons Alexander has for making room for this kind of arguments is that he finds evidence that Aristotle had a theory, in the *Topics* (*Top.* 2.6, 112a24 ff.), of such arguments, and (perhaps even more importantly) used them in his scientific writings, as Alexander's comments clearly show.[38]

Alexander's attitude in these texts suggests that he is not completely sure as to whether hypothetical *logoi* fail to comply with some structural requirements specified in the definition of *sullogismos*. In fact, other texts may suggest that, whatever reasons Alexander may have to exclude at least some hypothetical *logoi* from the class of *sullogismoi*, these may not be well pondered views about the logical structure of deductive arguments rather than more general views about what syllogistic and, more generally, logic is about and what a *sullogismos* is for. This point emerges, for example, in Alex., *in An. Pr.* 263,7–25:

[T 2.4] Alex., *in An. Pr.* 263,7–25

For if the co-assumption were not in need of proof (*deixis*),[39] but were evident and known as the conditional, such an argument (*logos*) would not be a *syllogism* (*sullogismos*) anymore. For it is not even possible that such an argument (*logos*) serves the function of a *syllogism*: for a *syllogism* must show (*deiknunai*) something which is not known without *syllogizing* (*sullogizesthai*). The conditional in the hypothetical arguments which are called 'tropical' is assumed and posited as known in those cases in which it is indeed like this. What is left as doubtful, as Theophrastus says, and in need of proof (*deixis*) is the co-assumption. The *syllogism* [having as its conclusion] that this is the case, then, will be categorical and deictic (*deiktikos*). So that also in hypothetical *syllogisms* from a tropical conditional what is established and in need of proof (*deixis*) is shown (*deiknutai*) through a categorical *syllogism,* and what was submitted at the beginning is not shown (*deiknutai*) through a *syllogism* but rather through the supposed hypotheses; and this was [the hypothesis] of the conditional. For it is not possible to show (*deikhthênai*) that something that is not known is this something or such and such or, more generally, it is not possible to establish something and to posit something strictly speaking if not through a categorical *syllogism.* And if the continuous [proposition] were in need of a syllogistic proof (*sullogistikês deixeôs*), that too would be shown through a categorical *syllogism.* For if one enquired into why, if virtue is knowledge, then it is teachable, a categorical *syllogism* comes about once the universal premise is taken: 'all knowledge is teachable'; and virtue is knowledge.

Alexander suggests that two aspects in particular should be taken into account in order to assess whether something qualifies as a *sullogismos*: whether the proposition which is supposed to figure as the conclusion of the deductive argument is in need of *deixis* and whether such a proposition expresses a *huparxis*. Neither of these aspects, as far as I can see, can be clearly extrapolated from the definition of *sullogismos* in *An. Pr.* or *Top.* More specifically, in order for a deductive argument to qualify as a *sullogismos* the conclusion of the argument must be something which is in need of *deixis* ('showing', but also 'proof') – a *deixis* which shows why the conclusion is the case. Alexander might also think that the basic form of something that can be proven is a *huparxis*, i.e. the predicative form expressing that something belongs to something else, rather than an *akolouthia*, i.e. a consequence or that something follows upon something else.[40] In other words, all questions about something that can be proven can be formulated as questions about whether or why something belongs to something else. There certainly are texts in Aristotle suggesting this idea, although unfortunately we do not have Alexander's comments on all of them: see, for example, *Metaph.* 7.17, 1041a10–30, claiming that one can only enquire into whether something belongs to something else; or *An. Pr.* 1.23, 40b23–5 (cf. *An. Pr.* 1.27), which spells out the basic forms of *huparkhein* that can be argued for through a syllogism. On a more general note, Alex., *in Top.* 62,30–63,19 at least recalls the well-known claim in *An. Post.* 2.1 that there are four questions one can ask and answer in a scientific enquiry. In particular, Alexander resorts to this four-fold distinction in the context of an argument in support of the completeness of Aristotle's classification of (dialectical) problems in *Top.* 1.8, i.e. a classification based on the type of predication (otherwise said: on the type of *huparkhein*) expressed in the problem. Alexander's reference to *An. Post.* 2.1 in this context might suggest that for Alexander the four types of questions distinguished in *An. Post.* and their corresponding answers exhaust the domain of enquiry in that they exhaust the basic types of questions one can ask about what is worth enquiring into.[41] Furthermore, the connection with the argument in *Top.* 1.8 might also suggest that for Alexander the proper answer to those questions can be typically constructed through one or more sentences in predicative form 'A is B' (or 'B belongs to A').[42] Finally, if it can be shown why some *huparxis* obtains, this can be done through a categorical syllogisms in which, presumably and ideally, the middle term expresses the cause explaining why the predicate of the conclusion belongs to the subject.[43]

In this respect, although *An. Post.* deals with a specific kind of *sullogismos*, the theory of demonstration there included determines for Alexander the goal of the whole logical enterprise at different levels. To start with, logical enquiries only make sense in so far as they are a tool for the attainment of truth; since knowledge of what is true comes about through demonstration, and demonstration is a *sullogismos*, the enquiry into *sullogismoi* must be praised as a basic tool of philosophy (*in An. Pr.* 4,30–6,12). The same assumption provides a justification for the practice of dialectical discussions as an exercise which aims at training the rational soul to find and discern the truth (Alex., *in Top.* 27,24–31; 28,23–29,16). On a similar note, since the *telos* ('end') and *skopos* ('goal') of logical enquiries is defined with respect to *apodeixis* ('demonstration') and *apodeiktikê epistêmê* ('demonstrative science'), all inferences which are useless in demonstrative sciences (e.g. because the conclusion is the same as the premises or because they assume that the conclusion follows from certain premises) or in discussions that are useful for attaining the correct habit of the rational soul (i.e. dialectical and sophistical arguments) should be left out (*in An. Pr.* 20,24–7; cf. *in Top.* 10,16–28).[44] This basic assumption plays some role in Alexander's discussion of the definition of *sullogismos* in *An. Pr.* 1.1 and *Top.* 1.1, a definition which, as we saw above, does not apply to some of the arguments idly analysed by Stoic logicians. And although *sullogismoi* do not differ from each other qua *sullogismoi*, the demonstrative *sullogismos* is, of all *sullogismoi*, *kuriôtatos* (*in Top.* 15,24–5). This idea seems to play a pivotal role when (as in [T2.4]) Alexander expresses explicitly his views about what counts and what does not count as a *sullogismos*. In fact, the emphasis on what can be 'shown' or 'proven' as something that can be expressed in standard predicative form also explains why wholly hypothetical syllogisms constitute a completely separate class of arguments: these arguments do not express any *huparxis* and they do not show that anything is (*einai*) or is not (*mê einai*) the case.[45] They do not make room for the use of a *deixis* as long as none of their parts (neither their premises nor the conclusion) is in predicative form. In this respect, the centrality and priority of categorical syllogisms (and, among those, of syllogisms in the first figure) is, at least for Alexander, also and perhaps primarily the result of more general and possibly not fully spelled out views about the goal of logical investigations rather than a specific logical thesis about the logical relations between different types of deductive arguments.[46] One important general feature of Alexander's approach to *sullogismoi* in *An. Pr.* and *Top.* is that his understanding (or lack thereof) of what a *sullogismos* actually is presupposes a broader logical theory than Aristotle's figure syllogistic in the *Analytics* and that this broader logical theory can accommodate the arguments discussed in the *Topics* which are not categorical syllogisms. One might wonder whether the very existence of the *Topics* forced

Peripatetic logicians to expand on and enlarge Aristotle's syllogistic of the *Analytics* in order to accommodate within Peripatetic logic the deductions discussed in the *Topics* or whether the development of Peripatetic logic made it possible to read the *Topics* as a part of the *Organon* in the way in which Alexander does. A combination of these two perspectives builds perhaps the likeliest scenario.

3. General theory and practice: Some examples

Both in the *Topics* and in the *Analytics* Alexander relies on the general picture outlined above to spell out points of detail. I shall confine myself to a few examples in order to illustrate Alexander's methodology and general attitude.

As I mentioned above, according to Alexander dialectical *sullogismoi* can be categorical as well as hypothetical. Accordingly, he thinks that the *Topics* includes examples of categorical as well as of hypothetical *sullogismoi*, both of which are explicitly analysed with reference to the standard Peripatetic accounts of both types of arguments expounded or alluded to in the commentary on the *Prior Analytics*. I shall start with a few examples showing how Alexander imports the theory of categorical syllogism in his reading of the *Topics*.

At the beginning of *Top.* 2 Aristotle gives the following *topos*:

[T 3.1] Arist. *Top.* 2.2, 109b30–5
    Another *topos* is: produce the accounts of the accident and of the subject whose accident it is, either of both separately or of one only, and then check whether anything which is not true in the accounts has been taken as true. For example, if [the claim at stake is whether] it is possible to do injustice to a god, what is doing injustice? For if it is to harm intentionally, then it is clear that a god cannot suffer injustice: for the god cannot suffer any harm.

In his commentary, Alexander clarifies that the arguments obtained from this *topos* are categorical syllogisms in the second figure:

[T 3.2] Alex., *in Top.* 142,2–17
    And it is clear that such arguments, having a negative universal conclusion, come about in the second figure. [...] e.g., if it were posited by someone that the indignant man is envious. For since in this case the indignant and the envious stand in the same relation to knowledge (for neither of them is obvious in itself), if we define both the indignant and the envious, in this way we will be able to demolish what is posited. For the envious man seems to be the one who feels

pain at the welfare of the good (since envy, too, is such a thing), whereas the indignant is the one who feels pain at the welfare of the bad (for indignation is such a thing). If, then, the indignant man is the one who feels pain at the welfare of the bad, but the envious man does not feel pain at the welfare of the bad (for, on the contrary, it is posited that he is the one who feels pain at the welfare of the good), it turns out that the indignant man is not envious.

This passage shows not only (and not very surprisingly) that in reading the *Topics* Alexander has the *Analytics* in mind, but also and more specifically that Alexander does not see any contrast between resorting to a *topos* to find the premises for a certain conclusion and resorting to the prescriptions of the *An. Pr.* 1.27–8 to find a suitable middle term. In fact, the direct application of the *topos* leads to the identification of four distinct terms: 'the envious man', 'the indignant man', and their respective definitions (respectively: 'the one who feels pain at good people's faring well', 'the one who feels pain at bad people's faring well'). In Alexander's reformulation of the argument as a figure syllogism, however, the definition of the envious man is taken to imply that the envious man 'does not feel pain at bad people's faring well'. This allows Alexander to find two standard syllogistic premises (with exactly three terms, one of which is in common between the two premises) for the following syllogism in the second figure (which for Alexander is the typical figure of dialectical syllogisms):[47]

[4]
[P1] The envious man does not feel pain at bad people's faring well.
[P2] The indignant man feels pain at bad people's faring well.
[C] Therefore, the indignant man is not envious.

This move, from two premises with contrary subjects and contrary predicates to two premises, one affirmative and one negative, with three terms, is not an isolated episode and might reflect Alexander's conscious effort to deal with this type of arguments by following systematically one and the same strategy. Some confirmation for this can be found at least in one other passage, i.e. Alexander's commentary on *An. Pr.* 1.28, 44b38 ff. (Alex., *in An. Pr.* 312,19–317,22).[48] In *An. Pr.* 1.27 and in the previous part of *An. Pr.* 1.28 Aristotle has sketched a method to find the appropriate middle term for building a syllogism with a given conclusion by looking at three different classes of terms linked to the subject and the predicate of the conclusion respectively (a method also baptized by medieval logicians *pons asinorum*).[49] Both for the subject and for the predicate of the conclusion one has to collect the terms that follow it (i.e. terms that are predicated of it), those which it follows (i.e. terms of which it is predicated), and those which cannot belong to it. Depending on the type of conclusion that one intends to establish (universal affirmative, universal negative, particular affirmative or particular negative) one has to find the terms in common between one of the classes linked to the predicate and one of the classes linked to the subject. For example, if one wants to establish a universal affirmative conclusion, one will have to find a common term (i.e. the middle term) belonging to the class of terms of which the predicate is predicated and the class of terms which are predicated of the subject of the conclusion.

In this context, at 44b38 ff. Aristotle remarks:

[T 3.3] **Arist.,** *An. Pr.* **1.28, 44b38–45a4**

It is also clear that when looking through the terms one must take those that are the same, not those that are different or contrary. This is so first of all because one is looking for the middle term, and one has to take a middle term that is the same, not different. Furthermore, even those cases in which a syllogism comes about by means of finding contraries or things that cannot belong to one and the same thing will all be reduced to the methods just described.

(Translation by Striker 2009)

In the commentary to *An. Pr.* 1.28, 45a4 ff. (*in An. Pr.* 314,9 ff.) Alexander specifies that the kind of argument Aristotle has in mind and intends to criticize are arguments in which one aims at reaching a universal negative conclusion (of the type 'E does not belong to any A') and, in order to do that, selects some predicate X of A and some predicate Y of E such that X and Y are contraries or, more generally, opposite to each other. Alexander explains that this procedure does not allow to reach the desired conclusion syllogistically. For in order to reach the conclusion syllogistically one has to find a middle term which is in common between some two classes, of which one is linked to A and the other is linked to E. In particular, if X is predicated of A and Y, which is contrary to X, is predicated of E, X itself will belong in the class of terms which cannot belong to E. Once this is acknowledged, it will be possible to produce a standard syllogism with the desired conclusion:

[T 3.4] **Alex.,** *in An. Pr.* **314,9–34**

He shows that, also when we show and deduce something by assuming that some of the selected terms associated to each of the two extremes are contrary, or more generally opposite, to each other, also in that case the deduction (*sullogismos*) does not come to be because the contraries or the opposites have been assumed, but because some of the selections of which we have spoken before hold true. [...] For if the white belongs to the snow and the black, which is the contrary of the white, belongs to the pitch, the snow belongs to no pitch; but this is so not on account of the things posited, since nothing common has been assumed. Rather, [the conclusion follows] because some term B, which follows A, is the same as some term Θ, which cannot belong to E, or, again, because some term Z, which, as we said, follows E, is the same as Δ, which cannot belong to A. For in this way the same thing will belong universally to one term and will not belong universally to the other term, and there will be a deduction, in the way we said, in the second figure. For, in order for there to be a deduction in this way, the white will have to be the same as some of the things which cannot belong to the pitch, and not just contrary to the black, which belongs to the pitch.

Alexander's way of spelling out Aristotle's rather cryptic text is very interesting for at least two reasons. Firstly, it shows how an argument originally formulated as an argument with four terms (A, X, Y, E) can be associated to a corresponding standard syllogism in three terms. The standard syllogism will have the same conclusion and a proper part of the same matter of the original argument (it will keep only three of the four terms). Secondly, from the example Alexander gives (314,30–4) it looks like he has in mind some arguments based on *topoi* such as e.g. the argument in [T 2.1] and [T 2.2], or in Arist., *Top.* 2.7, 113a24–32. In the latter passage Aristotle gives a *topos* to refute claims of the form 'S is P', i.e. a *topos* to establish 'no S is P'. The *topos* consists in checking whether the claim 'S is P' is such that it will follow from it that the contraries belong to one and the same object. For example, say that one wants to refute the claim 'Ideas are in us'. One can find out that contrary properties belong to the subject and the predicate of this claim: Ideas are unmovable, we are movable; Ideas are intelligible, we are perceptible; etc. The strategy of the *topos* is, presumably, that we can refute the claim by a *reductio*: if the claim 'Ideas are in us' were true, then Ideas would be movable and unmovable. But this argument is not a syllogism. However, the negative conclusion 'No Idea is in us' can be reached syllogistically in the way described in *An. Pr.* 1.27–8.

One further interesting case is given by Alexander analysis of Arist., *Top.* 2.4, 111a14–32. In this text Aristotle presents two *topoi* aiming at establishing that contrary properties belong to a certain subject once they belong to a genus of the subject or to a species of the subject:

[T 3.5] Arist., *Top.* 2.4, 111a14–32

In order to show that the contraries belong to the same thing, look at its genus; e.g. if we want to show that rightness and wrongness are possible in regard to perception, and to perceive is to judge, while it is possible to judge rightly or wrongly, then in regard to perception as well rightness and wrongness must be possible. In the present instance the proof proceeds from the genus and relates to the species: for to judge is the genus of to perceive; for the man who perceives judges in a certain way. But per contra it may proceed from the species to the genus: for all the [attributes] that belong to the species belong to the genus as well; e.g. if there is a bad and a good knowledge there is also a bad and a good disposition: for disposition is the genus of knowledge. Now the former *topos* is fallacious for purposes of establishing a view, while the second is true. For there is no necessity that all the [attributes] that belong to the genus should belong also to the species; for animal is flying and quadruped, but not so man. All the [attributes], on the other hand, that belong to the species must of necessity belong also to the genus; for if human being is good, then animal also is good. On the other hand, for purposes of demolishing a view, the former [*topos*] is true while the latter is false; for all the [attributes] which do not belong to the genus do not belong to the species either; whereas all those that are wanting to the species are not of necessity wanting to the genus.

(Translation by Pickard-Cambridge 1984, modified)

In his commentary Alexander spells out the reasons why the inference from the claim that a certain pair of contraries belongs to the genus to the claim that the same pair of contraries belongs to the species is invalid. In particular, he accounts for the relations between 'being in something' and 'belonging to all/each' in a way which is reminiscent of the mereological account of predication which can be found, for example, in the *dictum de omni et nullo* in *An. Pr.* 1.1, 24b 26–30:

[T 3.6] Alex., *in Top.* 159,21–160,3

For this reason, showing that the opposites belong to its genus is not sufficient for showing that the opposites belong to the species. However, the one who has shown that the opposites belong to the species of some genus will have shown, in general, that they belong to its genus too. For, since the species is under the genus, it is necessary that all things that belong to the species be also in the genus and under the genus: for it is universally true that things that are in the species are also in the genus. For if being in something were the same as belonging to the whole of it, it would not be true that things that are in the species are also in the genus: for example, rational and biped are in [the species] human being, but would not be in [the genus] animal any longer, since they do not belong to the whole animal. Nor would the white be in [the species] human being, since it is not in all of it: for then the contrary would be true, that the things that are in the genus are also in the species. But since [being in something and belonging to it all] are not the same (the species is in the genus in which it is, and the human being is in the animal, but it is not the case that every animal is a human being, nor that the whole genus is the species), it is necessary to agree that the things that are in the species are also in the genus, being contained by it.

All cases considered so far are regarded by Alexander as cases of *topoi* which lead to the formulation of arguments that can be easily turned into figure syllogisms. At several places in the commentary of the *Topics*, however, Alexander interprets the arguments based on *topoi* as standard syllogisms from a hypothesis: as we have seen in section 2, these arguments for Alexander are composite deductions made of a categorical syllogism and an inference from a hypothesis. Alexander sticks to this picture in that he systematically expands on Aristotle's text in order to make clear that the co-assumption (or the re-assumption) is supposed to be established by resorting to a standard categorical syllogism. One example may suffice to illustrate this point. In *Top.* 2.4, 111b17 ff. Aristotle says that one should check whether what is submitted is necessarily the case if something else is the case or, vice versa, whether something else is necessarily the case if what is submitted is the case. The *topos* can be taken as an early formulation of what will be known as *modus ponendo ponens* and *modus tollendo tollens*.[50] Say that the submitted claim is P. Then we have to check whether we can find anything Q such that, if Q is the case, then P is the case; or if we can find anything R such that, if P is the case, then R is the case. If we can argue that Q is the case, then we will have also established P; if we can argue that R is not the case, then we will have also removed P. This is how Alexander comments on this *topos* 'from consequence':

[T 3.7] Alex., *in Top.* 165,6–166,2

The *topos* is from consequence. And it is twofold: for it is both constructive and destructive. For once a certain problem, which we want to establish or to demolish, is submitted, he says that we have to consider and look for what this submitted thing follows upon and, the other way round, what things follow upon it in this way. And if we want to establish it, we have to show that something of those it follows upon is the case: for in general, if that is posited, this one will be too, since it follows upon the former; for if the antecedent, then also the consequent according to the first so-called indemonstrable, which is constructive from consequence. For example, if the problem is whether every pleasure is good or not, and we want to show that every pleasure is good, we have to look for what [the claim] that every pleasure is good follows upon, and we have to establish that: for example, if it follows upon [the claim] that every pleasure is according to nature, we have to show that the latter is the case: for once this will have been shown, also [the claim] that every pleasure is good will be shown together with it. Similarly if it were established that every pleasure is choiceworthy, that every pleasure is good would follow again. And in this way Plato, too, in the *Phaedo*, intending to show that souls are in Hades and survive, took that upon which he believed this to follow, i.e. that the living come to be from the dead; and he established this through [the claims] that the contraries come to be from the contraries, and that being alive and being dead are contraries. And indeed in the *Meno* again, intending to show that the virtues are teachable, he took that upon which this follows; and this is [the claim] that they are [forms of] knowledge: for if the virtues are [forms of] knowledge, then the virtues are teachable. And [the claim] which he took could be established in this way: the man who is in the best disposition with respect to the soul has knowledge of all appropriate and due things; but the man who has the virtues is in the best disposition with respect to the soul; therefore, the man who has the virtues has knowledge of all due things; therefore, virtue is knowledge of all due things. And it is possible to show the same [claim] in this way as well: the thing through the presence of which one has knowledge, this is knowledge; but it is through the presence of virtue that people come to know the things that are due; therefore, virtue is knowledge.[51]

We have seen above (p. 5) that Alexander distinguishes different types of *sullogismoi* from a hypothesis. In addition to *reductiones ad absurdum*, to which *An. Pr.* already testifies quite extensively, most types of *sullogismoi* from a hypothesis are (Alexander thinks) clearly represented by the arguments discussed in the *Topics*. Arguments from a hypothesis where the hypothesis is an explicit former agreement can be found in *Top.* 2.3, 110a32–b7;[52] arguments with a tropical hypothetical part can be found, for example, in Alex., *in Top.* 165,6–166,2; 166,2–167,2; 174,5–175,26; 187,10–188,3.[53] Syllogisms from a hypothesis based on quality are extensively dealt with in *Top.* 3, where Aristotle exclusively considers comparative arguments. The way in which Alexander deals with this last class is interesting in various respects. To start with, the account of syllogisms from a hypothesis 'from the more, the similar and the less' which he gives in *in An. Pr.* 265,30 ff. shows that the universal proposition which, in the *Topics*, corresponds to the general comparative *topos* turns out to be a universal premise that must be included in the formulation of the argument in *An. Pr.* The relevance of this point will become apparent in section 4. In his reconstruction, Alexander suggests that the 'replaced' premise or re-assumption (*to metalambanomenon*) is a specific categorical proposition which falls under the antecedent of the universal conditional proposition that corresponds to the *topos* in *Top.*:

[T 3.8] Alex., *in An. Pr.* **265,30–266,1**

And those from the more, the similar and the less fall under those from a hypothesis, too: for in these, too, one thing is subsumed while one thing is replaced – and it is with respect to the latter that a categorical syllogism is uscd; for all [arguments], in which something is replaced, are from a hypothesis. And in these, too, there occurs a replacement: for example, if what is a greater good than something else is not productive of happiness, neither will the lesser good be productive of it; but health, being a greater good than richness, is not productive of happiness; for this is what is replaced and is in need of a categorical argument. And similarly for 'if the lesser good is choiceworthy by itself, also the greater good is; but richness, being a lesser good than health, is choiceworthy by itself'; for in this case again this is what is replaced and is in need of a categorical argument. And [arguments] from the similar are of such a sort, too. And Aristotle uses the specific label 'based on quality' for arguments from the more, the less and the similar, while he uses the specific label 'based on replacement' for the so-called *kata proslêpsin* (which are the mixed one), as we will learn as the discussion proceeds.[54]

Other examples of *topoi* from the more and the less include propositions which may look like general principles of comparative logic: of two things of such and such a sort, the one which, when added to the same thing, makes it of such and such a sort to a higher degree is of such and such a sort to a higher degree than the other (Arist. *Top.* 3.5, 119a22–5).

One could think that Alexander's analysis of comparative arguments sketched above would also apply to arguments such as: A is equal to B; C is equal to B; therefore A is equal to C.[55] Alexander deals with these arguments and their structure at various places (Alex., *in An. Pr.* 22,3–7; 344,14–20; *in Top.* 14,20–8). There are reasons to believe that this kind of arguments was the object of a specific debate[56] and Alexander's way of dealing with them is relatively familiar from the literature on Alexander's logic,[57] so I shall confine myself to a few brief remarks on this case. In short, Alexander's idea about these arguments seems to be that they reach their conclusion in virtue of the fact that a universal proposition is true.

[T 3.9] Alex., *in Top.* **14,20–7**

And also the arguments which are said by the Stoics to reach their conclusion unmethodically are of this sort. For it is not the case that, if A is equal to B and similarly B is equal to C, it is shown syllogistically that A is equal to C on this ground. For the necessity is not in virtue of the things posited. For this conclusion follows the things posited in virtue of the fact that the universal [proposition] is true that things equal to the same thing are also equal to each another. For this reason, if that [proposition] is laid down and what was divided there is composed and brought together into one proposition, namely 'A and C are equal to the same thing B', one also infers syllogistically the conclusion that A is equal to C.

While the shortcomings of taking the argument as described in this passage as a categorical syllogism have been extensively exposed,[58] it is not clear why Alexander should think that this kind of argument radically differs in logical type, as it were, from the arguments from the more, the less and the similar, which he takes to be syllogisms from a hypothesis.[59] Be this as it may,[60] what is relevant for what we are going to discuss in the next section, is that it looks like in some cases, i.e. in the cases of syllogisms from a hypothesis based on quality, Alexander would construe the 'standard form' of the argument as a syllogism from a hypothesis in which the general *topos* plays the role of a general premise. This case contrasts with that of arguments such as in [T3.2], [T3.5] and [T3.7], where the reformulation of the arguments in standard syllogistic form would not include any mention of the *topos* on which the arguments as presented in the *Topics* are based.

4. *Topoi* as *arkhai* and *stoikheia* of deductive arguments

We have seen (p. 7) that the distinction between dialectical and scientific arguments is, for Alexander, primarily a distinction concerning the 'matter' of the premises rather than a distinction concerning their 'form'. There is, however, one prominent feature of the *Topics* and of the arguments there analysed which is not easy to place and analyse within the general picture sketched in section 2. The arguments discussed in the *Topics* are based on *topoi*. Whether this is supposed to be a feature of dialectical arguments only and, if so, what kind of feature this is supposed to be, is controversial. In fact, there is a general problem in Aristotle about how the whole topical approach in the *Topics* relates to the analytical approach of the *Analytics*. In contrast with the contemporary reader, who can only avail herself of the rather general account in *Rhet.* 2.26 (quoted on p. 2) and of sparse hints throughout the *Rhetoric* and the *Topics*, Alexander can (and must) address this problem based on a relatively informative and articulated definition of *topos* given by Theophrastus (whose authority for Alexander is comparable to that of Aristotle in this context). Theophrastus's account of *topos* includes some hints about the sense in which a *topos* is an *arkhê* ('principle') and a *stoikheion* ('element') of dialectical arguments. As a consequence, Alexander can, at least in principle, give a more precise answer than we can to two intertwined questions. First, what are *topoi*? For instance, are they patterns of inference, or inference rules, rather than general premises of dialectical arguments? Second: what is it for a particular argument (for an argument-token) to be 'based' on a *topos*? (Does it simply consist in being 'found' by using a *topos* as a starting point? Or is it the case that arguments based on *topoi* also display a more basic structural dependence on the corresponding *topoi* in that, e.g. they instantiate a pattern of inference or the application of a rule of inference or include the corresponding *topos* as a premise?)

In order to attempt an answer to these questions we can start from the explicit definition of *topos* which Alexander inherits from Theophrastus and mentions twice:

[T 4.1] Alex., *in Top.* **5,21–7**

A *topos* is, as Theophrastus says, a certain principle or an element, from which we take the principles about each subject, fixing our mind [on it]. It is determinate in its outline (for either it circumscribes the common and universal things which preside over the deductions, or it is possible to make clear and take such things from them), but it is indeterminate with respect to the particulars. For starting from these it is possible to supply a reputable premise for what is submitted: for this is the principle.

[T 4.2] Alex., *in Top.* **126,11–31**

A *topos* is a principle and a starting point for an attack (they call 'attack' the dialectical deduction). For this reason, Theophrastus also defines the *topos*, as we have already said in the first book, in this way: a *topos* is a certain principle or an element, from which we take the principles about each subject; it is determined in its outline, but is indeterminate with respect to the particulars. For example, a *topos* is: 'if the contrary belongs to the contrary, then also the contrary belongs to the contrary'. For this statement, i.e. this proposition is determined with respect to the universal (it makes clear that it is in general about contraries), but it is not further determined in it whether it is about these or these particular contraries.

However, starting from this, it is possible to lead an attack about any contraries: for if the enquiry is about the good, whether it benefits, we will take, starting from the given *topos*, a premise appropriate to the given problem, i.e. 'if the bad harms, the good benefits'. Both its being and its credibility will come to this premise from the given *topos*. If the object of the enquiry is whether the colour white dilates sight, we will again take a premise that is pertinent and appropriate to this problem from the given *topos*, i.e. 'if the colour black contracts sight, then the colour white dilates sight'. But, if one enquires about pleasure whether it is good, from the given *topos* the premise will be taken that says 'if pain is bad, pleasure is good'. For all these and similar things are potentially and indeterminately contained in the given *topos*.[61]

There is a third text, from which we can gather some further information about some differentiation among *topoi* and about their standard formulations. In this passage Alexander is commenting on the first *topos* in *Top*. 2.2. In Aristotle's text the *topos* is introduced in this way:

[T 4.3] **Arist.,** *Top.* **2.2, 109a34–5**
   One *topos* is to check whether [the interlocutor] has given as an accident what belongs [to the subject] in any other way.

Aristotle explicitly calls the prescription given in this text a *topos*. Alexander comments that Theophrastus introduced a distinction between *parangelma* ('precept' or 'prescription') and *topos* – a distinction Alexander rejects while retaining the idea that some *topoi* are given in the form of a prescription.[62] In this context Alexander also gives examples of the standard formulation of *topoi* (presumably according to Theophrastus) and this is relevant for spelling out the claim in [T 4.1] and [T 4.2] that *topoi* are *arkhai* and *stoikheia*.

[T 4.4] **Alex.,** *in Top.* **135,2–23**
   We must not ignore that Theophrastus says that there is a difference between a precept and a *topos*. For a precept is what is said to be more common and more universal and simpler, from which the *topos* is found: for the precept is a principle of a *topos* in the same way as the *topos* is [a principle] of an attack. For example, a precept is what is formulated in this way, e.g. that one must attack from the contraries, or from the coordinates. A *topos*, instead, is, for example: 'if one of the contraries is said in several ways, then also the other contrary is'; or 'if the contrary belongs to the contrary, then also the contrary belongs to the contrary'; and again 'as one of the coordinates, so also the others'. For the *topos* is already a certain proposition that has come to be from the precept. And seeing this difference between precept and *topos*, Theophrastus calls such things as the aforementioned first *topos* 'precepts' or 'preceptive *topoi*'. For that 'one must check whether [the interlocutor] has given as an accident what belongs [to the subject] in any other way' is preceptive. A *topos* deriving from it would be the one saying: 'if what has been given as an accident belongs [to the subject] in any other way, it has not been given well'; or even more appropriately: 'if what has been given as an accident is a genus or again a definition or a proprium [etc.]'. However, Aristotle calls these things '*topoi*' too because he already took the *topos*

together with the precept, and we always establish the ways in which we call things from the more specific ones: for example, we do not call substance 'being' rather than 'substance', or quantity 'being'; rather, we call it specifically 'quantity'. Since these things, then, are not external to the formula, he calls '*topoi*' also the precepts of this sort.[63]

From [T 4.1], [T 4.2] and [T 4.4] we can gather three important pieces of information about the nature and function of *topoi* in dialectical arguments. Firstly, *topoi* are characterized, among other things, by their generality (and, to a certain extent, by their topic-neutrality).[64] Under each *topos* there fall a plurality of topic-specific arguments in the same way in which under a precept there fall several *topoi* [T 4.4]. *Topoi* are or embed propositions whose terms are more general than the terms of the desired conclusion; by considering the pair of *topos* and topic-specific claim that one wants to establish (i.e. the desired conclusion),[65] one can find the topic-specific[66] premises for a deduction that will have the desired claim as its conclusion. In this sense, *topoi* are *arkhai* ('principles' or 'starting points') of *arkhai*. The latter 'principles', of which *topoi* are principles or for which *topoi* are starting points in turn, are the specific premises which we will need to establish the desired conclusion. [T 4.2] gives examples of *topoi* in relation to the corresponding specific premises: a *topos* is the general proposition 'if the contrary belongs to the contrary, then also the contrary belongs to the contrary'. Starting from this *topos* the appropriate premises for arguments about different things can be found: e.g. 'if the bad harms, the good benefits'; 'if the colour black contracts sight, then the colour white dilates sight'; 'if pain is bad, pleasure is good'. Alexander's remarks are too brief to get a clear view on the exact relation between the *topos* and the specific premises of the arguments based on the *topos*. The general idea seems to be that the *topos* is a sort of universal proposition under which more specific (and, therefore: particular) propositions fall. The way in which the specific propositions relate to *topos* in the examples suggests that the specific propositions share the same syntactical structure with the general 'topical' proposition and differ from the latter in that the terms appearing in them are less general.[67]

Secondly, 'both its being and its credibility will come to the premise from the given *topos*'. This suggests that the (general) *topos* is a source of trustworthiness for the (specific) premises: it is because the general *topos* looks credible or trustworthy that the premises deriving from it are trustworthy in their turn. From what we have seen so far, *topoi* turn out to have a special relation to the *premises* of dialectical arguments: they are or include a generalized version of the more specific premises which are needed to establish the desired conclusion. With respect to the more specific premises they are the source of their credibility – presumably because they are themselves more evident or likely to be accepted without further justification. Note that in dialectical arguments it does not matter whether the *topos* is or (if it is in the form of a prescription, which cannot be true or false) embeds or leads to a true general proposition: as long as the general proposition is endoxastic, it is fine for the purposes of a dialectical argument.[68] Alexander (*in Top.* 91,10–15; 92,15–19) says explicitly that, if a general proposition is likely to be accepted, one need not make it the object of an explicit question. This suggests that *topoi* as such (unlike the specific premises which are needed in order to establish the desired conclusion) will not be the object of any specific question in the course of the dialectical debate, while they might be made explicit if one attempts an analysis which fully displays the logical structure of an argument, including implicit premises.

As we have seen, what is distinctive of dialectical *sullogismoi* is not so much their structure, but the nature of their premises: dialectical *sullogismoi* are deductive arguments whose premises are endoxastic. Alexander's take on this requirement for dialectical *sullogismoi* is distinctive of his interpretation.[69] Alexander states clearly that the assessment of a proposition as *endoxon* is simply based on a different criterion from the assessment of a proposition as true. The assessment of a proposition as true is based on the relation between the proposition and the objects the proposition is about; the assessment of a proposition as *endoxon* is based on the interlocutors' views about the objects the proposition is about (Alex., *in Top.* 19,22–7; 21,31–22,6). Nothing prevents an *endoxon* from being also true or a true proposition from being endoxastic (in fact, the general principles of demonstration must be endoxastic), but Alexander's point is that a proposition can be used as a premise in a dialectical deduction only based on whether it is endoxastic and this does not have any direct implication as to its truth value.[70] Accordingly, the characterization according to which a *topos* is the source of 'credibility' for the subject-specific premises of the arguments that fall under it does not carry any implication as to whether *topoi* can be only used in dialectical contexts. If some *topoi* turn out to be true, there does not seem to be any obvious reason why, in principle, they cannot be used in scientific arguments. What one might wonder is whether in scientific arguments, in which premises are supposed to be true, primary and immediate (or, at least, prior to the conclusion and established through further premises that are true, primary and immediate), there would be any room for *topoi* in their 'warranting' function as sources of credibility for the premises.[71]

There seems to be, however, a sense in which *topoi* are responsible not just for the trustworthiness and being of the premises, but also for the validity (or, in cases in which the *topos* happens to be false) at least for the plausibility of the whole argument. This idea is captured by what Alexander says at the end of [T 4.1]: a *topos* 'circumscribes the common and universal things which preside over the arguments, or it is possible to make clear and take such things from them'. Readers of the commentary on the *An. Pr.* can hear in this formulation an echo of Alexander's insistence in *An. Pr.* that something universal is needed (in the case of categorical syllogisms: a universal premise) in order to get a deduction at all. One might wonder whether 'the common and universal things that preside over the arguments' only are universal premises or whether they might also include, for example, general inference rules which allow certain inferential steps[72] or general principles about the conditions a predicate is supposed to satisfy in order to be a predicate of a certain kind[73] (e.g. a genus rather than a definition etc.).

This takes us back to the discussion of comparative arguments and unmethodically conclusive arguments which, according to Alexander, reach their conclusion in virtue of the truth of one universal proposition and to the third and last point I would like to stress with respect to the nature and function of *topoi*. [T 4.2] spells out two ways in which *topoi* can relate to the appropriate premises in the corresponding arguments: 'for [a] either it [namely the *topos*] circumscribes the common and universal things which preside over the arguments, or [b] it is possible to make clear and take such things from them'.[74] Alexander does not expand on this distinction and any attempt at fleshing out the details is marred by some degree of speculation. I suggest that [a] and [b] are not equivalent and refer to different cases. [a] describes the case in which the *topos* appears (in a fully explicit version of the argument, which need not be the one which is put forth in the course of an actual dialectical debate) as a general premise (e.g. 'if the contrary belongs to the contrary, then also the contrary belongs to the contrary'), whereas [b] covers cases in which the *topos* gives a prescription about how to find the appropriate premises without being itself a premise (or the general version of the specific premises which are actually needed in order to establish the desired conclusion). Theophrastus' precepts, for example, would belong to case [b]. *Topoi* falling under [a] would include those discussed in [T 3.8], [T 3.9].[75]

The distinction between [a] and [b] turns out to be a distinction about two ways in which *topoi* can be said to be *arkhai* and *stoikheia* of the arguments based on them: if one thinks of *topoi* as in [b], *topoi* mainly have a heuristic function, but they are not meant to be parts of the argument, not even in its fully explicit (possibly: syllogistic) formulation. Rather, they help one find what is *kurios* of the argument. If one thinks of *topoi* as in [a], *topoi* turn out to play a more integral role: they may have to appear as premises in a fully explicit reformulation of the arguments based on them – a reformulation which will display the validity of the argument. In the latter case, the validity of the argument based on the *topos* may rest on the truth of a universal proposition. In this case, the *topos* turns out to be *kurios* of the argument.

These last considerations allow us to link the discussion about the nature and role of *topoi* in Alexander to two relatively well-known aspects of the logical debate contemporary and posterior to Alexander. First, the distinction between *topoi* thought of as something that is an integral part of the argument rather than general prescriptions which remain external to the arguments becomes standard in Boethius's treatment of topical arguments.[76] Second, we know from Galen[77] that Peripatetic logicians attempted a distinction (which, according to Galen, is misleading) between arguments that are valid in virtue of the truth of a universal proposition and arguments which are valid (presumably) just in virtue of their logical structure or form. In order to establish whether this distinction interplays with the analysis of *topoi* and topical arguments and their reduction to standard syllogistic form a much more detailed analysis would be needed than can be provided here by way of introduction. But the idea that in arguments such as the one in [T 3.1] and [T 3.2] the *topos* helps to find the premises for a deduction and yet remains external to the deduction, which is valid simply by being a categorical syllogism, does not seem completely implausible.

All this shows, I think, that Alexander's commentary on *Topics* 2 (and, more generally, on the *Topics*) is a fundamental source of material relevant to at least two general and crucial issues for the understanding of Aristotle's logic and, more generally, for the history and philosophy of logic: how the deductive arguments dealt with in the *Topics* relate to Aristotle's syllogistic and, more generally, to Peripatetic logical theory; and what the function of *topoi* as principles and elements of arguments is supposed to be. This source is still largely unexplored and unused. I hope that the translation and notes presented in this volume will encourage more scholars to make use of it.

5. Note on the translation

To conclude this introduction I provide here a brief discussion of my main translation choices with respect to the recurrent terminology used by Alexander to describe dialectical arguments and, more generally, dialectical practice in book 2. More specific points are discussed in the notes at the end of the translation. A useful discussion of the translation of Alexander's logical terminology mainly with respect to *An. Pr.* can be found in the introduction in Barnes et al. (1991).

In *Top.* 1.12, 105a11 ff. Aristotle distinguishes explicitly between *epagôgê* ('induction') and *sullogismos*. This opposition between *epagôgê* and *sullogismos* suggests 'deduction' as an appropriate translation for *sullogismos*. The alternative and, in a way, more technical translation 'syllogism' is widespread. One argument in favour of the latter is that Aristotle and, more importantly in our case, Alexander distinguish between *sullogismoi* and arguments which are valid deductions (in Alexander's terminology: they reach their conclusion) but cannot be said to be *sullogismoi*. As I have tried to argue above, it is not completely clear that Alexander has a firm grasp on the distinction. For this reason, I opt for the more general translation 'deduction' for *sullogismos*, 'to deduce' for *sullogizesthai*, whereas I use the more generic 'argument' for a *logos* which reaches its conclusion.

A similar difficulty concerns the use of the verb *deiknumi* and of the corresponding noun *deixis*. The verb (and, correspondingly, the noun) means, quite generally, 'to show', where the 'showing' or bringing to light can be achieved either by pointing at something, or by explaining it or, in the context of scientific explanation, by producing a proof or demonstration. I have decided to translate the occurrences of *deiknumi* with the rather generic 'to show' (rather than e.g. with the possibly more specific 'to prove') in order to leave room for some distinctions. For example, Alexander claims (see pp. 13–16) that a genuine *sullogismos* (as opposed to any other valid deductive arguments) is supposed to be of something that need be 'shown'. Furthermore, at least in the *Topics* Aristotle (and, therefore, Alexander) considers cases in which a claim is 'shown' by producing a deduction for a different claim. This is for example the case of arguments from a hypothesis, arguments from the coordinates and inflections. Suppose that we want to argue that justice is a virtue, but we do not have a deduction to this effect; we can, however, produce a deduction for the claim that the just man is virtuous or for the claim that acting justly is acting virtuously. Once we have established either of these claims through a deduction, we can draw the further inference that justice is virtue (for which we have not produced a deduction strictly speaking). It is hard to tell what Aristotle or Alexander thought about the nature of this sort of inference, which is certainly not syllogistic (at least not in the technical sense of figure-syllogistic) and, one could argue, not even deductively valid. Note that the distinction between these two inferential moments (the inference of the conclusion C of a deduction and the further inference of a further claim F from C) seems important independently of terminological differentiation: for certainly the inference of 'justice is a virtue' from 'the just man is a virtuous man' or from 'acting justly is acting virtuously' is not only not a figure syllogism, but not even a deduction if one shares the view (rather common among ancient logicians: cf. e.g. Alex., *in Top.* 8,14–9,19) that deductive arguments must have at least two premises. One disadvantage of 'to show' as a translation for *deiknumi* is that there is no cognate noun which can work as a translation of *deixis*, which I translate with 'argument' (which leaves the precise nature of the argument unspecified). As I mentioned above, I have also used 'argument' as a translation for *logos* whenever this seemed appropriate (whereas in other contexts *logos* has been translated with 'phrase', 'words', 'formulation' or 'account').

The aforementioned procedure of 'showing' a claim by producing an argument for a different one, from which the original claim can be derived, is regarded by Alexander (and, presumably, by Aristotle himself) as involving a sort of 'replacement' of the original claim with the one for which an argument is actually produced. This general procedure is admitted if the claim which is 'replaced' or shown instead of the original one is functional to establish the original one, whereas it is vicious, i.e. utterly sophistical, if this is not the case. With reference to this general procedure one can find in Alexander's commentary a terminology which refers to the practice of establishing (or removing) a claim by establishing (or removing) another one and a rather rich terminology for the practice of 'replacing' or 'shifting' from one claim to another. Examples of the first case are *sunkataskeuazein*, 'to establish at the same time' or 'to establish together with', and *sunanhairein*, 'to remove at the same time' or 'to remove with'. The terminology for replacement and shift includes a variety of expressions which are used (as far as I can tell) in a very similar way, if not interchangeably: *metabainein*, 'to pass over' (from one side to the other); *metabasis*, 'shift'; *metagein*, 'to drag'; *metalambanein*, 'to make a replacement'; *metalêpsis*, 'replacement';[78] *metapherein*, 'to divert'; *metathesis*, 'replacement'. *Apagein*, 'leading away', belongs to the same semantic area.

The specific word for dialectical deduction used by Alexander is *epikheirêma* (see 126,12–13; cf. Arist., *Top.* 8.11, 162a16), which I translate literally and systematically with 'attack'. The military flavour of the terminology to describe dialectical exchanges is retained in the use of *topos*, which is literally a 'place' for an attack (cf. Arist., *Top.* 8.1, 155b4–5), and of *aphormê*, which I translate 'starting point' and which also indicate the base of operations in war. The cognate verb *hormaô*, 'to make a move', carries a corresponding connotation. Similarly, *parangelma*, 'precept', also indicates a military order, and a *parangelmatikos* ('preceptive') *topos* is a *topos* which is given in the form of an order or prescription.[79] Note, however, that I have left *topos* untranslated throughout. The main reason behind this choice is that the natural translation 'place' may link in the mind of the modern reader to the notion of 'commonplace', which would be a misleading association. Since, as I spelled out in the Introduction, the nature and function of *topoi* is an extremely complicated and controversial issue, any less literal translation (such as e.g. 'scheme' or 'strategy' or 'rule') would imply the ascription to Alexander of views which he may not share.

The characteristic feature of dialectical arguments is that their premises must be *endoxa*, which is notoriously difficult to translate. I have opted for 'reputable opinions' when the adjective is nominalized, and for 'reputable' when this is not the case. I translate its opposite *adoxon* correspondingly as 'disreputable'. One advantage of this translation is that 'reputable' does not only mean 'having a good reputation' or 'respectable' but is also used in linguistic to indicate that an expression is 'standard' or 'acceptable as good use' (Collins, *s.v.* 'reputable'). I take it that 'standard' and 'commonly accepted as good' capture some connotations of *endoxon*.

As for the activities of the dialectician, the typical task of the dialectician is that of *anaskeuazein* ('demolish') something. Since what has to be demolished is (in Alexander's text) often a proposition, in the translation I occasionally supply '[the claim] [...]' to indicate what is supposed to be demolished. This is not a trivial point since there are texts in which what is established or demolished are rather things (e.g. Ideas)[80] or a certain type of predicate (e.g. the accident rather than the definition). The reader should bear this qualification in mind throughout. The activity opposite to that of demolishing is that of *kataskeuazein*, 'establish'. The same considerations concerning what can be demolished apply to what can be established. I translate the cognate expressions in the following way: *kataskeuastikon*: 'constructive'; *anaskeuastikon*: 'destructive'; *kataskeuê*: 'establishment' (but 'for constructive purposes' in the phrase *pros kataskeuên*); *anaskeuê*: 'demolition' (but 'for destructive purposes' in the phrase *pros anaskeuên*). The verb indicating the activity of assuming a premise in order to establish or demolish a claim is *lambanein*, which I translate, quite generally, as 'to take'. Note, however, that in a dialogical context the questioner can only assume the premises she needs once the answerer has given her assent to them; in this sense, assuming a premise in a dialectical context can also be described in terms of 'obtaining' a premise. In fact, 'to obtain' is also a possible translation of *lambanein*. I have opted for the weaker and more neutral translation because it is not always clear to me how much emphasis Alexander intends to put on the dialogical context and on the specific procedures of 'obtaining' a premise rather than on the more general necessity of assuming certain premises in order to deduce a certain conclusion.

What is supposed to be established or demolished is what is *prokeimenon*, which I render as what is 'submitted'. However, *to prokeimenon* occasionally also indicates the 'goal' or the 'aim' to be attained by following a certain argumentative strategy, whereas as an adjective it often simply means 'given' (e.g. 'the given *topos*'); in such contexts I translate accordingly. Alexander also uses *elenkhos* ('refutation') and *elenkhein* 'to refute', which typically have a person as their object, which is certainly not the case with *anaskeuazein* (one can 'refute' an interlocutor, but one can only 'demolish' a claim). For this reason, I prefer to avoid translating *anaskeuazein* and its cognates with 'refuting'. *Anhairein* ('to remove') is also used by Alexander – interchangeably with *anaskeuazein*, as far as I can see. Occasionally (115,7; 145,16; 148,5; 149,26; 169,11; 170,17; 171,27; cf. Arist., *Top.* 2.2, 110a10; 8.2, 157b3) Alexander uses the verb *enhistêmi* (in the participle form *enhistamenos*) in its (rare) meaning of 'making an objection' (cf. *enstasis*, 'objection').

6. Note on the Greek text

The translation is based on the Greek text established by Wallies (ed.), *Alexandri Aphrodisiensis in Aristotelis Topicorum Libros Octo Commentaria*, *Commentaria in Aristotelem Graeca*, vol. II.2, Berlin 1891. My attitude towards Wallies' text has been rather conservative. Anybody interested in the history of the text should read Gonzáles Calderón (2014). Roselli (2002) is fundamental for making sense of the text at 139,32–140,2. Departures from Wallies' text and philologically difficult passages are in < > in the translation and commented upon in the notes (whereas [ ] indicate possibly controversial words which do not correspond to anything in the Greek text and have been added to the translation for the sake of clarity). A list of departures from Wallies' text is appended.

One general problem with Wallies' edition is that it is not always clear what he takes to be a direct quotation rather than a paraphrastic reference to Aristotle's text. At different places he uses different devices (quotation marks or double-spaced words) to refer to it. In the translation I have only signaled what I take to be direct quotations from Aristotle's text by putting them into quotation marks. One further point of departure of the translation from the Greek text is due to the fact that Alexander's periods are often very long and relatively involute. In order to make the translation more readable and the text more intelligible I have occasionally split up Alexander's period into shorter ones. It does not seem to me that these interventions yield an alteration in the meaning of the text, but the reader should be aware of this departure from the Greek.

Acknowledgements

This book was written during my stay as a research fellow at the Munich School of Ancient Philosophy (MUSAPh) in the academic years 2015–2019. I am grateful to the Deutsche Forschungsgemeinschaft (DFG) for funding my research in those years. I am particularly grateful to my host in Munich, Christof Rapp, for his support, and to my other colleagues at MUSAPh for a most stimulating and pleasant working environment. Various parts of the introduction and commentary have been presented at workshops and conferences in Bergamo, Berlin (HU), Edinburgh, Munich, Oxford, and Paris. I am grateful to the audiences on those occasions for their questions and comments. For feedback on specific points I am indebted to Peter Adamson, Maddalena Bonelli, Alan Bowen, George Boys-Stones, Riccardo Chiaradonna, Matteo Di Giovanni, David Ebrey, Michael Griffin, Pieter Sjoerd Hasper, Inna Kupreeva, Alvise Lagnerini, Stephen Menn, Marilù Papandreou, Oliver Primavesi, Richard Sorabji, and to the four readers who commented on an earlier draft at the editors' request, Jakob Fink, Katerina Ierodiakonou, Mirjam Kotwick, and Chiara Militello. Special thanks go to Richard Sorabji and Michael Griffin for their precious feedback, support, and patience during the preparation of the volume, and to Marilù Papandreou for her invaluable and competent help in preparing the final draft for the press and for compiling the *Index of Passages*. Finally, I would like to express my gratitude to Georgina Leighton and, especially, Merv Honeywood at Bloomsbury for their precious and professional assistance in seeing this volume to press.

Notes

1 For a detailed account of the tasks involved in the two roles see in particular Arist., *Top.* 8.1–6.

2 Based on the type of predication expressed in the conclusion dialectical arguments are classified into arguments about the accident, arguments about the proprium, arguments about the genus and arguments about the definition. Arguments about the comparison of properties which belong to their subjects to a higher, lower or similar degree fall under the rubric of arguments about the accident. Arguments about the differentia and about sameness in genus fall under the rubric of arguments about the genus. Arguments about numerical sameness fall under the rubric of arguments about definition. According to Alexander there are further types of arguments – in particular: problems about 'unqualified being', i.e. about existence – which are not explicitly dealt with by Aristotle but fall under the arguments about the accident. On Alexander's views about the completeness of the classification of dialectical problems based on the type of predication see Castelli (2013).

3 Based on their general contents dialectical problems are divided into ethical, physical and logical. For some discussion of this partition and its relevance in Alexander see Castelli (2014).

4 I return to the issue of the translation of *sullogismos* on p. 31. The main issue is the following: *sullogismos* is introduced by Aristotle as opposed to *epagôgê*, 'induction'; this speaks in favour of the general translation 'deduction'. However, as we shall see, both Aristotle and Alexander acknowledge the existence of deductive arguments that are not *sullogismoi* and yet are valid deductive arguments. This speaks in favour of a more specific translation for the Greek term (this strategy is followed and argued for, for example, by Barnes et al. (1991)). Since one of the issues I intend to discuss is to what extent Alexander had clear views about the distinction between deductive arguments that can be said to be *sullogismoi* and deductive arguments that cannot be said to be *sullogismoi*, I leave the word untranslated wherever it seems that a choice between the general and the more specific translation may be confusing or misleading as to what the issue is.

5 I explain why I prefer to leave this expression untranslated in the Note on the translation, p. 33.

6 'Enthymeme' is the technical term to indicate the rhetorical *sullogismos*.

7 On the Academic background of the *Topics* see in particular De Pater (1965) and Hambruch (1904).

8 An important role in establishing this picture was played by Friedrich Solmsen, one of Jaeger's pupils, who completed his dissertation about the development of Aristotle's logic and rhetoric in Berlin in 1929. The dissertation was to be published in the same year under the title *Die Entwicklung der aristotelischen Logik und*

Rhetorik. Although, as in the case of Jaeger's studies, not all of Solmsen's theses met or keep meeting with scholars' consensus, Solmsen (1929) certainly confirmed and contributed to further establishing a relatively widespread picture. Before and after Solmsen (1929), various traits of this picture have been dealt with by Brandis (1835), Prantl (1853), Maier (1896–1900, II 2, 78 ff.), Hambruch (1904), Kapp (1931), Gohlke (1933; 1936), Sainati (1968).

9 For example, textual evidence has induced some scholars to introduce the hypothesis of the distinction between a dialogical phase and a non-dialogical phase in Aristotle's approach to dialectical syllogism in the *Topics* as well as in his general theory of syllogism in the *Prior Analytics* (Barnes 1969: 142; Primavesi 1996: 59–67). Or, to give another significant example, Aristotle's theory of predication in the *Topics*, far from being simply superseded and abandoned in the *Analytics*, might turn out to be the key to understanding Aristotle's modal syllogistic (Malink 2013). A fuller and detailed account of Aristotle's approach to *sullogismoi* in the *Rhetoric* and in the *Topics* is given in Castelli and Rapp, 'The logical branch of Aristotle's dialectic. Traces of an early project' (in progress).

10 Interpreters tend to take only the first four books of Alexander's commentary on the *Topics* as authentic. It is perhaps worth noticing that, even if books 5–8 stem from Alexander's commentary through the intervention of an epitomist, they are mainly paraphrastic in character and do not offer many elements to speculate over the more general views of their author. For some discussion see Brandis (1835) and Wallies' introduction to the critical edition of Alexander's commentary.

11 It might be worth emphasizing that the commentary on the *Topics* has not received much attention in the general reconstructions of Alexander's logic. Moraux (2001) does not consider the commentary on the *Topics* in his account of Alexander's logic in the first part of the volume; Flannery (1995) makes some use of the commentary, but he mainly relies on the commentary on *An. Pr.* 1 also in the choice of the general topics to which he devotes the single chapters of the book; Gili (2011a) gives a reconstruction of Alexander's syllogistic based on the commentary on *An. Pr.* 1. Similarly for Lee (1984).

12 A more specific if concise summary of the contents of *An. Pr.* 1–2 can be found in Alex., *in An. Pr.* 6,15–29. Although the description is supposed to cover the contents of the two (6,29) books of the *Prior Analytics*, it mainly focuses on book 1. Book 2 is presumably supposed to fall under the third rubric of Aristotle's division of the enquiry into *genesis* of the *sullogismos*, *heuresis* and *anagôgê* of *sullogismoi* (note that the division of *An. Pr.* 1 into three sections about the generation, the heuristic and the reduction of deductive arguments to figure syllogisms, is standard in the Greek commentaries: cf. e.g. Phil., *in An. Pr.* 387,18–388,2). Alternatively, according to Alexander *An. Pr.* 2 might fall, even more generically, under the generic rubric 'all

things that are pertinent to the syllogistic enquiry' (Alex., *in An. Pr.* 6,28–9). For an overview of the reception of *An. Pr.* see Ebert and Nortmann (2007: 112–75).

13 Aristotle speaks of these arguments in *An. Pr.* 1.44, 50a39 as of arguments that reach their conclusion through a hypothesis (*peiranontai ex hupotheseôs*), but he then refers to them as *sullogismoi* (50b3); cf. 50a16.

14 Theophrastus's logic has been the object of important studies and its most original features as well as its shortcomings are relatively well known: Bochenski (1947), Repici (1977), Barnes (1983; 1985), Bobzien (2000, 2002a). A collection of the sources with English translation and commentary can be found in Huby (2007).

15 Alexander refers to the Stoic terminology by saying that the *neôteroi* have adopted specific labels: for example, they call the second premise of some hypothetical syllogisms *proslambanomenon* (Alex., *in An. Pr.* 262,9; 263,26 ff.) and identify a specific class of hypothetical arguments (*hoi dia tropikou [. . .] kai tês proslêpseôs ginomenoi*) as the only *sullogismoi*; these are the arguments that the *arkhaioi* used to call 'mixed' from a hypothetical premise and a categorical one (*ibid.* 262,28–32). About the use of different terminology by old and recent logicians cf. Galen, *Inst. Log.* III–IV. For some discussion of arguments from a hypothesis in Galen and the use of Stoic indemonstrables in Alexander see Bobzien (2002a and 2014 respectively).

16 About the differences between *metalêpsis* and *proslêpsis* see Alex., *in An. Pr.* 263,26 ff.; 324,16–19.

17 This partition can be found consistently throughout the commentary on the *Prior Analytics* (Alex., *in An. Pr.* 262,6 ff; 325,33–326,10; 386,15–30; 389,31–390,19). About wholly hypothetical syllogisms and on why they constitute a separate class see p. 14. The partition seems to be based on different criteria, which makes the partition itself somewhat untidy: distinctions (3) and (4) are based exclusively on structural features of the premises and conclusion; (1) and (2) on different sorts of features of the premise that counts as the hypothesis (it is opposite to the conclusion that one wants to establish in (1); it is assumed only based on previous explicit agreement in (2)). However, Alexander presents all of (1)–(3) as based on differences of the hypothesis. One might wonder whether this indicates anything about Alexander's understanding of what a 'hypothesis' is.

18 More generally, Alexander tends to obliterate important distinctions which are nowadays taken for granted: in particular, that Aristotle's *sullogismoi* from a hypothesis are something quite different from Stoic *sullogismoi* is a relatively well-established result of modern scholarship: see in particular Striker (1979), Crivelli (2011). For a radically different account of arguments from a hypothesis in Aristotle see Strobach (2001). Similarly, the label 'hypothetical syllogisms' for Stoic syllogisms is Peripatetic and does not reflect the Stoic conception of hypothesis: on the Stoic conception of *hupothesis* see Bobzien (1997).

19 The idea that the *Topics* contain (among other things) evidence about what Aristotle calls *sullogismoi ex hupotheseôs* is, nowadays, not particularly controversial. However, what Alexander adds (and we should not add) in reading Aristotle is a full theory of such arguments and their relation to categorical syllogisms which is likely to be post-Aristotelian. A reading of Aristotle's *Topics* along the lines of Alexander's commentary has been given by Slomkowski (1997). I have just explained why I think such a reading is not adequate.

20 Frede (1974), Barnes et al. (1991: 64 n. 67), ascribe to Alexander the views which Alexander explicitly ascribes to Aristotle. I am inclined to think that Alexander clearly identifies what he takes to be Aristotle's position on the matter, but it is not so clear to me that Alexander also endorses that position without qualification.

21 Alex., *in Top.* 1,19–2,16: 'Aristotle and his followers, instead, do not share the same views about dialectic [*scil.* as the Stoics and the Platonists]. Rather, they posit that it is a certain syllogistic method. And since they believe that *sullogismoi*, in the respect in which they are *sullogismoi*, do not differ from each other, while they differ with respect to the forms of their premises, with respect to modes and figures, and with respect to the matter about which they are – and, of these, the first difference makes some of the *sullogismoi* deictic (which we call "categorical"), and some hypothetical; the second difference is that based on which some *sullogismoi* are perfect and some imperfect, some in the first, some in the second and some in the third figure, as is spelled out in the *Prior Analytics* [. . .]; and the third difference, based on the matter, makes some of them demonstrative, some dialectical, and some eristic.'

22 A well-known discussion of the issue of whether this presentation of the debate is appropriate is Frede (1974). In this article, Alexander is singled out as the standard orthodox Peripatetic. This implies that Alexander himself cannot really raise a question of priority between the two types of syllogism given that (if Frede is right) hypothetical syllogisms, i.e. Stoic arguments i.e. what I called hypothetical *logoi*, are not really *sullogismoi* in the first place. It seems to me that this picture needs some refining along the lines I specify above. For an overview of the sources and of the main aspects of the debate see Sorabji (2004, chapter 8).

23 Frede (1974) refers to this passage as one of the very few that might testify to the existence of a debate.

24 cf. Alex., *in Top.* 7,24–8,14, quoted on p. 10.

25 The formulation of the definition in *Top.* 1.1 is slightly different, but Alexander takes the two to be equivalent. Translations are mine unless otherwise indicated.

26 For the sake of clarity and uniformity, in translating this text I adopt the same translation choices as in Barnes et al. (even if I depart from them in my translation of Alexander's commentary on *Top.* 2). In particular, I render *sullogismos* with 'syllogism' and *sullogizesthai* with 'syllogizing'. However, I italicize these expressions

in order to emphasize that I take them as calques of the corresponding Greek terms, without endorsing any specific interpretation. Cf. Alex., *in Top.* 10,19–28.

27 Of course, this does not exclude that hypothetical *sullogismoi* may fail to comply with other clauses of the definition (a point to which I shall return). In fact, even inductive arguments comply with the first part of the definition of *sullogismos* – but fail to comply with the rest of the definition (Alex., *in An. Pr.* 18,8–12).

28 One could speculate that in standard Peripatetic hypothetical *sullogismoi* the definition applies in that the clause about what is 'posited' only refers to the premises of the categorical syllogism which is included in the larger argument. However, I am not sure this is a viable option: what follows from the premises of the categorical syllogism is the conclusion of the categorical syllogism, i.e. the co-assumption or re-assumption, and not the desired conclusion of the whole argument. But the point of the definition of the syllogism seems to be that the conclusion of the whole argument follows necessarily from what is posited.

29 The distinction Alexander alludes to is certainly the one Aristotle draws in *Top.* 2.11, 115b29 ff. (Alex., *in Top.* 215,18–216,10).

30 Alex., *in An. Pr.* 18,12–22; *in Top.* 9,20–10,6.

31 Alex., *in An. Pr.* 18,18–19.

32 Alex., *in Top.* 10,7; cf. *in An. Pr.* 18,16.

33 This is the example in Alex., *in Top.* 10,11–12.

34 Alex., *in An. Pr.* 18,17–18; *in Top.* 10,9–10.

35 Alex., *in An. Pr.* 19,19 ff.

36 Alex., *in Top.* 12,29–13,10.

37 Castelli (2015).

38 Alex., *in Top.* 174,26–175,2 analyses Arist., *Cael.* 1.5 in light of Arist., *Top.* 2.6, 112a24 ff.

39 For the issues involved in the translation of this and similar passages see the general comments on the translation at the end of the introduction, pp. 31–32.

40 cf. Alex., *in An. Pr.* 330,28–30.

41 Alexander's argument seems to be the following: one might object to Aristotle's classification of problems in *Top.* 1.8 that it is not exhaustive since it leaves out problems of the form 'why is S P?' and 'what is S?'. But these two types of questions do not belong in the province of dialectic (which rather deals only with two other questions: 'whether something is the case' and 'whether something is'). They rather belong to scientific investigation.

42 Note that for Alexander the question 'whether something is' and its answer are in predicative form and, in particular, express an accidental predication: see Alex., *in Top.* 53,2–10.

43 At least some questions about whether something is or what something is will not be answered by resorting to a syllogism but to sense perception or intellect or induction.

44 Alex., *in An. Pr.* 18,22–19,3; cf. *in Top.* 10,26–8: indifferently concluding arguments would not be used in scientific, dialectical or sophistical contexts. Since these three contexts exhaust the domain of syllogistic, and the genus is nothing over and above the species, if they do not fall under any species of syllogism, they will not fall under the genus either; therefore, they will not be syllogisms.

45 See e.g. Alex., *in An. Pr.* 326,12–17. This feature seems to be the reason why either these arguments are not *sullogismoi* at all or, if they in any sense are, their reduction to categorical syllogisms will be of a different nature than the reduction which is available for other types of hypothetical arguments: cf. Alex., *in An. Pr.* 326,6–10; 326,21 about the claim that these arguments can be reduced *allôi tropôi*, 'in another way', i.e. as Theophrastus did. What this reduction is about is controversial (see n. 46), but it seems clear that Alexander regards them as building a class of their own.

46 This is not to deny that Alexander also seems to endorse a logical thesis about the reducibility of other types of deductive arguments to categorical syllogisms – see in particular Barnes (1983) about the reducibility of wholly hypothetical syllogisms. Note, however, that Alexander is aware of the fact that, whatever the operation of reduction turns out to be, the way in which wholly hypothetical syllogisms relate to categorical syllogisms is different from the way in which arguments that establish a categorical conclusion relate to categorical syllogisms. For some discussion of Barnes's reconstruction and an assessment of the different ways in which ancient logicians of different schools may have come up with different understandings of wholly hypothetical syllogisms see Bobzien (2000).

47 Alex., *in An. Pr.* 49,7–17 associates each figure to one species of syllogisms: the first figure, which is the only one that can prove universal affirmative conclusions, is typical of scientific syllogisms; the second figure, which characteristically proves negative conclusions, is typical of dialectical syllogisms, which usually aim at refuting a claim; the third figure, leading to particular conclusions, is typical of sophistical syllogisms.

48 In this as in all other cases I am mainly interested in Alexander's views emerging from his commentaries. Unless this is directly relevant for the appreciation of Alexander's views, I do not discuss whether Alexander's comments are a reliable exegesis of Aristotle's text. However, I give some assessment of Alexander's general views about the relation between *An. Pr.* and *Top.* as a viable (or non-viable) option for the modern reader, on pp. 1–5.

49 *Pons asinorum* ('the bridge of asses') indicates a problem, a test or a stumbling block which will be tackled and solved by the smart minds and not by the fools who, like asses (whose reluctance to cross a bridge apparently used to be proverbial) will not

be able to move on to the other side. The proof of the theorem that the angles at the base of an isosceles triangle are equal is a well-known *pons asinorum* in Euclidean geometry. Logic had its own 'bridge' in the discovery of the middle term. One alternative account of the label could be that the method given by Aristotle in *An. Pr.* 1.27–8 was meant to facilitate the task of finding a middle term and, in this way, built a 'bridge' to help the slower students.

50 On the dialectical origins of the terminology see Bobzien (2002b).

51 cf. also Alex., *in Top.* 166,2–167,2; 174,5–175,26; 187,10–188,3. On [T 3.7] see notes on p. 159.

52 It is important to stress that Alexander seems to be right in isolating this type of argument from a hypothesis as distinct from other types of arguments from a hypothesis in that this is the only type of argument from a hypothesis where the explicit assent of the interlocutor to a proposition in conditional form is necessary in order to legitimate the inferential step from the established conclusion to the desired conclusion. Interestingly enough, all examples Aristotle gives of arguments based on explicit *homologia* are cases in which the desired conclusion does not actually follow from the established conclusion. A thorough discussion of these cases can be found in Castelli and Rapp (in preparation).

53 Slomkowski (1997) takes Alexander's interpretation of these arguments as hypothetical syllogisms as basically correct. I hope to have shown that Alexander's reasons for this exegetical move are part of a much broader picture relying on his general views about Peripatetic (and not just Aristotelian) logic, which includes significantly more than Aristotelian logic. In particular, scholars tend to agree that the development of a Peripatetic theory of hypothetical syllogisms was Theophrastus's rather than Aristotle's achievement.

54 A similar account with further examples is given in Alex., *in An. Pr.* 324,18–325,24. See, for example, 324,24–31: 'For the one who shows that being happy does not consist in being rich by showing that it does not even consists in being healthy subsumes (*hupotithetai*) the claim: "if what seems to be more sufficient for happiness is not sufficient, neither will what seems less sufficient than it"; but health, which seems to be more sufficient for happiness than richness, is not sufficient; therefore, neither richness is. For it is laid down (*hupokeitai*) that richness is not sufficient for happiness if health is not sufficient either. And that health is not sufficient for happiness can be shown through a syllogism in this way: [. . .]'.

55 In fact, Alex., *in Top.* 275,28–276,1 suggests that the primary application of comparative arguments concerns quantities (lengths, numbers, weights etc.), which also provide the paradigmatic case for the use of arguments such as A is equal to B; B is equal to C; therefore, A is equal to C.

56 Gal., *Inst. Log.* XVI–XVIII singles them out as arguments based on the relatives (Kalbfleisch p. 38, ll. 13–14: *kata to pros ti*). Alexander refers to them by saying that

Top. 3 is 'about comparative problems' (*in Top.* 217,6–7: *peri tôn sunkritikôn problematôn*) and explicitly says that 'every comparison falls under what is relative' (*in Top.* 218,16: *pasa men oun sunkrisis upo to pros ti*). These arguments are one type of deductive arguments that are 'unmethodically conclusive' (*amethodôs perainontes*).

57 See especially Barnes (1983).

58 *ibid.*

59 I give a fuller account of the possible ways of analysing these arguments and of the problems connected with them in the introduction to the translation and notes of Alexander, *in Top.* 3, in preparation for this series.

60 By saying this I by no means imply that the matter is of secondary importance in order to give a consistent picture of Alexander's views about Peripatetic logic. For the purposes of this introduction, however, it is enough to acknowledge that, despite the troubling existence of this treatment of unmethodically conclusive arguments in Alexander, there are texts which clearly link to some arguments in the *Topics* and it is not always clear that a reduction to categorical syllogisms along the lines of [T 3.8] is part of the picture.

61 For some comments on the text see below and notes on pp. 141–2.

62 The two terms, *parangelma* and *topos*, appear in an Aristotelian text (*Insom.* 1, 458b20–5), where Aristotle illustrates some aspects of dreams with reference to some mnemonic devices used as aids in remembering things by storing them in mental places each associated to an image. The text is unclear, but it may make room for a distinction between *parangelma* and *topos* in that the former would be a sort of label for the latter (where the *topos* would be the 'place' where images and possibly rational thoughts linked to the images are stored; in this sense the *topos* would include more than the *parangelma*). The mnemotechnical use of *topoi* (without any mention of *parangelma*) is alluded to by Aristotle himself in *Top.* 8.14, 163b28–32.

63 See notes on p. 148 for more specific points about Alexander's commentary and the translation.

64 Topic-neutrality is for Aristotle a feature of dialectical arguments that are based on 'common things' (*koina*), in contrast with scientific arguments in which all terms must belong within the same kind which is the subject genus of a specific science. See e.g. *Rhet.* 1.1, 1355a27–9; 1355b8–9.

65 Note that both interlocutors of the dialectical debate know what sort of conclusion the questioner tries to establish: a proposition which contradicts the claim endorsed by the answerer.

66 I take this to be the point of finding premises that are 'for what is submitted' in [T 4.1] and 'appropriate' or 'proximate' (*prosekhês*)' or 'pertinent and appropriate' (*oikeia kai prosekhês*) to the problem at stake in [T 4.2].

67 In this sense the relation between *topos* and the specific premises is not cast in terms of the opposition between universal (e.g.: All A are B) and particular propositions

(e.g.: Some A are B) as spelled out in *An. Pr.* (and in *Top.* 2.1, 108b34 ff.) through the use of quantifiers. See notes on pp. 141–2 for more details and some assessment.

68 In the course of the commentary on *Top.* 2 Alexander emphasizes whether a *topos* is true or merely reputable without being true. See e.g. 97–8, 109, 126, 130, 138–9.

69 By way of contrast: Later Neoplatonic commentators (e.g. Ammonius, *in An. Pr.* 2,29–3,30; Philoponus, *in An. Pr.* 2,22–4,20) see in the endoxastic character of the premises of (Peripatetic) dialectical syllogisms an allusion to the kind of object dialectical syllogisms are about (the objects of *doxa* – as opposed to the objects of knowledge) and the faculty of the soul (*doxa*) responsible for the production of such syllogisms; on this interpretation, the claim that dialectical syllogisms are *from endoxa* receives a fundamentally pejorative connotation. Nothing could be farther from Alexander's views on the matter.

70 Note that for Alexander the scientific syllogism is not only characterized by premises that are true, but by premises that are true, primary and immediate (Alex., *in Top.* 16,1–25) or by premises that are true, prior to the conclusion and proven through primary and immediate premises (Alex., *in Top.* 16,31–17,26). Alexander even asks the question whether syllogisms with true premises that are posterior to the conclusion (and which, therefore, cannot be regarded as scientific syllogisms or demonstrations) should be regarded as dialectical syllogisms or scientific syllogisms in a secondary way (*deuterôs*) (Alex., *in Top.* 16,25–31).

71 I deal with this problem in further detail and with the relation between *topoi* and principles of proof in 'Alexander of Aphrodisias on deductive arguments and their principles', in preparation.

72 For example, in arguments from agreement in which one wants to establish a universal claim (e.g. every soul is immortal) but can only establish a particular claim (e.g. the human soul is immortal) one needs the explicit agreement from the interlocutor that, if she manages to produce an argument for the particular case of human souls, the interlocutor will grant the universal conclusion that every soul is immortal. See pp. 75–7 for Alexander's comments on this procedure. It is not clear whether in these arguments and, more generally, in arguments from a hypothesis in which the interlocutor agrees that if something holds in one of several similar cases, then she concedes that the same holds in the other similar cases, what is granted is a general premise or rather the resort to a controversial inferential rule.

73 See e.g. the 'elements' about genus and differentia which Aristotle gives in *Top.* 5.6, 128a20–9.

74 The plural here is puzzling, but I take it to refer (*ad sensum*) to *topoi*.

75 One might wonder where such things as the *stoikheia* and *theôrêmata* about genus and difference in Alex., *in Top.* 365,25–366,13, would belong: 'the genus is said of more than the difference'; 'even if the difference seems to be predicated in the what it is of the species, still the genus is more appropriate than the difference if one is asked

to spell out what the species is'; 'the difference indicates a quality of the genus whose difference it is, but not vice versa'.

76 See e.g. Boethius, *De Top. Diff.* 2, 1185B–D: 'Such a proposition is sometimes contained within the boundaries of an argument, and sometimes it supplies force to the argument and makes [it] complete from without. Here is an example of an argument which contains such a maximal proposition. Suppose there is a question whether rule by a king is better than rule by a consul. We will say this: rule by a king lasts longer than rule by a consul, when both are good; but a good that lasts longer is better than one which lasts a short time; therefore, rule by a king is better than rule by a consul. This argumentation contains its maximal proposition, that is, [its] Topic, which is "Goods that last a longer time are of more worth than those which last a short time." This is so known that it needs no proof from without and can itself be a proof for other things. And so this proposition contains the whole proof; and since the argument arises from it, it is rightly called a Topic, that is, the foundation of an argument. Let this be the example that a maximal proposition posited outside [the argument] brings force to the argument. Suppose the task is to demonstrate that an envious man is not wise. An envious man is one who disparages the good of others. But a wise man does not disparage the good of others. Therefore, an envious man is not wise. The maximal proposition does not appear included within this argumentation, but it gives force to the argumentation, for belief for this syllogism is provided by that proposition by which we know that things whose definitions are different are themselves also different. But in the definition of the envious man there is that – to pine at others' good – which is not found in the wise man; and therefore the wise man is separated from the envious man'. (Translation by Stump 1978).

77 Gal., *Inst. Log.* XVI–XVII.

78 cf. p. 5 about 'what is replaced' in the structure of hypothetical syllogisms.

79 See, however, n. 62 about the use of the terminology of *topoi* with reference to mnemonic devices.

80 See e.g. Alex., *in Metaph.* 79,4 and 80,9 about the *kataskeuê* of Ideas and 80,16 as well as 82,11 about arguments that 'establish' (*kataskeuazein*) Ideas.

List of Departures from Wallies' Text

I provide here a list of the passages in which my departure from the text in Wallies' edition makes a difference for the translation. See Introduction: pp. 34–5, and the notes for further comments on Wallies' text.

128,25:   I follow Wallies' suggestion in the apparatus and read *panta katholou ta problêmata <alêthôs> dunatai lambanesthai* instead of *panta katholou ta problêmata † allêlois dunatai lambanesthai*.

139,32:   I read *metekhein* instead of *metekhei* and I do not adopt Wallies' addition of *ou* before *khrê*. On both points, see Roselli (2002).

140,2:   I follow Roselli (2002) and read *sunalgôn* instead of *sunagôn*.

154,30:   I read *aporein* with B instead of *euporein* in Wallies' edition.

156,8:   I depart from Wallies, who prints *autos houtôs deiknusi*, and follow the reading of the manuscripts: *auta houtôs deiknuousi*.

157,17:   Wallies signals a lacuna after *spoudaiou*. Wallies' proposal in the apparatus that the missing text should be something like *anankaia, oud' an pasa hupolêpsis tou spoudaiou* seems likely and I translate this text.

162,12:   Wallies prints a *crux* after the parenthesis. Some integration, possibly along the line of the one suggested in the translation '<check whether>' is required; Wallies suggests *skeptein* in the apparatus.

183,14:   The text seems damaged; I translate the text suggested by Wallies in the apparatus: *hai ou monon têi aretêi enantiai eisin*.

195,9–10:   I depart from Wallies' text in that I omit *anaskeuasomen*.

205,9:   Wallies signals a lacuna in the text. I translate the text he suggests in the apparatus: *ean men gar tôi mallon to mallon huparkhêi*.

Alexander of Aphrodisias

On Aristotle Topics 2

Translation

Alexander of Aphrodisias's commentary on the second book of Aristotle's topical investigation

In the first book of the *Topics*[1] he talked about the things it was necessary to discuss before the presentation[2] of the *topoi*,[3] and these were: [*Top.* 1.1] what is the objective of this investigation, what is a deduction, what are its differences, in what respect the dialectical one differs from the other [kinds of] deductions, and what a reputable opinion is; he also preliminarily set down to what extent one can expect precision in these discussions. And he said [*Top.* 1.2] for how many things and for what things this investigation is useful. Furthermore [*Top.* 1.3], he made clear what accomplishment in this [investigation] amounts to.[4] And, after these things, having said in what things this [investigation]'s being resides [*Top.* 1.4], namely in problems and premises and the tools through which it is possible to have a great supply of such deductions, he first discussed premises and problems in general.[5] And he showed that these are one thing in substrate, just as conclusion and assumption are (for all these things, i.e. problem, premise, assumption and conclusion, are propositions with respect to their genus, and their difference is based on their mode of expression and on the sort of relation they bear to some things).[6] In what follows, he said how many the kinds of problems and premises are, and having shown that they are four and what they are, he said [*Top.* 1.5–6] what each of them is. He talked about the things that are pertinent to and belong together with each of them, which are ordered together with them based on similarity, but he also showed through induction and through deduction [*Top.* 1.8] the reason why the kinds [of problems and premises] are in this number. After these things, he [*Top.* 1.7] made a division of [the ways in which] the same [is said], since there are some problems from the same, too, that are ordered together with those concerning definition.[7] After this, he defined [*Top.* 1.10–11] the dialectical premise and the dialectical problem and showed how they differ from each other; and he talked about the thesis,[8] since the thesis, too, is a certain problem, but he also discussed [*Top.* 1.12] induction and showed what it is, and said that induction, too, like deduction, is a part of dialectical arguments.[9] After these things, he said [*Top.* 1.13–18] what the tools are, and how many, through which one can have a great supply of dialectical arguments; and, having gone through each of them separately, he also showed what utility derives to dialectic from each of them.

Having discussed these things in the first book of the *Topics* as necessary to know in order to use the *topoi* that are to be presented, in the second book he begins the presentation of the *topoi* that are useful for each problem.

125,3

10

20

126,1

10

A *topos* is a principle and a starting point for an attack (they call 'attack' the dialectical deduction). For this reason, Theophrastus also defines the *topos*, as we have already said in the first book,[10] in this way: a *topos* is a certain principle or an element, from which we take the principles about each subject; it is determined in its outline, but is indeterminate with respect to the particulars. For example, a *topos* is 'if the contrary belongs to the contrary, then also the contrary belongs to the contrary'.[11] For this statement, i.e. this proposition[12] is determined with respect to the universal (it makes clear that it is in general about contraries), but it is not further determined in it whether it is about these or these particular
20   contraries.

However, starting from this, it is possible to lead an attack about any contraries: for if the enquiry is about the good, whether it benefits, we will take, starting from the given *topos*, a premise appropriate[13] to the given problem, e.g. 'if the bad harms, the good benefits'. Both its being and its credibility will come to this premise from the given *topos*. If the object of the enquiry is whether the colour white dilates sight, we will again take a premise that is pertinent and appropriate to this problem from the given *topos*, i.e. 'if the colour black contracts sight, then the colour white dilates sight'. But, if one enquires about pleasure whether it is
30   good, from the given *topos* the premise will be taken that says 'if pain is bad, pleasure is good'. For all these and similar things are potentially and indeterminately[14] contained in the given *topos*.

Again, a *topos* of one about two is: 'If the thing that seems to belong to
127,1 something to a higher degree does not belong to it, the [same] thing that seems to belong to [something else] to a lesser degree will not belong to the that either'.[15] For this statement, too, is determined with respect to the universal (it makes clear that it is about what belongs to a higher and to a lesser degree, just as the [statement] before it made it clear that it was about the contraries); however, it is indeterminate with respect to the particulars. For it is not made clear in it what the thing is in which the higher degree occurs: one can take the higher and lesser degree in colour or in taste as well as in goodness. By starting from the aforementioned *topos* it is possible to have a great supply of pertinent[16] premises for each of the problems admitting of the use of the more and the less. For if one happens to be enquiring into whether richness is good or not, if one wants to
10   show that it is not good, starting from the aforementioned *topos* he will take a premise appropriate to the given problem, through which he will deduce that richness is not good. For if health, which is good to a higher degree than richness, is not good, then richness will not be good either. Once this premise is taken, if a further premise were taken in addition, saying that health is not good (because,

say, for some people it leads to something bad, and nothing good becomes a cause of what is bad), then it would be shown, based on the given *topos*, that richness is not good.

He begins with the presentation of the *topoi* relating to problems from the accident, both because this is more common and has priority in this sense (for the [property of] belonging [to their subjects] belongs to all [kinds of predicates]),[17] and because in this way the presentation of the *topoi* becomes ordered and articulated.[18] For the accident is – as he said in the previous book   20
– that 'which is neither a genus nor a definition nor a proprium, and still belongs to the thing'.[19] However, the [property of] belonging follows upon the other [kinds of predicates] too: for nothing can be a genus or a definition or a proprium of something without belonging to it. For this reason, if the belonging – through which the accident is defined – is removed, then also each of the others is removed; on the other hand, it is not the case that, if one of the others is removed, then also the accident is removed at the same time. So the accident is, in this sense, prior in nature to the other [kinds of predicates].[20] Furthermore, [he begins with the accident] because starting from the accident, the presentation of the *topoi* will become ordered and articulated, assuming that some [*topoi*] relate to the accident, some to the genus, some to the proprium and some to the   30
definition. For, since the definition must not only signify the essence – rather, firstly, it has to belong to the thing whose definition it is; and then it has to be predicated in its what-it-is; but it also has to be predicated instead[21] of it – if he had started the presentation of the *topoi* from the definition, it would have been necessary to mention, as concerning the definition, the *topoi* which are   128,1
constructive and destructive of what belongs to the thing (which are pertinent to the accident), and those showing that [the predicate] is predicated in the what-it-is (which, in their turn, are pertinent to the problems concerning the genus), as well as those capable of showing that [the predicate] is predicated instead [of the subject] (which are pertinent to the problems from the proprium). In this way, he would have considered also the *topoi* that are pertinent to other problems as concerning the definition. But then, talking about them and mentioning them, he would have still said that some of them are from the genus and some from some other [kind of predicate], as if the same *topoi* were pertinent to several [kinds of problems]. Now, instead, starting from the accident, which is the most common and the simplest, he presents the *topoi* about belonging or not belonging   10
as specific to the accident. Next, when he mentions the *topoi* relating to the genus, he presents as specific to the genus those that go beyond the [mere] belonging and reach out[22] to the genus; and as pertinent to the proprium those

that go beyond the genus and reach out to the proprium; and as relating to definitions those that go beyond the latter and reach out to the definition.

For these reasons, then, he starts from the *topoi* relating to the accident. But first he provides a certain division of problems which can be made with reference to the other [kinds of problems], too, but is particularly relevant to the problems from the accident. And the division is that some of the problems are universal

20   and some are particular. For in the other kinds of problems, even if one took some particular as true per se, that has something universal in it nonetheless. For it is clear that the one who says: 'the animal is the genus of some ensouled thing' speaks in particular, but the [expression] 'some this and this' does not indicate an individual, but a universal. In the case of accidents, though, also the particular understood as individual can be taken as true per se. For in problems from the other kinds [of predicates] it is possible to take all the problems as <in truth> universal:[23] for neither a genus nor a definition nor a proprium belongs to some individual without belonging to some other of the same species;[24] rather, it either belongs to all or to none. Only the accident can belong to some particular thing, understood as an individual, and not to some other – e.g. the white or the musical, as well as any other of its accidents, [can belong in this way] to the human being: for some particular human being is musical, whereas

30   some is not.

He will set the order of the presentation of the *topoi* through this division. For, having provided the aforementioned division, he will first show that one does not have to look for some specific *topoi* in order to demolish or establish all

129,1 particular problems: for the *topoi* establishing the universals at the same time establish the particulars falling under them, too, so that these would be enough for both. Similarly, universally destructive *topoi* at the same time also remove the particulars together [with the corresponding universals]. Furthermore, the one who shows that 'what is universally constructive or destructive is common',[25] will take that one has to start from the presentation of the *topoi* that show [something] universally, for the reason that these things at the same time establish also the particulars and are useful for establishing those, too. And again, since, of the common and universal *topoi*, some are constructive, while some others are destructive, he will take that one has to start from the destructive ones

10   based on the consideration that those who posit problems posit that [something] belongs [to something] and [does so] affirmatively, and the goal of the discussants is to show the opposite of what is posited; and the opposite of the affirmative is the negative.[26] Therefore, since universally destructive *topoi* are more useful and more necessary for the dialecticians, he will start from these.

<Chapter 1>

108b34 Of the problems, some are universal and some are particular.

He now seems to call 'problems' not those that are submitted for discussion (for those encompass the contradiction), but those that have already been determined according to one side of the contradiction and with respect to which one always must have a great supply of attacks. For as some of the premises are in interrogative form and encompass the contradiction, while others are already taken as parts of   20
a deduction and consist in one of the two parts of the contradiction (and these are those that are reputable, i.e. not the interrogative ones, but those that have already been conceded and laid down, through which the dialectical deduction comes about),[27] in the same way some of the problems, too, are proposed for debate, while others are already determined – and now he talks about the latter.

And now he calls 'universal' the problems which, in the treatise *On expression*, he called 'universal as universal'.[28] For everything that is common is universal, even if it is expressed indeterminately; and such a universal is the opposite of the particular [individual] – e.g. human being is universal, whereas Callias is a particular [individual]. But the universal is said as universal when 'every' or 'none' is added to the universal – e.g. 'every human being is biped'; 'no human being is winged'. In this passage he calls 'universal' without qualification the   30
problems that are expressed in this way; particular problems are the opposite of these, and particular problems, too, are about universals: e.g. 'some human being is musical', 'not every human being is musical'.

109a1 Things that are universally constructive or destructive are common to both   130,1
kinds of problems.

These are useful for establishing and demolishing particular problems as well. And he shows again that one does not need to look for some *topoi* that are fully specific with respect to particular problems. For – he says – the *topoi* from which we will establish something universally or demolish universally are common to both kinds of problems (in this context by 'kinds of problems' he intends the universal and the particular). And he says this because he will provide the presentation of the *topoi* [by formulating them] without qualification and universally, without adding 'in particular' or 'to some'.[29]

In order to make it plain, then, that the same *topoi* will be useful to us, even   10
if a problem is particular, he declares this preliminarily. But he will say this very

same thing again, and even clearer, towards the end of the third book.[30] Things that are universally constructive are useful, then, both for universal affirmative problems and for particular affirmative problems, whereas things that are universally destructive are useful both for universal negative problems and for particular [negative] ones. For not only universal affirmative problems, but also particular affirmative problems are shown through the *topoi* leading to a universal affirmative conclusion.[31] For the one who shows that every human being breathes has also already shown that some human being breathes. And, if the aim is to show that some pleasure is good, one could also avail himself of the universal argument that every pleasure is good: for once one has shown that

20   every pleasure is good, he would have also shown that some pleasure is good.[32] Similarly, the one who shows that being four-footed does not belong to any human being or that being good does not belong to any pleasure would have also shown that it does not belong to every pleasure. However, the vice versa does not hold: for it is not the case that the one who showed that it belongs to some also showed that it belongs to every, nor is it the case that the one who showed that it does not belong to some also showed that it does not belong to any.

It has to be noted that he says that 'things that are universally constructive or destructive' are useful 'for both kinds of problems',[33] but he does not say: 'things that are destructive of the universal'. For it is not the case that the one who has shown that not every pleasure is good has also [thereby] removed [the claim] that some pleasure is good; and yet he has demolished the universal. But it is also not the case that the one who has demolished [the claim] that no pleasure is good by showing that some pleasure is good has already also removed [the claim] that some pleasure is not good: for 'none' is appropriately demolished by

30   'some', by the positing of which [the claim] that some pleasure is not good is not
131,1 removed, just as it is also not the case that the one who has shown that some pleasure is good has also already shown that every pleasure is good.

Since, then, universal things are common (for we use them also with reference to particular things), and common things are first, he says that one has to talk of universal *topoi* first. And since, of the universal things, some are constructive and some are destructive, he says further that, among universal things, one should talk first of the destructive ones: for these in their turn are more useful for the dialectician than those showing a universal affirmative [claim]. For since, as we have already recalled[34], discussants for the most part introduce affirmative theses and problems, but the goal of the dialectician is to demolish what is posited and

10   to carry out an attack that leads to the opposite [claim] (for such is the exercise[35] in arguments),[36] it is clear that the affirmative will be demolished by way of

negation. Accordingly, the negative has priority over the affirmative, because it is much more useful to the dialectician, while the universal negative has priority over the particular negative because the universal is common and can be used with reference to the particular as well.

That the activity of demolishing rather than that of establishing, is more characteristic of the dialectician has been said in the first book of the *Analytics* entitled *Eudemian* (the same work is also entitled: Eudemus's *On the Analytics*),[37] in which it is said so, i.e. that 'the things that are established by the dialectician are few, while the biggest part of his power resides in removing something'.

He calls 'thesis'[38] the problem more generally.

109a10 It is most difficult to convert the proper name from the accident.   20

He probably says 'most difficult' because it is not as simple and straightforward as it is in the other cases. And in this passage he talks of a conversion which is different from those considered in the *Analytics*: for, of those, one was with respect to the terms and the other was with respect to the affirmative and the negative, as possible propositions were said to convert.[39] But the conversion he talks about now is with respect to the name: for he calls 'converting' the procedure of calling the subject with the name of what is posited as belonging to something. For example, by converting 'animal belongs to human being' we say 'human being is animal': for we say that the subject is that which we took to belong to the subject. And this procedure would be a conversion as long as we first start from   30
the predicate and then, after these [moves], we start from the subject. When, then, once we have made this replacement, what we say is true and it is correct to   132,1
name the subject with the name of what belongs to it absolutely and without any addition, then he says that, when this situation obtains, things convert with respect to the name. The [conversion is said to be] with respect to 'the [proper name] from the accident' instead of 'with respect to the formulation naming the subject through the name proper to its accident'. Alternatively, he said 'to convert the proper name from the accident' [in this sense]: in such a conversion the subject is named with the name of the predicate as if it were [its] proper [name]. The cases in which this is not true anymore do not convert according to this conversion with respect to the name. The things, then, that belong to some things as genera or as definitions or as propria convert: for the thing of which 'animal'   10
is the genus is [an] animal;[40] and the thing of which 'biped terrestrial animal' is the definition is [a] biped terrestrial animal; and the thing of which 'capable of

laughing' is the proprium is capable of laughing. For this reason, if it turns out that what has been posited as belonging in some of these ways does not convert, then it will not belong in the way in which it was posited. But this is not anymore true of the accident without qualification. For it is not the case that, if the white belongs to something, in all cases this thing is also white; nor is it the case that, if it is not possible to say that it is white, then it is already the case that the white does not belong to it: so that it is not possible to demolish the accident by resorting to this [move]. The reason for this is that the accident can belong to something in a certain respect and that to which something belongs not as a whole but in a certain respect and in some way, this thing cannot be named without qualification with the name of the thing that belongs to it in this way.

20   For it is not the case that what is black in a certain respect is already also black, nor that what is white in a certain respect is already also white: so the Ethiopian, despite being white in a certain respect (i.e. with respect to his teeth), is not white. This sort of qualified belonging finds application only in the case of the accident; for neither the genus nor the definition nor the proprium considered strictly speaking[41] admit of belonging to something in a qualified way, just as they cannot belong in some part or to an individual only. It follows that, if the qualified belonging to the subject is the reason why there is no conversion, and this is only possible in the case of the accident, it would be true of the accident only that it does not always convert: for it will not be possible to say that the subject is this accident (which belongs to it in a certain way and not without qualification). For sure [the claim] that something is an accident of something else is not removed by the fact that it does not convert: for it is not the case that,

30   if it does not convert, then for this reason it is not an accident. But, on the other hand, if something has been shown to be an accident of something else, it is not also [thereby] shown that the subject is called with the name of the accident.

              Since he is about to provide the presentation of the *topoi* relative to the
133,1   accident, he first set out what the characteristic features of the problems from the accident are compared with the other [types of] problems. One of these was that, in this case,[42] some problems are universal and some particular, if one understands 'particular' in the sense of what is said with reference to individuals; the second was that not all problems from the accident convert in the aforementioned mode of conversion. And we acknowledge the latter feature as useful for attacks: for the one who has shown that the human being is not [an] animal or [a][43] mortal rational animal or capable of laughing has also shown at the same time that the given [predicate] was not its genus or definition or proprium – for, [if it were,] it would convert. But the one who has shown that the human being is not pale or

dark or any other of its accidents has not yet removed [the claim] that some of 10
these properties belongs to it incidentally.[44] For some of them can still belong to
it incidentally in some way or in some respect. For 'being without qualification'
and 'being in some qualified way' [can be found] in the accident in the same way
as the universal and the particular can. There is a certain analogy in the way in
which being without qualification stands to the universal on one side, and being
in some qualified way stands to the particular on the other side, both of which
are in the accident, as he will mention himself: for what is in some qualified way
is also not universal. Being without qualification is opposed to being in some
qualified way as the universal is opposed to the particular; so he set the universal
in opposition to what is in some qualified way, thinking that the former bears a
certain resemblance to what is without qualification. Justice would belong to
someone in some respect – as he said – if one has by nature a suitable
predisposition to this disposition; similarly, also if one has a certain inclination
towards some just things merely from habit: for someone in this condition is not 20
yet just without qualification, even if a certain justice belongs to him.

*109a27 We also have to define the mistakes that occur in problems; and these are
of two types: saying what is false and deviating from the established use of language.*

It has been a matter of enquiry how it is possible to say that a problem is false: for
if every problem encompasses a contradiction, how could being false or being
true apply to problems? As I have already said earlier,[45] then, he is not talking
anymore of the problem which is submitted and proposed for debate, but of the
problem as already determined and laid down, as he has already said at the
beginning. And this is the problem of which someone, whom the dialectician
tries to refute, undertakes the defence.[46]

And he says that in the first place the mistakes concerning the problems must
be defined and be known before the presentation of the *topoi*. For since the 30
demolitions of problems come about based on the mistakes that are present in
them, it is clear that such mistakes must be known and agreed upon: for the
things in accordance with which their[47] refutation must occur through the 134,1
attacks must be known.

And he says that two mistakes occur in problems. It is clear that the one who
has exposed such mistakes will have removed the problem: for either something
false is posited through them[48] or the linguistic formulation in them[49] deviates
from the established use of language. The one who posits that pleasure is an end
and defends[50] it says what is false for he claims that what does not belong to

pleasure belongs to it. Similarly, the one who says that motion occurs through the void says what is false, too; and also the one who posits atomic magnitudes as well as the one who generates bodies from surfaces, the one who posits the

10 soul as separate and immortal, and the one who says that only the fine is good, just as the one who says that twice two is five.

A deviation from the established use of language occurs when someone who knows the underlying nature, whatever it is,[51] does not call it with its usual and established name, but coins new names and uses them in an idiosyncratic way, just as those who say that only the wise is rich or beautiful[52] or noble or an orator.[53] For these people call the [features] belonging to the wise 'richness' or 'beauty' or 'nobility' not ignoring what these are, but by deviating from the established use of language. For richness and beauty are not attributed based on virtue, but the former based on possessions and belongings, and beauty based on the symmetry of the anhomeomerous parts in the animal.

If doing this is a mistake, the one who has explained that something like this

20 occurs in the problem would have refuted it. But he[54] resorted to a blatant and striking example for this mistake, calling the plane tree 'human being':[55] for if one allows himself to deviate from the established use of language completely, he will also call the plane tree 'human being'. And the one saying that the plane tree is human in the belief that it is [a] mortal rational animal would say something false and would be caught in the first mistake we talked about; whereas the one naming such a tree in this way would deviate from the established use of names. And he mentioned this to show that this, too, – and not just saying something false – is a mistake; and demolitions of problems based on this mistake may occur as well.[56]

<Chapter 2>

109a34 One topos *is to check whether [the interlocutor] has given as an accident what belongs [to the subject] in any other way.*

31 Having said that one must begin with universally destructive *topoi*, he presents

135,1 the first *topos* of this sort. For through this *topos* one shows that what has been given as an accident is not an accident: for it is not possible that any of the [properties] belonging to something in any other way belongs to it as an accident.[57]

We must not ignore that Theophrastus says that there is a difference between a precept and a *topos*. For a precept is what is said to be more common and more universal and simpler, from which the *topos* is found: for the precept is a principle of a *topos* in the same way as the *topos* is [a principle] of an attack. For example, a precept is what is formulated in this way, e.g. that one must attack from the contraries, or from the coordinates. A *topos*, instead, is, for example: 'if one of the contraries is said in several ways, then also the other contrary is'; or 'if the contrary belongs to the contrary, then also the contrary belongs to the contrary';[58] and again 'as one of the coordinates, so also the others'. For the *topos* is already a   10 certain proposition[59] that has come to be from the precept. And seeing this difference between precept and *topos*, Theophrastus calls such things as the aforementioned first *topos* 'precepts' or 'preceptive *topoi*'. For that 'one must check whether [the interlocutor] has given as an accident what belongs [to the subject] in any other way' is preceptive. A *topos* deriving from it would be the one saying: 'if what has been given as an accident belongs [to the subject] in any other way, it has not been given well'; or even more appropriately: 'if what has been given as an accident is a genus or again a definition or a proprium [etc.]'. However, Aristotle calls these things '*topoi*' too because he already took the *topos* together with the precept, and we always establish also the ways in which we call things   20 from the more specific ones: for example, we do not call substance 'being' rather than 'substance', or quantity 'being'; rather, we call it specifically 'quantity'. Since these things, then, are not external to the formula,[60] he calls '*topoi*' also the precepts of this sort.

Given that there are two mistakes that occur in problems, as he said before,[61] i.e. either the mistake of saying something false or that of deviating from the established use of language, the *topos* presented here seems to be rather said with reference to those who deviate from the established use of language, unless one thought that also what belongs to the subject in another way belongs [to it] incidentally. And the *topos* is this: one must check – he says – whether the one who is undertaking the defence of the problem has given as an accident what belongs to the subject in any other way; for who says that what belongs to the subject in any other way 'belongs incidentally'[62] to it does not speak correctly   30 (and it is clear that 'in another way' is understood as: in one other way of those previously spelled out). For it has been shown that anything that belongs to something belongs to it either as a definition or as a proprium or as a genus or as an accident.[63] Therefore, if someone said that what belongs to something as a   136,1 genus or as a proprium or as a definition belongs to it as an accident, it is clear that he should be refuted as making a mistake. In what follows he explains how it is possible to recognise such a mistake. And he says that this mistake mainly occurs about genera. And this is because genera, more than the other [kinds of predicates], seem to bear a certain resemblance to the accident: for proprium and definition belong only to their subject and to all of it, which is also the reason why they convert with the things of which they are [a proprium and a definition respectively]. The genus and the accident, instead, have a greater extension of the thing they belong to and for this reason they are also not predicated instead [of it].

The one who speaks in this way, then, because he really thinks that what belongs to something as a genus belongs to it as an accident would be refuted as someone who says something false. But the one [who speaks in this way]
10   knowing the difference between them[64] and still using language in this way, has to be refuted as someone who deviates from the established use of language. We will recognize that someone is clearly giving as an accident what belongs [to the subject] in some other way if they add 'belongs incidentally' to what is said to belong [to the subject], for example: 'being an animal belongs incidentally to the human being', or 'being a colour belongs incidentally to the white' or 'being a virtue belongs incidentally to justice'; for some people use these expressions in this way, as we have just clarified. But [the same applies] even if 'belongs incidentally' is not added and the predicate is predicated of the subject paronymously as in 'whiteness is coloured': for 'is coloured' is a paronym of colour, which is the genus of whiteness; or again as in 'walking changes': for
20   'changes', too, is a paronym of change, which is the genus of walking. But no predication from the genus is paronymous: for genera are predicated synonymously of the species. For only in the case of accidents the predication is paronymous, as has been shown in the *Categories*:[65] for it has been shown that, of the things that are in some subject (and these were the accidents), some are predicated paronymously and some homonymously. For example, the surface is said to be whitened, the body is said to change and the human being is said to be a grammarian[66] from grammar. Indeed the one who predicates something's genus of the thing [whose genus it is] paronymously would say, through such a predication, that the genus is an accident of that of which it is a genus. For he would not express the genus, given that [the predicate he gives] is predicated paronymously. And still much less will he express a proprium or a definition, given that the predicate can belong to more things [than the subject], if indeed it
30   is a genus, while the proprium and the definition do not belong to anything else. And if what is said is not given as a genus nor as a definition nor as a proprium, it is clear that it has been given as an accident. For the predication from the genera becomes paronymous not if [the genus is predicated] of some of the species or of the individuals falling under the genus, but if it is about some of

those things of which the species of some genus are accidents: for instance, 137,1
'being coloured' is predicated of what has whiteness, and 'changing' of what is
walking and 'being just' of what has justice, but they are not predicated of
whiteness or walking or justice; rather, 'colour' is predicated of the first, 'change'
of the second, and 'disposition' of the third.

*109b9 Nor as a proprium or as a definition: for the definition and the proprium do
not belong to anything else.*

He says that these are distinct from the accident because they belong to their
subject only, not as if he were conceding that the proprium and the definition are
predicated paronymously; rather, he means that it would be shown most clearly
that what has been given is not a proprium or a definition also in virtue of the 10
fact that what has been given is predicated of more things [than the subject],
whereas neither of them is.

For this reason, being is not a genus of things that are either, i.e. because 'to be',
which is paronymous of being, is properly predicated of each of the things that
are: for substance as well as quality and quantity are said to be, and similarly for
each of the other genera; and things that are predicated paronymously of
something are accidents and not genera.[67]

We should also check whether it is ever the case that the predication from
propria, too, occurs paronymously: for [predicates] such as 'capable of laughing'
or 'capable of receiving knowledge' seem to be of this sort. Or, if the proprium is
predicated in conjunction with the genus – as it seems to him[68] –, then the
proprium, too, would be an account and not a name; but paronyms derive from
the name. [We should check this] since, if 'to laugh' or 'to have knowledge' were a
proprium of the human being, then 'capable of laughing' and 'capable of receiving 20
knowledge' would be said paronymously from the proprium. But actually these
things, i.e. those said paronymously, are propria of it, whereas those of which
they are paronyms[69] are not its propria. And indeed the walk is not predicated
of the human being, but 'capable of walking' is predicated of it and is not a
proprium. These cases show that what is predicated paronymously[70] of something
is predicated of it in no other way than as an accident.

Making a move from here, we can refute those who say 'the human being
animalizes', or 'Socrates humanizes', or 'the triangle assumes a certain form', or
'magnitude extends' or 'the animal animates'. And difference, too, is of the sort
of the genus[71] and is not predicated paronymously; still 'rational', despite being
paronymous, is a difference.

138,1   *109b13 One other [topos] is to check the things to all of which or to none of which it was said to belong.*

This *topos*, too, is preceptive. And it takes the attack from division: for – he says – if some problem has been proposed for debate and has been posited either as an affirmative universal or as a negative universal, we have to make a division of the things of all of which or of none of which it has been posited that the predicate is an accident and belongs[72] to them. And we have to check for each of them separately if what has been posited in the problem as belonging to them belongs to them. For if we find out that what has been posited as belonging universally does not belong to some or to all of them, then we will have removed

10   the affirmative universal . For the affirmative universal is removed by the negative particular and by the [negative] universal.

And he also sketches out the way in which the division of what is submitted must be carried out. For he says that we should first make the division into the more general and more proximate species; then, if what we are looking for is not yet known with respect to these, he says that we should divide further each of them into what first falls under them and check. And if it is still not known at this stage, we should proceed further with their division, taking the more general and proximate species, and then keep on doing the same descending down to the indivisible things.[73] With this method, the division will be well articulated and not confused, and the enquiry will not be about everything at the same time, but

20   about fewer and determinate things. In this way, none of the things that ought to be divided and inquired into will be missed by escaping notice. For example, if someone says that the same science is of all opposites, one has to divide the opposites, since these are said in many ways; and, in dividing, one should not proceed directly with the division into the indivisibles (by 'indivisibles' he means the [indivisible] species) – e.g. not into white and black, and double and half. Rather, since there are four types of opposites, we must divide the opposites into these first and see whether what is said is true with respect to each of them. And if still no counterexample comes up, we must further divide each of them, the contraries separately into the indivisible species of contraries, and the relatives separately in turn, and similarly for the opposites according to privation and

30   possession and those according to contradiction. As examples of the division of the contraries he gave the just and unjust things, of the [division] of the relatives the double and half, of the opposites according to possession and privation blindness and sight, of those according to contradiction to be and not to be. And

139,1   if we found out that things are not in that way with respect to some of them, by

showing this we will have demolished [the claim] that the same science is of all opposites. For example, since there is no science of the unlimited, and the unlimited is opposed to the limited (either as contraries or as possession and privation), but there is a science of the limited, it will not be the case that the same science is [of both] of them. But also if we took that there is no science of what is not, since what is and what is not are opposed as affirmation and negation and there is a science of what is, it would not be the case that the same science is [of both] of them. And it is also not the case that the same science is of what is knowable and of what is unknowable, which are opposites according to possession and privation: for it is not possible that there be a science of what is   10
unknowable. But there is no [one and the same science] of what is false and of what is true (which are contraries) or of what is possible and of what is impossible. However, with respect to all relatives, it is necessary that, if one knows one of them, he knows its opposite too, since being for the relatives is the same as being somehow relative to something.[74]

By resorting to this *topos* we will also demolish the problem saying 'every animal breathes'. For we will divide the animal into winged, footed and aquatic, and again each of them; and finding that, of winged animals, insects do not breathe, and, of aquatic animals, fish do not breathe either (these are those having gills: for none of those having gills breathes), we will have removed [the claim] 'every animal breathes'. We will also show that not every virtue is knowledge by dividing virtue into dianoetic and ethical, and by showing that the being of   20
ethical virtues does not consist in cognition. And we will also demolish the problem that no love is noble, which is [a] negative universal, because not every love is mean, by dividing love into eager desire of sexual intercourse (as Epicurus says), which cannot be noble; impulse of making friends caused by the manifestation of beauty (as the Stoics say), or recollection of the once seen beauty (as Plato says);[75] for the latter [two kinds of] love are noble.

One must divide not only the subject term in the problem, but often also the predicate if it admits of division in this way, as in problems of this sort: 'the wise man will not get involved in politics', 'the wise man will not participate in strife'. For if 'to get involved in politics', which is not simple, were divided, one will show   30
that in some sense getting involved in politics is appropriate to the wise man, whereas in another sense it is foreign to him. Similarly 'not <to participate> in strife' can have two meanings, too: either [in the sense that] one should suffer from the illness of a fatherland which is ill, as Solon required,[76] for it is the role of the statesman not to subtract himself from the common misfortune and, in   140,1
this sense, possibly to put an end to a part of a strife, if he appears to be <suffering

together>[77] [with the fatherland] and [to be] in the same situation[78] [as those who are at strife]; or it means that the wise man should not start a strife and become its leader.

Having said: 'for if it has been shown that in some case [the science] is not the same, we will have removed the problem',[79] he added: 'and similarly if it is does not belong to any',[80] showing that the affirmative universal is not removed by the negative particular only, but also by the negative universal; for the universal removes both, i.e. both the universal which is its contrary and the particular which is its contradictory opposite. It is possible that what is said through the [words] 'and similarly if it does not belong to any' is that, in a similar way as the affirmative universal is demolished once one finds something falling under the universal which is not in this way,[81] in the same way, then, if what is posited is a negative universal, one would demolish it if one found that what is posited as not belonging to any belongs to some of the things falling under the universal.[82] In fact, he said before that one should 'check the things to all of which or to none of which it was said to belong'[83] – for example, if it was posited that no animal is rational: for having shown through a division that some [animal] is rational, we will have removed it.

He also says that the aforementioned topos is useful not only for the demolition of an affirmative universal, but also for its establishment. For if having carried out the division it appears that things are in this way in all cases, we would have established the affirmative universal. And if it appeared that things are not in this way in all cases but in most cases (for it is not possible to go through all cases), we will require [from the interlocutor] that either [he] concedes the universal or, in case he does not concede it, that he produces an objection [spelling out] in which case he thinks that it is not so. For it would appear absurd if [the interlocutor] neither conceded the universal nor produced an objection [spelling out] in which case of those signified by and falling under the common term he thinks that it is not so: for example, if the object of the enquiry is whether every animal moves the lower jaw, if we show that this is so in most cases and require that [the interlocutor] either concedes the universal or says in which case this is not so, while he does not do either.

By 'demolishing' and 'establishing'[84] he meant: the affirmative universal. And it is clear that one will establish the affirmative universal when the one who posits the problem says that the predicate belongs to none or not to all – for example, if one posits that not everything that is just is advantageous, or that not every pleasure is good: for it is against such theses that one needs to establish the universal.

And it must be noted that this *topos* is not universally destructive (he said that   141,1
one should first talk only about them);[85] rather, it is destructive of the universal,
but it is also useful for establishing, as he said.

109b30 One other [topos] is to produce the accounts instead of the names of the
accident and of the thing it is an accident of, either of both separately or of one of
them.

This *topos*, which is universally destructive from the definition, is like this: since
the problem against which we make the attacks is, with respect to its genus, a
predicative proposition (for we want to establish or demolish a proposition of   10
this sort), and every predicative proposition is composed of a subject term and a
predicate, and in the problems from the accident the predicate term indicates an
accident, he says that, taking apart the terms of the problems, i.e. the subject and
the predicate, we have to define each of them separately: the accident, which is
the predicate, on its own, and the subject on its own (for this is what 'both
separately' means: [he says this] so that we avoid linking together the definitions
of both – as if, with reference to 'human being walks', we said: 'biped terrestrial
animal moves by using its legs' – and we rather give the definition of each by
separating them). Or, if one of them is obvious, we should define only the other
one, which is not obvious (and this is what 'or of one of them' means), and then   20
see whether anything of what is in the definitions conflicts and cannot belong to
that to which it was posited to belong. For if this is the case, we will demolish the
problem universally. For example, if it is posited by someone that a god can
suffer injustice, if the one who suffers injustice suffers injustice from someone
who commits injustice, one has to define what it is to commit injustice. And,
having taken that it is to damage voluntarily, since it is not possible that the god
be damaged by anybody (for this is reputable and evident), one has to show that
it is not possible that the god suffers injustice either. And having said at the
beginning 'whether it is possible to commit injustice against a god',[86] he made
clear that he took 'committing injustice' instead of 'suffering injustice' by adding
'it is clear that it is not possible that a god suffers injustice'.[87] Again, if there were
someone claiming that the excellent man is envious, one should define who the
envious man is. And we would do this if we first defined what envy is. If envy is   30
indeed pain at the apparent welfare of some fair man, it is clear that the one who
feels pain at the apparent welfare of fair men will be envious. Once this is posited,
since it is patent that feeling pain at the welfare of good men (for the fair are   142,1
good) is foreign to the excellent man, the excellent man would not be envious.

And it is clear that such arguments, having a negative universal conclusion, come about in the second figure.[88] And in this way, if the subject of the problem is known, we will demolish the problem universally by defining the accident of the subject. But we will define both terms of the problem in those cases in which neither is known in itself, as in such cases: e.g., if it were posited by someone that the indignant man is envious. For since in this case the indignant and the envious

10   stand in the same relation to knowledge (for neither of them is obvious in itself), if we define both the indignant and the envious, in this way we will be able to demolish what is posited. For the envious man seems to be the one who feels pain at the welfare of the good (since envy, too, is such a thing), whereas the indignant is the one who feels pain at the welfare of the bad (for indignation is such a thing). If, then, the indignant man is the one who feels pain at the welfare of the bad, but the envious man does not feel pain at the welfare of the bad (for, on the contrary, it is posited that he is the one who feels pain at the welfare of the good), it turns out that the indignant man is not envious. This problem can concern the definition if one enquired into whether the indignant and the

20   envious are the same or not: for he said that problems concerning sameness must be ordered under the definitions.[89]

In this way, it will be shown that the tyrant is not happy, too. For if the tyrant is an unlawful ruler, and happy is the one who is active[90] in accordance with virtue, it is not possible that the tyrant is happy: for ruling unlawfully does not belong to the one who is active in accordance with virtue. And [in the same way it will be shown] that the wise man is not rich, if richness consists in the possession of money, whereas wisdom consists in the possession of virtue.[91]

Since it is often the case that, once the definitions are spelled out, the difference between the defined things is still not obvious because there have been used some words in them which do not indicate the same in each of them but are homonyms, [he][92] requires that one does not stop there, but rather goes on to

30   take the accounts of these very words which appear in the definitions. For in this way the difference obtaining between them[93] will be known, if one comes to know what this common word has been used to signify in each of the definitions.

And he has already said this, in the first book, in the instructions about the *topoi* which he presented for finding the things that are said in many ways. For

143,1 he said so: 'And it often escapes notice that homonymy attends to the accounts themselves; and for this reason one ought to examine the accounts too. For example, if one said that what is a sign of health as well as what produces health is what stands proportionately with respect to health,[94] one should not stop, but should check what he took 'proportionately' to mean in each of them – for

example, if in one case it means being of such quantity[95] as to produce health, whereas in the other case it means being such as to indicate of what sort the disposition is'.[96] If what is posited is that what produces health is a sign of health, if one wants to demolish this claim and, by defining each of them, he finds that each of them is what stands proportionately with respect to health, it will seem that, as far as those accounts go, the given things[97] are the same. But he will find   10
out that this is not the case if he goes on to provide the account of the proportionate in each of them. For he will find out that what is said to be proportionate in the sense of what produces health is proportionate in that it is of a certain quantity, whereas what is a sign of health is proportionate in that it is of a certain quality.

And now he says that one ought to take the accounts given in place of names in the [first] accounts without stopping until one gets to something that is known, not only with reference to those accounts that involve homonymy, but in general whenever the difference between the given things is not yet clear or known because some of the words included in the definitions are unclear. For he prescribes not to stop, but to define the very same words and parts of the account as well as the whole: in this way what is enquired will be known. For example, if someone says that pleasure is good, if the one who wants to demolish this claim   20
defined pleasure as 'smooth change', it would not be known from this account whether it is good or not. But if he went on to define the change which is included in the definition of pleasure and gave as its account 'incomplete actuality', he would be able to show that pleasure is not good because no good is incomplete; but pleasure is incomplete, given that it is change, since every change is incomplete actuality.[98] In this problem, again, the subject term is defined.

And it is clear that we ought to have a great supply of reputable definitions about each thing if we intend to resort to the given *topos*. For in this way we will be able to provide a rendition of the terms in a way that is useful for what is set before us.[99] For example, if it is posited that the wise man will be loved: if we   30
want to demolish this, we will define 'being loved', and will take that it is to take someone's love. And since what is submitted is not yet known, we will proceed to defining love. And for sure if, in defining it, we take that it is an irrational desire of the pleasure deriving from corporeal beauty or that it is an eager desire for sexual intercourse, we would have demolished the problem: for it is clear that   144,1
these things are foreign to the wise man. Similarly, if we define it as strong desire, since 'strong' is unclear, we will replace this in turn with an account; and if 'strong' is what is in contrast with right reason, we would have demolished what is posited in this way as well. If, on the other hand, we give as an account of love

'impulse at making friends caused by the manifestation of beauty'[100] or 'divine inspiration and desire of friendship caused by the appearance of the once contemplated beauty', as Plato wants in the *Phaedrus*,[101] we would have established the problem.

And it is clear that the *topos* will be occasionally useful for the establishment
10   of a universal affirmative claim, too, and not only for demolition.[102] Using this *topos* we will show that god is not angry nor does he feel pain, if being angry is a desire of getting revenge on someone who seems to have committed injustice, and feeling pain is contracting at a present bad, as fearing is contracting at an anticipated bad; but god does not seem to suffer injustice nor does it seem to be the case that something bad can be with him or that he anticipates anything bad. But also, if one is enquiring into whether the soul is immortal, if we defined the soul as intelligible or perceptible breath,[103] we would have shown that it is not immortal: for every breath is perishable. But one would also show that it is not separate from the body, if one defined it as 'actuality of an organic natural
20   body':[104] for no actuality of a body is separate from it. And again, if we took after Plato[105] that its definition is that it is self-moving substance, we would have shown that it is immortal, because the self-moving seems to be always moving, and what is always moving is eternal. But we would also show that the law is excellent if we defined it as 'right reason for the safeguard of those who use it'. And similarly one would show that virtue is teachable, if virtue's definition is 'knowledge about life': for every knowledge is teachable. Whereas it is not yet necessarily the case that every virtue is teachable if its account is 'excellent disposition' or 'disposition from which the thing whose disposition it is is excellent and brings its characteristic actualities to excellence'.

110a10 Furthermore one [ought to] make objections [to a problem] by turning the problem into a premise[106] on his own.

30   This *topos*, too, is preceptive. What it says is this: having changed the problem into
145,1 a universal premise, by submitting this premise to oneself one ought to try to move an objection against it, as we would make objections if someone else submitted it and required to take it. For the very objection which we find against the premise would become a principle and a starting point of an attack for the demolition of the given problem: and this is so since objections against premises are more customary than attacks against problems. And since an objection against universal premises arises from some of the things that fall under the universal, and this is found by looking at the things that fall under the universal, he says that

this is almost the same *topos* as the one mentioned a little earlier,[107] from the 10
division of the universal, in which he said that one should 'check the things to all
of which or to none of which it was said to belong'. For as in that case we demolish
the problem once we have found the thing, of those falling under the universal, to
which it does not belong [starting] from the division of the universal into the
things that fall under it, in the same way in the given case, too, the objection is
raised against the universal premise. For we make an objection once we have
surveyed in thought the things that fall under the universal and having found in
this way the thing, of those falling under the universal, to which it does not
belong. However, this *topos* and that one are not exactly the same; rather, they
differ with respect to their mode,[108] as he said: for in that case we directly carried
out the division of the universal into its proximate species, whereas in this case we
[first] make a premise with the intention of making an objection to that premise.
Since objections against premises are more customary than attacks against 20
problems, we make the objection a principle[109] of the attack against the problem.
For example, if what is posited by someone is that virtue is knowledge, we will
change what is posited into the premise 'is every virtue knowledge?', and, having
submitted this to ourselves, we will look for an objection to it by considering the
species of the virtues. And once we have found that the virtues of the emotional
part of the soul are not of this sort (for they do not come about from teaching, but
through habits, nor does being in them and having them consist in knowing what
they are), turning this objection into an attack, we will use it for the demolition of
the problem by saying: 'Ethical virtues do not consist in knowing what one ought 30
to do nor do they come about through teaching; but every knowledge consists in
knowing what falls under it and comes about through teaching; therefore, no
ethical virtue is knowledge. And, if so, not every virtue is knowledge'. Again, if 146,1
what is posited by someone is that every pleasure is good, we will change the
problem into a premise and we will ask ourselves 'is every pleasure good?'. And
once we have found an objection through the division of pleasures, e.g. that the
pleasures of the immoderate are not good, we will have the objection (which we
found in looking for an objection against the premise on our own) as a starting
point for an attack for the demolition of what is posited in that we ask 'are the
pleasures of the catamites, which are pleasures, also good?'. Perhaps nobody would
concede this, which is at the same time false and disreputable. For once we have
taken this, we would have shown that not every pleasure is good and [that pleasure
is not good] without qualification. We will do something similar also if the 10
problem is that only what is fine is good: for once we have found this as an
objection against the corresponding premise, namely that health, which is good,

is not fine, by using this objection we will demolish the problem. This *topos*, as he said himself too, is only destructive.

110a14 Furthermore, one should determine what things one should call and what things one should not call as the many do.

This *topos*, too, is preceptive. So, he says that one starting point for our attack against problems will also be from the previous determination and agreement about what things we should call by following the use and custom of the many and what things we should not [call in this way]. And this is useful 'both for establishing
20   and for demolishing'[110] problems. For if we have agreed in advance that we should use the names that are customarily used and already given to things and those which the many use (for names are conventional, and it is not the case that everyone is in charge of assigning a name to each thing and to change names as they please: for in this way the common language would be removed, if we were not using some common and customary names to refer to things), whereas [when it comes to establishing] what things (of those for which the common and customary names are used) are of such and such a sort, and why they are so, and what is their measure, then 'we should no longer conform to the many',[111] but to the experts – [if we have agreed in advance about all this], then we would have starting points from this agreement 'both for demolishing and for establishing'.
30   And he made clear what is said through the example. For 'one has to call
147,1 "healthy" what is productive of health, as the many'[112] and custom want: in fact, the many use this word with reference to such a thing. However, one should no longer believe that what is productive of health is what the many think to be such, but rather what doctors do. We have to call 'healthy', then, following the common use of the word, whatever doctors regard as productive of health. Now, if someone, while agreeing that something is productive of health, yet does not call that thing 'healthy', but rather with a different name,[113] he would be refuted based on the presented *topos*, which requires that one use the names of things as the many do. On the other hand, the one who requires that 'productive of health'
10   is said to be what it seems to the many and to random people, this one too would be refuted, because we had agreed in advance that such things should not be discerned and spoken of as the many do, but rather as doctors do.

        From this *topos* one could also attack those things that are called 'paradoxes' by the Stoics. For, given that the many call 'rich' only the one who owns much, if someone uses this word not with reference to this and does not call 'rich' the one who owns much, but rather uses the word with reference to the wise man and the

one who has the virtues, this person would transgress the established boundaries of the use of words. For knowing who is the one who owns much is not a task for the many but for those who investigate such things; but that one has to use the word 'rich' to refer to the one who owns much, [for this] the use of the many is enough. Certainly the one who agrees that someone owns much and yet does   20
not call this 'rich' would not use this word as one should. And neither would the one who uses it with reference to the person who has the virtues. And again, the many call 'lucky' the one who thrives in the goods of fortune; whereas they[114] call 'lucky' the one who has virtue, which is not a good of fortune. Therefore, these people, too, deviate from the appropriate use of words.

And when he said 'one should call "healthy" what is productive of health,'[115] he added 'or[116] as the many say', which is equivalent[117] <to 'or>[118] in whatever way the many may happen to speak'; in fact, the many use the word 'healthy' also with reference to other things, i.e. not only with reference to what is productive of health, but also with reference to what is a sign of it. Alternatively, he said 'in whatever way   30
the many may happen to speak' as to indicate that [this] does not apply to this very word but rather to using the word that the many use: for even if [the word that the many use] were not this one but some other word, one should use that. Alternatively, [the phrase] is not after 'or' and stands separately, i.e. he says 'as the many say': for it is customary for the many to call 'healthy' what is productive of health.

And in the same way in which the aforementioned *topos* is useful for   148,1
demolishing it is also useful for establishing. For if one does not want to concede that those who own much are rich, we will establish this by using [the *topos*] that one should name things as the many do; and the many call these people 'rich'. Similarly, one could object to the one who denies that health is good: for this is the custom. And if, again, someone said that health is good as happiness or as a part of happiness, because this is what the many think, we could demolish this by resorting to the agreement that the many are no longer in charge of this: for such a judgement about health is the task of the excellent.

<Chapter 3>

110a23 Furthermore, if it is said in many ways, and it is posited that it belongs or   10
that it does not belong.

These three *topoi* (i.e. this one and the two that follow) take the starting point of the attack from the things that are said in many ways. Of these [*topoi*], the first one is from the homonyms. For if it is posited that [something] belongs incidentally or that it belongs or does not belong to something absolutely and without specification, he says that, once we have carried out the division for ourselves (and he presented the *topoi* through which we will be able to recognize and divide the things that are said in many ways in the previous book),[119] if we are not able to show the opposite of what is posited with respect to all the things that are signified, we should show it with respect to some of them, i.e. with respect to one case in which [what is posited] does not hold. For having shown

20   [the opposite of what is posited] with respect to this, we will seem to have demolished what was posited because the homonymy escapes notice and what was posited was expressed as if it were said absolutely. For example, if someone posits that the one who is asleep does not have perception, once we have divided for ourselves 'having perception' into 'having perception in actuality' and 'having perception in potentiality', we have to show that the one who is asleep does have perception: for those who have the capacity to perceive are said to have perception. And again, if it is posited that it is appropriate for the excellent man to get involved in politics: having divided for ourselves 'appropriate', which signifies what is fine, what is advantageous and what is necessary (what is necessary, when we say 'it is appropriate that all that comes to be perishes'; what is advantageous, as when we say 'it is appropriate to resort to walks or to

30   such and such a regime'; and what is fine, when we say 'it is appropriate to do just things' or 'to obey the laws' or 'to obey one's parents'), given that it[120] signifies these many things, if we show that getting involved in politics is not advantageous for the excellent man or that it is not necessary for him to get involved in politics, we have to[121] remove what is posited on the ground that 'appropriate' signifies these things.[122] But also if one says that it is not appropriate for the excellent man to get involved in politics, having shown that this is fine

149,1 (for supporting and running in aid of the homeland and providing counselling for the best things is fine: and 'appropriate' signifies this) we would remove what was posited.[123] And again, if someone posits that the virtues entail each other or that they do not entail each other, having divided virtue for ourselves and having taken both natural virtue and virtue based on reason, if we show with reference to the natural virtues that they do not entail each other, we will remove that the virtues entail each other; if, on the other hand, we have shown with reference to the virtues based on reason that they do entail each other, we will remove that they do not entail each other. For since it escapes notice that [one term] is said in many ways, it seems that what is said is said with reference to the same nature with respect to which what was posited in the problem was said too;

for which reason [what is said] is also believed to be capable of removing the latter.[124]

There are, however, cases in which, even if one takes all things that are signified 10 [by an expression that is said in many ways], it is possible to demolish what is posited with respect to all of them: for example, if one says that one should not do philosophy, since both the enquiry into such a thing, i.e. whether one should do philosophy or not (as he himself said in the *Protrepticus*),[125] and the pursuit of philosophical contemplation are said to be doing philosophy, once we have shown that either of these things is pertinent to the human being, we will remove what is posited from every side. In this case, then, it is possible to show what is submitted in both ways; in the first examples, instead, [it was not possible to show the submitted claim] from all or from either case, but rather <from one> or from some [only].[126] And it is clear that in those cases in which it is possible to show the opposite of what is posited with respect to all things that are signified, we have to draw an explicit[127] division of [the term] that is said in many ways.

And he says that one has to resort to this *topos* 'in those cases in which it 20 escapes notice'[128] that what is posited is said in many ways and that, with respect to some of the things that are signified, things are as it is posited, whereas with respect to some other [of the things that are signified] this is not the case. For if it does not escape notice, the defender of the problem will easily object that the opponent does not move the objection against the problem and does not carry out the demolition with reference to what is posited, but rather with reference to something else, giving a reply[129] which only addresses the verbal formulation and is sophistic. Therefore, the one who objects to the one who posits that the animal is ensouled and shows that the painted ones are called 'animals' and yet are not ensouled, turns out to be easy to catch since the ambiguity of the name is obvious and it is utterly clear that the one who posits the claim had not predicated the ensouled of the animal said in this way.[130]

And he says that this *topos* converts: for it is useful both for establishing and 30 for demolishing. In fact, it is not only possible to demolish the posited problem, be it posited affirmatively or negatively, by resorting to it; rather, it is also possible to establish something, i.e. to show in general what is posited, that things are in 150,1 such a way as they are posited. For in this context he calls this 'establishing', i.e. showing in general[131] and not removing what is posited; for 'establishing' is mainly said with reference to what is posited affirmatively. Having said, then, that it is possible to establish and to demolish, and that we will demolish what was posited if we show that it does not belong to some [of the things to which it was posited to belong], and we will establish it if we show that it belongs to some, since the affirmative universal is not established through the particular (for both the affirmative universal <and the negative universal>[132] are demolished through the opposite particulars,[133] but neither the affirmative universal nor the negative

10   universal is established through any of the particulars [falling under them]), he sets out a certain difference between the procedure to establish [the universal] and the procedure to demolish [it]. For it is possible to show some affirmative particular or negative particular, as was said before, by resorting to the division of what is said in many ways. But since the negative particular is sufficient for demolishing the affirmative universal in the same way as the affirmative particular is sufficient for demolishing the negative universal, whereas the affirmative particular is no longer sufficient for establishing the affirmative universal, how will we be able to establish the universal through it? Indeed he says that one has to try to show [it] and to take [it] 'from agreement'.[134] 'From agreement' is what he called towards the end of the first book[135] 'from a hypothesis'

20   (for saying what the enquiry into similarity is useful for, he said 'for inductive arguments and for deductions from a hypothesis'). For [deductions] from agreement are from a hypothesis, as he has shown in the *Prior Analytics*;[136] however, the vice versa is not true.[137] And he spelled out how they come about by adding 'for the reason that it is reputable that, whatever is the case in one of [several] similar cases, the same will be the case in the remaining cases too'.[138] What he called there more generally 'from a hypothesis', then, the same thing he has now called more appropriately 'from agreement'. For since what is shown with respect to some one particular of those falling under something common is not sufficient to establish what is common and universal (in fact, the particular does not show the universal), he says that one has to agree in advance and to establish by convention[139] that, as it is in one case, so it is also in the other cases. For if, having conventionally established in advance that what holds true for

30   some soul, the same also holds true for every soul, we show that some soul[140] is
151,1 immortal, in virtue of the agreement we would have that every soul is immortal, too. Similarly, if we take beforehand that the same that holds for one [type of] perception holds for all, once we have shown for one, e.g. for touch, that it carries out the reception through affection, we would have also that the same holds similarly for the others. The same account applies to the opposites, too: if it is agreed that what applies to some of the opposites, the same will apply to the others as well, once we have shown that the same science is of the relatives or that the contrary comes about from the contrary, it would be posited that the same holds for the other opposites as well.

And he says that one should do this, i.e. dividing and enquiring in what case this is not so and showing from agreement in this way, 'when we do not have the   10 resources'[141] to carry out the argument through something common and applicable[142] to all things that fall under the universal. For if it were possible, one ought to show in that way, as the geometer shows universally that the triangle has angles equal to two right angles, and one ought not to take this through agreement and convention. For if one could show universally that the soul is immortal through [its being] self-moving, one ought to show it in that way. In the same way in which he showed that the affirmative is established from agreement, so it is possible to establish the negative from agreement, too. For if the aim is to show that no soul is immortal, in establishing this we will take that, if whatever soul is mortal, then all souls are as well; and once we have shown that the souls of plants or of irrational animals are mortal we would have that every   20 soul is such, too, in virtue of the agreement.

This is what one ought to do if it escapes notice that [some term] is said in many ways. 'If, on the other hand, it does not escape notice',[143] and it is rather known that [some term] is said in many ways, he says that, once one has carried out its division, one should either show that what is said holds in the same way for all things that are signified and demolish what was posited in this way (as was shown in the case of whether one should do philosophy),[144] or that it does not hold in any of them – if what was posited is affirmative, e.g. if what was posited is that it is appropriate for the wise man to get involved in politics, being known that 'appropriate' is homonymous, having divided it into the things that are signified, 'the fine and the advantageous', by showing that the wise man will not get involved in politics in either of these senses; if, on the other hand, [what was posited is that] it is not appropriate, by showing that it is appropriate for the wise man to get involved in   30 politics in both senses. Or, if it is not possible either to establish or to remove what was posited according to both senses, then one ought to divide and show that, in some sense,[145] things are like this, whereas, in some other sense, things are in the opposite way; but they are not [like this] without qualification, as was posited. For example, it is appropriate for the wise man to get involved in politics in the sense   152,1 that it is fine, but it is not appropriate in the sense that it is advantageous: in this way we will have shown that neither [claim holds][146] without qualification.

And having said with reference to the case in which two things are signified that 'in one sense [it is so], in the other [it is] not [so]',[147] he added: 'and the same account applies even if the ways into which [the term which is said in many ways] is divided are more than two'; for we will say similarly: 'in some senses it is the case, in some other senses it is not the case'.

110b16 And again, as for those things that are said in many ways not based on homonymy, but in another way.

Since of the things that are said in many ways some (which we call 'homonyms') present an ambiguity in single words and some (which they used to call 'amphibolous') in a phrase,[148] having said how one has to lead the attack against
10   the problems in which some homonym is posited, he now talks about those that have an ambiguity in their phrase, i.e. the amphibolous ones, and sketches how we will demolish or establish a problem also in these cases. For since the phrase saying 'the same science is of many things' signifies more than one thing and is amphibolous[149] – for one and the same science is of many things in the sense that it is of the end and of the means for that end: e.g. domestic economy is a science of both the house as its end and of the things through which a house comes to be, which are means to an end; the same [science] is, then, of many things. Similarly, medicine is of health and of the things that produce health, e.g. regime, surgery, cauterizations. And again, one science is said to be of many things also in the sense that it is of many ends, as we say that the same science is of the
20   contraries: medicine is of health and disease, music of the attuned and of the out of tune, gymnastics of good and bad physical condition; for the one who has knowledge of both good and bad physical condition does not know the two of them the one as what produces [an end] and the other as an end, but knows both of them as ends. For in the same way in which good physical condition is the end of things that relate to good physical condition, so bad physical condition, too, is the end of things that relate to bad physical condition. If, then, gymnastics is the science of both these things, it would be a science of two ends; for even if the knowledge and production of bad physical condition is not the end of training, nonetheless bad physical condition is an end; so that the person who has knowledge of it will have knowledge of it as an end, too. For good physical condition is not more of an end for things relating to good physical condition than bad physical condition is an end for things that bring about bad physical condition. And again, in a different sense one science is said to be of many things
30   when it is of one thing in its own right and of another thing incidentally:[150] for a science is said to be not only of the things of which it is principally, but also of the things that belong to the latter[151] incidentally. For example, medicine is,
153,1 principally, knowledge of health, but, incidentally, it is also [knowledge] of good complexion and of easiness in breathing, which belong incidentally to health and to the person who is healthy – and [, incidentally, it is also knowledge] of being: for this belongs incidentally to health too.[152] And again, medicine knows,

in its own right, that the one who cannot breathe has to relax or that the one who is ill has to eat light food, whereas it knows incidentally that one should take some of these things as relaxing means, e.g. honey and milk, or that one should be nourished with these things since they are light, e.g. fish: for being relaxing belongs incidentally to that drink and being light and easily digestible belongs incidentally to this food. And the geometer knows, 'that the triangle has' its angles 'equal to two right angles in its own right',[153] whereas he knows 'that the equilateral triangle [has its angles equal to two right angles] incidentally':[154] for it does not have its angles equal to two right angles insofar as it is equilateral, but insofar as it is a triangle, and [being a triangle] belongs to the equilateral one.   10 Knowing, then, that [this property belongs to it] in its own right in as much as it is a triangle, he knows that the equilateral [has this property] incidentally:[155] for being equilateral belongs incidentally to the triangle.

Since, then, this phrase[156] signifies more than one thing and is amphibolous, as has been shown, one has to proceed in the case of such a phrase and, in general, in cases of amphiboly in the same manner as in cases of homonymy. For if we have shown that the science of these things, which are many, is not one in any sense,[157] we would have removed universally [the claim] that the same science is of many things. Or, having shown that it is not of these things, which are many, in some sense, we would have removed [the universal claim] that every [science is of many things] in this way too. And again, if what was posited was that this science is not of these things, which are many, once we have shown that in some sense this very science is of these things, which are many, we would have   20 removed what was posited again. For example, if someone says that medical science is of health and good physical condition, if we show that it is not of the one of them as of what is productive of [the end] and of the other as of an end, nor of both of them as ends (for good physical condition is not contrary to health nor is it the end of things opposite to the healthy ones, which are precisely the unhealthy things: but the same science is of many things understood as ends in this way); nor in the sense that it is of the one in its own right and of the other incidentally (for good physical condition does not belong incidentally to health), we would have removed what was posited. Again in a similar way, if someone says that the art of building is knowledge of the house and of health. And one should proceed in all cases of amphiboly which are of some interest[158] as in the   30 case of this example.

So, he says that, in drawing the division of things of this sort and said in this way, one does not have to carry out the division into all the things that are signified, but [only] into those that are useful for what is submitted. For if our aim is to establish the problem, we have to carry out the division into the things with respect to which we will be capable of showing what is submitted and of establishing it. If, on the other hand, [our aim is] to demolish, again we have to

154,1 take the things with respect to which we would be able to show that what is posited as belonging [to them] does not belong [to them]. For if it is posited that medicine is of health and of good complexion, one has to demolish the problem by dividing [the phrase] that the same science is of many things either in the sense that it is of many ends or in the sense that it is of one thing as an end and of another thing as a means to an end (for medicine is of both health and good complexion in neither of these senses).[159] If, on the other hand, someone says that medicine is not of health and good complexion, [one has to remove the problem] by showing that one science is of several things and that, when [one takes this claim in the sense that it is] of one thing in its own right and of another thing incidentally, in this way, then, medicine is of the given things too.

One can also understand [the words] 'to divide into as many ways as it is

10 useful'[160] as if this were said in general about all things that are said in many ways, as it seemed to some people, and not as just about [the claim] that one single science is of several things. For given that [the claim] 'I know of everybody who got more pebbles that he won'[161] can be taken in either of two senses (for either the respect in which this is determined is universal or [the claim is that one knows] everybody [who got more pebbles] individually, which is not possible), leading the argument to this one has to show: 'and yet you do not know this particular person who won; therefore, you do not know all those who won and got more pebbles'. This is similar to what Theophrastus mentions in his work *About the number of ways [things are said]*,[162] 'to know of every triangle that its three angles are equal to two right angles': for 'every' is taken either universally[163] or individually with reference to each single triangle.[164] If, then, we want to demolish [the claim] that the geometer knows of every triangle that it has its

20 three angles equal to two right angles, we have to drag the argument to [the claim] about each single individual (for [the original claim] signifies this too) and, taking that of the object of which one does not know that it is a triangle one does not know that it has angles equal to two right angles either, having produced a certain particular one has to say: 'But you do not know this; therefore, you do not know whether it has angles equal to two right angles; therefore you do not know every [triangle]'. He says that one has to carry out the division in these cases, too, as in cases of homonymy, 'if it escapes notice in how many ways it is said'.[165] For if it is known in how many ways [something] is said, we will be caught in the act of diverting something and of carrying out the division aiming at what is useful

to us. When, then, the things that are signified are known, if we set out all things with respect to which we will show that this holds and the things with respect to which it cannot hold, as he said in the case of the homonyms, if it is not possible   30
to show that this holds in all cases, in this way we will not give the impression that we <lack resources>[166] in arguments about the problem.

110b33 And one should establish that this is or is not of this from the same topoi.   155,1

Having used an example of amphiboly, i.e. that the same science is of several things, and having shown in how many senses it is possible to say that the same science is of several things (i.e. either because it is of an end and of the means to an end or because it is of the opposites as ends or because it is [of several things] in the sense that it is of what is in its own right and of what is incidentally'),[167] he says that, in general, one should establish or demolish [the claim] that 'this is of this,'[168] too, from these *topoi*. For example, if we want to establish that medicine is productive of health or, more generally, that a science is[169] of something, we will show, based on some of these [*topoi*], that medicine, being a science, is   10
productive of health – or whatever the object of the argument[170] is. For either it is [of it] in the sense that it is of an end, e.g. of health (and it would be of disease in the same way, in as much as the latter is the contrary of the end), or in the sense [that it is of what is] with respect to an end, e.g. of some of the things that bring about health, or in the sense that [it is of something] incidentally, e.g. of good complexion.[171] So, if medical science is not of what is submitted as of what contributes to the end nor as of an end nor incidentally, then medical science would not be of what is submitted to start with. That medical science is certainly not of melodies and rhythms, [this] we show through [the claims] that neither do these things contribute anything to the end of medicine nor are they its ends nor do they belong incidentally to any of them, i.e. either to the end or to some of the means to the end. Similarly, if one says that rhetoric is a science of   20
just things, having shown that [it is not a science of them] as of an end (for this is not the end of rhetoric) nor as of what is productive of an end (for just things are not productive of the end of rhetoric), we would have demolished the problem; for they are not even its concern incidentally: being just does not belong incidentally to the end of rhetoric. Again, if desire is said to be of something, it would be [of something] either as of its end or as of the means to an end or incidentally: for desire would be of this thing 'either as of an end (e.g. of health), or as of the means to an end'[172] (e.g. of surgery and purgation, through which health comes about), or incidentally (e.g. as the sugar-addicted desires

wine: not in as much as it is wine, but because it is sweet, and for this reason he
30   desires it as a sugar-addicted; for being wine belongs incidentally to the object
which is desired by him – and this was the sweet. For that he does not desire
it in that it is wine is clear from the fact that the sugar-addicted does not desire
156,1 dry wine, although this very thing is wine nonetheless. The same point
would be shown through [the claim] that he desires something sweet which is
not wine).[173]

[The words] 'and [about] all other things that are said of several things'[174] are
added so that the account does not apply to science only or to desire or to those
things only that are of several things in the ways spelled out before (i.e. either as
of an end or as of the means to an end or incidentally), but also in case some
other things are of several other things of some sort and not of these, as
perception is: for, while being of several things, it is of things other [than those
mentioned before]. In fact, perception is of several things because it is of what is
proper or of what is common or of what is incidental. And <these very things
show>[175] in this way, say, that hearing is not receptive of colours: for neither it is
[receptive of them] as of its proper perceptible (sounds are its proper perceptible)
10   nor as of a common perceptible (colour is not a common perceptible: for what is
proper to some perception is not common), nor incidentally (colour does not
belong incidentally to sounds). You could also show that the void is not a cause
of change: for, given that 'cause' is said in four ways, the void is not a cause of
change in any of these ways.

And he says that this *topos* is useful 'in the case of relatives':[176] for we say that
something is of something and that one thing is of another in the case of relatives.
In this way, even if someone says that someone desires disease, we will demolish
[this] once we have shown that it is not possible that someone desires disease as
an end or as the means to an end or in some incidental way.

<Chapter 4>

111a8 Furthermore replacing with a better known word.

20   The *topos* is from replacement. For since everything becomes easier to attack
once it has become clearer, he says that one has to replace what is less clear with
what is clearer and try to attack in this way: for the attack against what is clear
can avail itself of more resources. And the replacement with what is clear is
similarly useful for destructive as well as for constructive purposes: for if we

want to demolish or to establish something we will show [it] more easily once we have carried out the replacement with what is clearer. For if we want to demolish [a claim] and show that the excellent man is not engaged with many things,[177] we will demolish what is submitted more easily once we have replaced 'engagement with many things' with 'meddlesomeness'. For the man who is engaged with many things does not quite seem to display an obvious fault, if 'engaged with many things' is the one who loiters around several things, but this can also 30 happen to someone by chance; the meddlesome man, instead, already displays a disposition and a peculiarity about things and a zeal and a choice which is 157,1 foreign to the excellent man. And again, if we want to establish that every conception[178] of the excellent man is exact, since it is not quite known what being exact is (for it seems that it signifies also what is necessary: for an exact [conception] seems to be one which comes about through what is necessary, which is a property that not every conception of the excellent man has; for the excellent man also has conceptions about possible things), by replacing 'exact' with 'clear' or 'true' we will show what is submitted more readily; for every conception of the excellent man is clear and articulated and true. Similarly, against those who set out some of their own conceptions about something, e.g. about pleasure, [saying] what sort of thing this seems to be to them. The one who says that his own conception is exact does not quite speak intelligibly; but if 10 he replaces 'exact' with 'clear', he would make what he says intelligible.

It is also possible to show that the excellent man is meddlesome by replacing 'meddlesomeness' with 'engagement with many things' (for enquiring and investigating into the celestial bodies and natural beings is engaging with many things: but this is what the excellent man does), and that the conception of the excellent man is not clear by replacing 'clear' with 'exact': for if what is exact is necessary, and not every conception of the excellent man <is necessary, then not every conception of the excellent man>[179] would be exact, so that it would not be clear either. By using this *topos* it is possible to show that the excellent man is not moderate once we have replaced 'moderate' with 'self-controlled': for if the parts of 20 the soul of the self-controlled are not in harmony with each other, whereas those of the excellent man are, it would turn out that the excellent man is not self-controlled: so that he would not be moderate either, if moderation and self-control are the same. And again, one will be able to show that the excellent man is self-controlled once he has replaced 'self-control' with 'moderation',[180] if the being of the excellent man consists in the mutual agreement of the powers of his soul, and the mutual agreement of the powers of the soul is moderation. In this way, Demosthenes too, when he wanted to establish that no gratitude was due to Philip for the things he had given, replaced 'gave' with 'gave back'.[181] And Thucydides, too, when he wanted to urge the Athenians against the inhabitants of Mytilene, replaced their 'revolt' with a 'rebellion'.[182] And the customary use [of language] provides ample evidence of this procedure,[183] since we always replace words with more emphatic ones: 'cut' with 'cut up', 'eat' with 'devour', 'smile' with 'laugh'. People also turn the cunning into the wise, the reckless into the courageous, and the mild into the idle and inactive, the liberal into the profligate, and the frugal into the stingy. In this way, too, Callicles in Plato's *Gorgias*[184] turns the wise into the foolish.

158,1

111a14 And in order to show that the contraries belong to the same [subject].

10 He presents us a *topos* which we will be able to use for the problems in which one aims at showing that the contraries belong to the same subject, for example [if one aims at showing] about perception that correctness and mistakenness[185] belong to it or about conception that truth and falsehood belong to it. And this *topos* says that one should check whether the contraries belong to the genus of what is submitted, whatever its genus is. And if this is the case, we should use it[186] to show that the contraries apply to what is submitted as well. For example, since perceiving is a certain kind of discerning (discernment is the genus of perception: for we discern not only through perception but also through intellect), and it is possible to discern correctly or mistakenly, it would turn out that both belong to perceiving as well. Again, if there is false and true conception, so there would be [false and true] opinion: for opinion is a species of conception. In this way, then,

20 it is possible to show about the species that the contraries belong to it by making a move from the genus.

And it is also possible to produce an argument the other way round, from the species about the genus. For if one enquires into whether disposition[187] is poor and excellent,[188] once we have found that both these [contraries] apply to some species of disposition, we would show that they both belong to the [genus] disposition too. For example, since craft is a species of disposition (for not only sciences and crafts, but also virtues are dispositions), and being poor and being excellent belong to the craft (for, of crafts, some are poor and some are excellent: he uses himself the word 'science'[189] in a rather general sense, instead of 'craft'), both being poor and being excellent would belong to the [genus] disposition, which is the genus of craft. Again in a similar way: if false and true belong to

30 opinion, they would also belong to conception.

And having said that one can establish that the opposites belong to something, i.e. both to the species starting from the genus and to the genus starting from the

species, he says that the one[190] which moves from the genus to the species and 159,1
requires that, since the opposites belong to the genus, then they will also belong
to its species, is false, whereas the one moving from the species to the genus is
true.[191] And he gives the reason for this. And the reason is that it is not necessary
that 'the things belonging to the genus also belong to the species';[192] and for this
reason the first one is not true. For the things that are in the substance[193] of the
genus and cover up[194] its being, these things necessarily belong to the species as
well, since genera are predicated synonymously of the species. But the things
which belong as accidents to the genus, it is not at all necessary that these belong
to each of its species as well. For also those things that belong incidentally to one
determinate species of the genus or are in its substance are said to belong 10
incidentally to the genus: for example, the white belongs incidentally to the
animal, since the swan, which is an animal, is white, but it is not the case that, for
this reason, it belongs to all things that fall under the [genus] animal. And indeed
it is not necessary that things that are said to belong incidentally to the genus in
this way also belong incidentally to the species. But it is also not [necessary] that
the things that belong to the genus in virtue of being in the substance of some
species [also belong] to some [other species] falling under it. But the opposites,
too, belong to the genus as accidents: for it is not possible that the opposites
belong in the substance of some genus (for in this way the opposites would
be together and inseparable from each other); rather, it is because, of the things
that fall under the genus, some are of this kind and some of that kind (e.g.
some are excellent and some are poor, or some are white and some are black)
that the opposites are said to be in the genus. But also being divided by opposite 20
differences belongs to the genus in this way: for being quadruped and not being
quadruped are in the genus in this way.[195]

For this reason, showing that the opposites belong to its genus is not sufficient
for showing that the opposites belong to the species. However, the one who has
shown that the opposites belong to the species of some genus will have shown, in
general, that they belong to its genus too. For, since the species is under the genus,
it is necessary that all things that belong to the species be also in the genus and
under the genus: for it is universally true that things that are in the species are
also in the genus. For if being in something were the same as belonging to the
whole of it, it would not be true that things that are in the species are also in
the genus: for example, rational and biped are in [the species] human being, but 30
would not be in [the genus] animal any longer, since they do not belong to the
whole animal.[196] Nor would the white be in [the species] human being, since it is
not in all of it: for then the contrary would be true, that the things that are in the

genus are also in the species. But since [being in something and belonging to it all] are not the same (the species is in the genus in which it is, and the human being is in the animal, but it is not the case that every animal is a human being, nor that the whole genus is the species), it is necessary to agree that the things that are in the species are also in the genus, being contained by it.[197]

160,1

And having shown that, with respect to establishing a claim, the *topos* establishing something about the species from the genus is false, whereas the one establishing something about the genera from the species is true, he says that things are the other way round with respect to demolitions. For the one[198] showing that what does not belong to the genus does not belong to the species either is true: what is not in the animal at all is not in the human being either. On the other hand, the one trying to show that what does not belong to the species does not belong to the genus either, is false: the quadruped or the irrational does not belong to [the species] human being, but it is nonetheless not true that, for this reason, it does not belong to [the genus] animal either.

10

And the reason for this is that the genus has a larger extension than the species: for it is not necessary that what belongs to what is more extended than something else also belongs to what is less extended and falls under it, if it does not belong to the whole of what is more extended. But it is necessary that what belongs to what is less extended and belongs under something common, this belong also to what is more extended and encompasses it. Vice versa, what does not belong to what is more extended would not belong to anything that falls under it either: for if it belongs to what is less extended, it is necessary that the species be in that which is precisely the genus.[199] And if something does not belong to what is less extended, it is not necessary that it does not belong to what is more extended: for it is possible that it be in the latter[200] by belonging to some other of the things that fall under the genus. For example, since being inanimate does not belong to the animal, it does not belong to any of the things under the animal either; similarly, since being without perception does not belong to the animal, it does not belong to any of its species either. And if someone, trying to dispute what has been said, claims that being under the animal belongs to the human being while it does not belong to the animal (for the animal is not under the animal), one must say that being under the animal belongs to the animal as well. For if it belongs to some animal, then it belongs <to the animal>[201] as well: and being under the animal, too, belongs to the human being, which is a certain animal; so that [it will belong] to [the genus] animal as well; for it was not posited that this, i.e. that which is in the whole of it, is in something.[202]

20

111a33 And since it is necessary that also some of the species be predicated of the things of which the genus is predicated.

The *topos* is of this sort: since genera are not in their own right, but have their being in the very species of which they are predicated,[203] it is necessary that, if the genus is predicated as a genus of something, then also some of its species be predicated of it, if it is not a proximate species[204] of the predicated genus: for example, the animal is predicated of the winged animal, but it is not the case that also one of the species is predicated of it, since it[205] is itself a proximate species of the animal. [Aristotle] omitted this addition because it was not useful for the presented *topos*. Alternatively: the species is predicated of it also in this case,[206] if it is true that it is predicated of itself, and this is itself a species of the animal. So, since genera are of such a nature, he says that necessarily, with respect to the things that are said to have a certain genus, i.e. the things to which a certain genus is said to belong and to belong incidentally, in general also some of the species of the genus belong and belong incidentally to these things. But also with respect to the things that are said paronymously from some genera[207] (and the things to which a certain genus belongs incidentally are said in this way), it is necessary that these things be said paronymously from some of the species of that genus, too. For example, if knowledge is said to belong to something, it is necessary that also some species of those falling under knowledge belong to it, either music or grammar or some other [species of knowledge]: for if no species of knowledge belongs to something, neither does knowledge belong to it in general. But even if someone is called paronymously from knowledge, as the one who is knowledgeable, it is necessary that this, too, be said paronymously from some of the species of knowledge: for this person is either a grammarian or a musician or a geometer or is called after some other [species of] knowledge. For if he is not called after any, he will not be called knowledgeable to start with.

Having taken the universal and having said 'e.g. if knowledge is predicated of something, also grammar or music or some other [species of knowledge] will be predicated',[208] he moved on to the things that are predicated as accidents, where he says 'and if someone has knowledge or is spoken of paronymously from knowledge':[209] for when knowledge is predicated of something in this way, i.e. by belonging to it incidentally and by being something that the thing has,[210] it is necessary that also some of the forms of knowledge which are species of knowledge be predicated of it. For since this is universally true, i.e. that of the object of which some genus is predicated also some species is predicated and it is not possible that some genus be in existence[211] unless some of its species is, it

30

161,1

10

20

30

turns out to be also true that to the thing to which some genus is said to belong incidentally also some of [the species] of that genus belongs incidentally, and [this is so] either if one formulates the predication of the genus by adding that

162,1   it belongs and belongs incidentally, or if one does not add that it belongs[212] and rather uses paronymous expressions from the genus: for paronymous predications, as he said also at the beginning of this book,[213] are from accidents.

111b4 If, then, [the interlocutor] posits something said from the genus in whatever way.

'In whatever way'[214] means 'either paronymously or by adding that the genus belongs[215] to it'. And he resorted to a case of paronymy as an example: for the one who says 'the soul changes'[216] predicates changing, which is a paronym of change, of the soul. Similar considerations apply if someone says that changing belongs

10   or belongs incidentally to the soul. So, if the problem is of this sort , by looking at the species of change (and these are increase, decrease, locomotion, alteration, generation and corruption: he now calls these, too, 'changes' more generally, in the same way in which [he] also [says] that change itself is a genus),[217] one has to <check whether>[218] it is then possible to make a paronymous predication of the soul from some of these (for then it would be established that it changes), e.g. whether the soul comes to be or passes away, whether it increases or decreases, whether it is altered, whether it moves. If none of these is possible, then what was posited at the beginning would be removed too, i.e. that it changes. If, then, as according to Xenocrates, the soul is a self-changing number, it would either increase itself or decrease or alter or move or corrupt or generate [itself]. But neither does something increase itself (for what is increased is increased by

20   something which is added and which is external to what is increased; furthermore, the [number] which is increased or decreased or altered would turn into another number and would abandon its proper substance and its being the number that it was).[219] Nor is it possible that something generates or corrupts itself; nor is it possible that something is moved by itself. So that [it is] not [possible that] that number [does this] either. Alternatively, in this way the definition of the soul would be demolished and the problem would concern the definition.[220] And if someone says that changing belongs incidentally to the soul, which is a substance, once we have shown that it does not increase nor decrease nor move in place nor come to be or pass away (for it is not possible that any incorporeal object be

163,1   affected in any of these ways), if we have shown that it is not altered either (for alteration concerns perceptible differences, which the soul does not receive since it is incorporeal), we would have demolished what was posited. But also if someone said that the god feels emotions, then he has to feel pleasure or pain or fear or desire; if, then, it makes sense that none of these belongs to the god, it would also be removed that he feels emotions. Again, if someone says that the one who errs errs involuntarily, then they have to err either through coercion or through ignorance; for these are the species of the involuntary.[221] And if through coercion, the cause [of the action] has to be external and [the agent] does not have to contribute anything to it, for such is [acting] through coercion; if through ignorance, then [the agent] has to be ignorant concerning the particular circumstances in which the action takes place: for the one who errs in ignorance   10 of the universal, even if he errs without knowing [something], does not err through ignorance but through himself, for he himself is responsible for this type of ignorance, as he has shown in the third book of the *Nicomachean Ethics*.[222] For this reason [such an agent] is not excused. If, then, the acratic man does not err through coercion or ignorance, he does not err involuntarily. In this way [the claim] that mistakes are involuntary would be removed.

It is furthermore clear that the *topos* is useful both for destructive and for constructive purposes. For having shown that none of the species of the genus belongs to the submitted subject, we would have removed the problem; if, on the other hand, it is shown that some of the species of the genus belongs to the submitted subject, it would be established that the genus belongs to it.

111b12 For the one who does not have the resources for an attack against the   20 *thesis.*

It seems that he has mentioned the *topos* from the definitions already in what was said before, where he said 'another [*topos*] is to produce the accounts of the accident and of the thing of which it is an accident, either of both separately or of one of them'.[223] For in that *topos* he required to make attacks from the definitions as from things that are more evident, and here he says the same. But this [procedure] does not concern the definition; rather, it consists in demolishing or establishing the accident through a definition, whereas [the problems that] concern the definition are those in which one enquires into whether what was posited is a definition; but the use of the definition does not concern the definition. What is added by means of this *topos* would be that one has to resort to several definitions of the same thing, not in the sense that there are several   164,1 definitions of the same thing in truth, but rather according to opinion: for this reason he added 'or of those that seem [to be such, i.e. definitions]'.[224] For [the *topos*][225] requires that, having taken (among the available definitions of what is posited) the definition that is more useful for what is submitted, we have to lead the attack against the posited problem (which he called 'thesis'[226] again) starting from this, whether one is establishing it or demolishing it.

And the attack from the definitions is simple and has several starting points. For example, if what was posited is that infinite things are equal, we have to define the equal in such a way that it is useful for us with respect to what is submitted. For this reason, if one is demolishing the problem, one has to define 'equal are the things which are [made] of equal units of measure'; for it is not possible that infinite things be equal in this way, since they are not measurable to
10   start with. If we want to establish it, instead, [we have to define] '[equal] are the things which neither exceed [each other] nor are deficient [with respect to each other]':[227] for also infinite things stand in this relation to each other.

And [the *topos*] requires that those who do not have the resources for attacks take several definitions of the same thing: for the discovery of the [means] relevant to what is submitted will be easier if one starts with several [definitions]. For example, if one is enquiring into whether pleasure is good, one has to provide several definitions of pleasure, e.g. that it is smooth change,[228] that it is a perceived coming to be to nature,[229] that it is irrational diffusion,[230] that it is unimpeded activity of a disposition according to nature[231] or that it is the end that follows upon complete activities.[232] For once several definitions have been given, it will be easier for us to find the resources for establishing or for demolishing [what was submitted]. It is therefore possible, starting from the given definitions about
20   pleasure, to attack both that it is not good and that it is good.

It is possible that 'for the one who does not have the resources for an attack'[233] was said not to recall some other *topos* but to add [something] to what was said before. For if by dividing the genera into the species we are not yet able to remove the problem clearly because there remains some controversy about the species as well (at least, those who claim that the soul changes deny that they have to accept the claim of those who say that it does not go through alteration: for it does go through alteration when it gets angry or is in pain and in pleasure, when it learns, remembers and formulates an opinion) – since, then, this seems to be controversial, whether it is the soul itself which is affected by these things or the bearer of the soul (i.e. the man who gets angry or is in pain), as we claim, he says
30   that, leaving this aside, we have to define 'changing', whatever it is. And having taken the given definitions of changing and having selected among them the most useful for what is submitted, we have to lead the attack starting from this
165,1   – e.g., that changing is shifting from one place to another: for if it is posited that

changing is such a thing, it is not possible that the soul changes, for a shift in place is a prerogative of bodies.

111b17 And one should consider, with reference to what is submitted, what is such that, if it is the case, what is submitted necessarily is.

The *topos* is from consequence. And it is twofold: for it is both constructive and 6
destructive. For once a certain problem, which we want to establish or to demolish, is submitted, he says that we have to consider and look for what this submitted thing follows upon and, the other way round, what things follow upon 10
it in this way. And if we want to establish it, we have to show that something of those it follows upon is the case: for in general, if that is posited, this one will be too, since it follows upon the former; for if the antecedent, then also the consequent according to the first so-called indemonstrable, which is constructive from consequence.[234] For example, if the problem is whether every pleasure is good or not, and we want to show that every pleasure is good, we have to look for what [the claim] that every pleasure is good follows upon, and we have to establish that: for example, if it follows upon [the claim] that every pleasure is according to nature, we have to show that the latter is the case: for once this will have been shown, also [the claim] that every pleasure is good will be shown together with it.[235] Similarly if it were established that every pleasure is choiceworthy, that every pleasure is good would follow again. And in this way 20
Plato, too, in the *Phaedo*,[236] intending to show that souls are in Hades and survive, took that upon which he believed this to follow, i.e. that the living come to be from the dead; and he established this through [the claims] that the contraries come to be from the contraries, and that being alive and being dead are contraries. And indeed in the *Meno*[237] again, intending to show that the virtues are teachable, he took that upon which this follows; and this is [the claim] that they are [forms of] knowledge: for if the virtues are [forms of] knowledge, then the virtues are teachable. And [the claim] which he took could be established in this way: the man who is in the best disposition with respect to the soul has knowledge of all appropriate and due things; but the man who has the virtues is in the best disposition with respect to the soul; therefore, the man who has the virtues has 30
knowledge of all due things; therefore, virtue is knowledge of all due things.[238] And it is possible to show the same [claim] in this way as well: the thing through the presence of which one has knowledge,[239] this is knowledge; but it is through 166,1
the presence of virtue that people come to know the things that are due; therefore, virtue is knowledge.[240]

In fact, the rhetoricians resort to this *topos* on several occasions. For example, if they are accusing someone of murder, they show the things upon which this follows, e.g. that the accused is hostile, that he is treacherous, that he was seen carrying a sword at that time and at that place on several occasions. And when they accuse someone of adultery, they establish that the accused makes an effort to look good; for that seems to follow. In this way also those who establish that there is void in the conviction that this follows upon [the existence of] change take that there is change. So, if we establish the problem upon which the submitted claim follows, we will have shown the latter.

If, on the other hand, we intend to demolish [what is submitted], we will take for demolition the things that follow upon what has been submitted to us, and,
10 having shown that those things are not the case, we would have demolished what was submitted as well. For if not the consequent, then neither the antecedent, according to the second so-called indemonstrable, which is destructive from consequence. For example, if our task is to show that not every pleasure is good, once we have shown that what follows upon [the claim] that every pleasure is good is not the case, we would have shown what was submitted. For example, that also the pleasures of the catamite are good follows upon [the claim] that every pleasure is good; if we take that the former is not the case, we would have removed that every pleasure is good. And again, if we intend to show that the diagonal is not commensurate to the side, once we have taken what follows upon
20 [the claim] that it is commensurate and shown that this is absurd, we remove that the diagonal is commensurate to the side. For that the odd are equal to the even follows upon it, as it was shown in the commentary on the *Analytics*.[241] But this is impossible; therefore, also the [claim] upon which this one follows is impossible. And again, one we have shown that [the claim] that objects of unequal weight turn out to move at the same speed follows upon [the claim] that there is void, since this is absurd, we remove [the claim] that there is void. In this way Plato, too, in the *Republic*[242] removes that injustice is good counsel having taken what follows upon this, namely that justice is poor counsel, and having shown that this is not the case. But also that self-control is not virtue is shown through the removal of what follows upon [the claim] that self-control is virtue; for if self-control is virtue, then it would be a disposition based on agreement;[243]
30 but it is not of this kind; therefore, it is not virtue. And that the definition of colour is not 'proper perceptible of sight' is shown in this way: for if its being consists precisely in this, then colour is a relative; but it is not a relative; therefore, it is a quality. Or perhaps such an argument concerns the definition.[244] And if
167,1 [the claim] that suicide is not rational follows upon [the claim] that virtue by

itself is sufficient for happiness, if suicide is rational, then virtue would not be sufficient by itself for happiness.

111b23 Furthermore one should look at time and check whether there is any discrepancy.

Having talked about the *topos* which is destructive from consequence, which comes about from the removal of the consequents,[245] he adds to the aforementioned one a destructive *topos* from time as well. The *topos* is: if what has been posited to follow upon something from necessity presents a discrepancy with respect to time in such a way that, when one of them is the case, the other is not – for [if this is so] it is no longer the case that things that obtain in this way are equivalent.[246] For example: if it is posited that growing follows from necessity upon things that are nurtured,[247] we will remove this once we have shown that 10 some things are nurtured, and yet do not grow. For old animals are fed (otherwise they would not be); still, they do not grow. And also that remembering does not follow upon knowing nor does the one who knows remember at all, can be shown from time, if it is true that memory is only of things past, whereas knowledge is also of things present and future. The astronomer, for example, has knowledge of the eclipse which will occur. And [one can show from time] that recollection does not follow upon learning either: for recollection is of past things only, whereas one can learn future things; for one can learn that there will be an eclipse. And scientific knowledge does not follow upon perception: for perception is there from birth, whereas sciences are acquired later. Nor will choice follow upon desire for the same reason: for choice occurs later, whereas 20 desire is already there from birth. And perceiving will not follow upon being capable of perceiving either: for we are capable of perceiving even when we are sleeping, but we are not perceiving then.

\<Chapter 5\>

111b32 Furthermore there is the sophistic mode, which consists in leading [the discussion] towards such a thing about which we have plenty of attacks.

The *topos* which he presents now consists in diverting[248] the problem and the discussion towards that 'about which we have plenty of attacks'[249] – which he said to be a 'sophistic mode',[250] since dragging the arguments and diverting [them]

towards that about which they have plenty of attacks while setting aside the
production of arguments about the submitted claim is typical of the sophists, as

30   Protagoras does in Plato's *Protagoras* in that sometimes he tells some tales, some

168,1   other time he talks about poems, about which he was in a position to have plenty
of discourses, refraining from producing arguments about the submitted
problems in the form of question and answer.

The practice of passing over from the submitted problems to something else
about which one has plenty of attacks and discourses is not useful for the submitted
problem: it is outright sophistic. Sometimes, however, the replacement and the
shift are necessary, i.e. when they are towards such a thing which, once established,
is useful for what was laid down at the beginning. And it is for this reason that he
puts this *topos* among the dialectical ones, despite its being, in general, a sophistic
one: for the replacement with such things which, once they have been shown, what

10   was laid down at the beginning is established at the same time,[251] is a task of the
dialectician. For, as he says, sometimes there occurs such a replacement which is
with what is necessary[252] and useful with respect to what was laid down at the
beginning, whereas sometimes it is with 'what seems to be necessary'[253] without
being necessary, and sometimes with what is plainly foreign to and not necessary
for what is submitted and does not even give the appearance of being necessary,
which is clearly a sophistic mode of replacement. The replacement, then, is with
what is necessary when, if one has asked for a premise which contributes to
showing the submitted [claim], the answerer does not concede it, and [the
questioner], passing over, produces an argument about this very same proposition[254]
and finds himself in the position of having plenty of attacks about it. For it is clear
that the establishment of such a proposition contributes something to the initial

20   problem, if indeed the questioner had submitted it with the intention of showing
what was submitted by means of it. For example, if someone, while establishing
the problem that every pleasure is good, takes that everything that is according to
nature is good in order to show that, but the answerer does not concede it;
the questioner, however, has more resources for establishing it [than the
original claim that every pleasure is good] and, passing over, produces a deduction
about [the claim] that everything that is according to nature is good, showing
this (on the one hand) [by saying] that what is according to nature is proper to
each thing, and what is proper to each thing is good, and (on the other hand) [by
saying] that what is against one thing's nature is bad for it and corrupts it, and
if what is against nature is bad, then what is according to nature is good: for if
the contrary belongs to the contrary, then also the contrary belongs to the

30   contrary.[255] Now, such a shift is useful for the initial thesis: for if this is not conceded,

it is also not possible to show what was submitted.[256] So, showing this[257] is necessary   169,1
for the initial thesis. And again, if someone, intending to show that the soul is
immortal, takes that the soul changes in order to show that it changes by itself, but
one does not concede that it changes; the other, however, has plenty of attacks in
support of the latter [claim] and, replacing [that] with this, produces arguments
showing that it changes. It changes in one respect in that it thinks, and in another
respect in that it learns, and in another respect in that it experiences pleasure and
pain, and in another respect in that it perceives, and in another respect in that it
hopes, and in another respect in that it fears: such a replacement is with what is
necessary for what was submitted. And this mode of shifting is a 'leading away', as
he said in the second book of the *Prior Analytics*.[258]

And [the meaning of the words] 'similarly also when one undertakes the   10
removal [of a claim] having carried out[259] an induction about something for the
sake of what is submitted'[260] would be this: the one who makes an objection to
the premise which is asked for as useful for showing the submitted claim can
simply not concede it,[261] saying that the proposition stating that everything that
is according to nature is good[262] is not true. But he can also remove it through
induction, saying that dying is according to nature and yet is not good, and
similarly for being in pain and being ill: for none of these things is according
to convention, but they are all according to nature.

The [words] 'for the sake of what is submitted'[263] would mean 'for the sake of
the very premise which is posited', i.e. the premise is 'everything that is according
to nature is good'. And the induction which is carried out for the sake of this very
same proposition seems to show that it is false: for it takes particular cases of   20
things that are according to nature and yet clearly seem not to be good. The one
who passes over to what is shown and posited through induction and removes
this makes a replacement with what is necessary for what was submitted – for
example, in case he shows by carrying out a division that not everything that
comes to be naturally is according to nature, but only the best of the things that
come to be naturally [are according to nature], while none of the cases taken for
induction is of this sort.[264] The same considerations apply also in case one,
intending to establish [the claim] that no pleasure is good, takes the premise that
no good is a process of coming to be, taking as an additional premise to this that
pleasure is a process of coming to be. It is possible, then, to object to this premise
simply by not conceding it; but it is also possible to falsify the premise through
induction, making use of the given [*topos*],[265] by saying: 'getting healthy, which is   30
a process of coming to be, is good; and so is learning'.[266] Passing over from the
submitted problem to showing this premise[267] and removing the things posited

through the induction, by showing that they are not good without qualification ,
170,1   is necessary for showing what is submitted if precisely, once this premise[268] has
been removed through induction, it is not possible to show what was initially
submitted, i.e. that no pleasure is good. For if this, i.e. that no process of coming
to be is good, is removed, then also the submitted claim, which was 'no pleasure
is good', is removed. In such cases, then, the replacement of the problem with
such things is necessary for the sake of what was submitted.

Alternatively, it is possible that these things concern the answerer, in the sense
that he leads away [the argument] for the sake of the objection towards [a claim]
about which he has plenty of resources by using induction. For it will seem that
10   this person is not doing anything absurd if he removes the thesis by resorting to
an induction for which he has plenty of arguments.[269]

Or rather what is said through these words[270] is something like this: 'And
similarly also when one undertakes the removal [of a claim] once [the other
interlocutor] has carried out an induction about something for the sake of what
was submitted: for once this has been removed, what was submitted is removed
too', as if the reading was *poiêsamenou* and not *poiêsamenos*.[271] For this would
mean: 'And similarly, in case [the questioner] has carried out an induction about
something for the sake of the submitted claim (i.e. clearly: for the sake of this
thing with which the replacement occurs and for which he has plenty of attacks),
the answerer undertakes the removal of this by moving an objection to it. For
once this thing is removed [, i.e. that] through which the submitted problem
20   was established – which he calls 'submitted' too – the problem is removed'. The
replacement of the argument with the establishment of this [claim] turns out to
be necessary for the questioner: for if some problem is established by the
questioner through induction (for showing what is submitted through induction
is not less dialectical than [doing the same] through deduction), since, having
[the questioner] taken also something of this sort (i.e. something with respect to
which he has plenty of arguments) in the inductive argument as useful for
showing [the initial claim], the discussant will move an objection against this,
the replacement of the argument with this becomes necessary for the one who is
establishing what was submitted. For if, while the answerer says that what is
according to nature is not good, the questioner could establish this through
induction, by taking with respect to each animal that the things that are according
to nature for each of them are good (for the horse the things that are according
30   to nature for the horse, for the dog those that are so for the dog, and for the lion
those that are so for the lion), but when he takes that also things that are
according to nature for the human being are good for the human being, the

interlocutor who defends the opposite of what is being shown[272] would move an objection to this, while the other[273] one has plenty of attacks to show this claim – [if this is the case], he will make a replacement in this way with the claim for which he has plenty of resources – and yet also necessarily, precisely if what was being shown initially, i.e. that everything that is according to nature is good, is removed if this[274] is not shown. And he shows this having taken that everything that is according to nature for the human being is either fine or pleasant or advantageous and having secured each of them, and then by taking as an additional [premise][275] that all these things are good. For through this he will have shown that against which the objection was moved – and once this has been conceded, he shows that everything that is according to nature is good.[276]

As for the possibility of making a replacement with something that seems to be necessary but is not necessary, this happens when the questioner produces an argument about some of the things mentioned in the problem, which, however, does not contribute to demolishing or to establishing the problem. For the one who makes a replacement with such a thing gives the appearance of producing arguments about something useful for the thesis, i.e. the problem. For example, if the problem is about the universe's being spherical, and he discusses about whether there is one or there are several universes or about whether it is eternal or generated. Or again, if the problem is whether pleasure is according to nature, and someone discusses about nature, showing either what nature is or that everything that comes to be by nature is for the sake of something, and does this either once the answerer, i.e. 'the defender of the argument'[277] is asked and 'denies'[278] this very thing (e.g. if the one asks [the other] whether it seems to him that everything that comes to be by nature is for the sake of something and the other denies this, and the first one, setting aside the submitted problem,[279] shows this, since he has plenty of attacks about it), or also if one resorts to some reputable induction which does not lead to show what was submitted as if it did show it,[280] and then, having used in the induction also the thesis with which the replacement occurs as if it were useful for showing what is submitted (e.g. that everything that comes to be by nature is for the sake of something),[281] the other objects to this, trying to remove it. For the replacement with this is a replacement with what seems to be necessary for the questioner, because he used this as a means to show the submitted problem. For example, if the one shows through reputable induction that everything that comes to be by nature comes to be for the sake of something, which was not necessary to show with respect to [the claim] that everything that is according to nature is good (which was the original problem), and yet it seemed [to be necessary], since, having resorted to [the

171,1

10

20

30

172,1

claim] that breathing comes to be for the sake of something in the course of induction, the interlocutor does not concede it, and he produces arguments about this, since he has plenty of attacks about it. And the replacement with this sort [of claim], as well as the use of this *topos* for the purposes of the replacement with this sort [of claim], would be dialectical.[282]

But there are also cases in which the replacement is not with what is necessary nor with what seems to be necessary, but rather with something arbitrary; for example, if the goal is to show that only the fine is good, if someone asks the answerer whether it seems to him that the void exists, and, once the other has

10   assented, he attacks that it does not exist having a great supply of attacks in support of this [claim] and eventually carrying out a side-refutation of him.[283] For the difference from the problem is obvious as it is obvious that neither [of the claims], once they are shown, can contribute to an argument in support of the other: for neither says anything necessary or useful [for the other], when one, leaving aside what was submitted, shows that some things were said incorrectly or were said against the given information[284] (for the side-refutation would be about such things). And he says that one has to keep guard against this sort of shift as being utterly sophistic and foreign to the dialectical method. He requires that in such shifts (i.e. when the questioner intends to take something foreign to the submitted problem by diverting the problem) the answerer concede to him that this is so (even if it does not seem to him to be so), by specifying that it does not satisfy him,

20   but that he posits it for the sake of the argument which concludes to what is submitted. For it so happens that those who ask such things get into difficulties when [the interlocutor] does not make a fuss about them – with which aim they propose them in the first place – but concedes them. For it becomes evident that they cannot use any of the given [claims] for the sake of what was submitted.

112a16 Furthermore everybody who has said whatever thing in a certain way has said several things.

This *topos* is the same as the one mentioned a little earlier,[285] the one which is destructive from consequence: for he said that one has to investigate 'what is the case from necessity if what is submitted is the case',[286] and to demolish this; for once this is removed, also what is submitted, upon which this follows, would be removed. And now he says the same thing: since several things follow upon any posited thing, no matter what of those that follow upon it we removed, we

173,1 would have removed it too. The difference between what is said now and that [other *topos*][287] might be that, there, he said that one has to enquire into what follows upon what was posited, whereas here he also sketches the discovery of the things that follow. For he said 'everybody who says[288] whatever thing in a certain way has said several things':[289] for the one who says one thing potentially says the definition of the thing said and its genus and its specific differences and the propria.[290] But if the one who says the thing potentially says these, too, it is clear that these will follow upon what is said; so that, no matter about which one of these we show that it is not the case, we will have removed also what was posited at the start. For example, the one who says 'human being' has also said 'animal', 'ensouled', 'biped' and 'rational'.[291] So that if it has been shown that one   10 of these is not the case, neither will the human being be. In this way, since from saying that virtue is sufficient for happiness it follows that suicide is not rational and that health or anything besides virtue is not choiceworthy, if any of these has been removed, also that virtue is sufficient for happiness would be removed. Again, since from saying that the soul is a body it follows that a body can penetrate through a body and that the soul is either an element or out of elements, if any of these is not the case, that is not the case either. And since from saying that motion comes about through void it follows that things with unequal weight move with equal speed and that the void is comparable to the full and that something covers the same distance in the same time through a full medium or through void,[292] if these things are absurd, then so is what was posited.   20

One has to be careful not 'to make the replacement'[293] with something 'more difficult'[294] and harder to attack: for it is often the case that it is easier to remove the thing itself[295] than what follows upon it. For example, the one who intends to show that injustice is not advantageous would have an easier time if he made an attempt to show this than if, taking what follows upon it, i.e. greediness, he produced arguments about this. For greediness seems to be more abject but expedient and advantageous. And one can show in a reputable way that injustice is not advantageous, either, as Plato did,[296] from [the claims] that it is the disease of the soul and no disease is advantageous, or from [the claims] that every vice is damaging for the one who has it and injustice is a vice. Passing over from   174,1 injustice to greediness to produce arguments about the latter is, therefore, not appropriate for the dialectician,.

<Chapter 6>

112a24 As for those things to which it is necessary that only one of two [properties] belong, e.g. either disease or health belongs to the human being.

Having set out some *topoi* that are constructive and destructive from consequence, after these things he presents a *topos* which is both constructive and destructive from conflict.[297] The *topos* applies to contraries without intermediates: for since contraries without intermediates are those such that it is necessary that one of them belong to what receives them,[298] if the problem posits that some of such contraries belongs to something, if, by taking what is receptive

174,10 of the contraries without intermediates of which the one [contrary] is predicated, we show that the other of them does not belong to it, we would have shown that the former (which was posited) belongs to it; if, on the other hand, we show that one contrary belongs to it, we would have removed that the other belongs to it. He requires, then, that in such problems in which it is necessary that one of two belong to the subject and is impossible that both of them belong to it, one carries out the discussion with reference to the one of them about which one has the resources. For the one is shown through the other: for if it has been shown that one belongs to the subject, the other one will be removed, whereas if it is shown that the one does not belong [to the subject], the other will be established. When the predicate of something in the problem is of this sort, then, we would establish or demolish what is submitted by showing that its contrary belongs or does not

20 belong to the subject. For example, since even and odd are predicated of number, if one leads the attack with reference to one particular number and says that it is even, if it was shown that it is not odd, it would be even; if, on the other hand, it has been shown that it is odd, it would be shown that it is not even. Similarly also if what is submitted is a body of an animal and it is said to be healthy: if it has been shown that it is ill, it will have been shown that it is not healthy, whereas if it is shown that it is not ill, it will have been shown that it is healthy. In this way, if it is posited that there is some infinite magnitude, since every magnitude is either finite or infinite, once we have shown that every magnitude is finite we would have removed [the claim] that there is some infinite [magnitude], as

175,1 Aristotle showed in the first book of *On the heavens*, showing that every body, be it simple or composite, is finite.[299]

The *topos* could be applied to the case of contradiction, too: for this is also an opposition without intermediates which is characterised by the aforementioned necessity not with respect to things that are receptive [of them] (as contraries without intermediates are), but rather with respect to all things.[300] For it is necessary with respect to anything that either the affirmation or the negation is the case, so that, if the affirmation is the case, the negation is not the case, whereas if the affirmation is not the case, then the negation is the case: if one has shown that richness is good, the corresponding negation would be removed; if one has shown that richness is not good, then the affirmation would be removed.

With respect to the contraries that have intermediates, however, the *topos* is no longer useful for both purposes, i.e. both for destructive and for constructive purposes, but it is useful only for demolishing the one contrary that is posited. For if it was shown that the other of them (i.e. not the one which is posited) belongs to what is receptive [of them], then it has been removed that the other belongs to it: for it is not possible that contraries belong at the same time. However, it is not the case that, if the other does not belong, then the remaining contrary will belong, since it is possible that some of the intermediates belong to it. For example, take a body: if it is white, from necessity it is not black; but if it is not white, it is not necessarily the case that it is black. And if someone is happy, this man is not unhappy; but it is not the case that, if he is not happy, he is necessarily unhappy: for happiness and unhappiness are not opposed to each other without intermediates, since it is possible that an excellent man is not happy. And if he is excellent, he is not bad; but if he is not excellent, it is not necessarily the case that he is bad: for virtue and vice are not without intermediates. And the one of sound mind is not mad; but it is not the case that the one who is not of sound mind is mad. So that contraries of this sort are no longer useful both for constructive and for destructive purposes. And it is possible that, in the case of contraries without intermediates, it is rather the argument through the fifth so-called indemonstrable that applies (this is the one which, from a disjunction and the opposite of one of the members of the disjunction, concludes to the other member of the disjunction).[301] In the case of contraries with intermediates, instead, [it is possible that] the argument through the fourth [applies] (this is the one which, from a disjunction and one of the members of the disjunction, removes the other member of the disjunction).[302]

112a32 Furthermore attacking by changing the name according to the account.

He presents us a *topos* from etymology. For if we change words into their etymological accounts (this is what 'by changing the name according to the account' means) as if they rather signified these and as if it were appropriate to understand words in this way 'rather than as it is common',[303] we will have plenty of attacks with respect to what is posited. For example, if we intend to show that the one who has any virtue, and not only the courageous man, is *eupsukhos*[304] [etym.: 'well-souled'; commonly: 'stout-hearted'], we will replace the word *eupsukhos* with its etymological account: this man is the one who has 'the soul in a good disposition' (*eu psukhen ekhon*), and this is the man who has a good soul. But if *eupsukhos* is the one who a good soul, and also the just man and the moderate and the wise have a good soul, then the courageous man would not be the only one who is *eupsukhos* nor would *eupsukhia* be courage.[305] And we will show that the *eupsukhos* is the one who has his soul in a good disposition through a comparison of similar cases:[306] the man 'in-good-hopes' (*euelpis*) is the

10   one who hopes well (*eu elpizôn*), i.e. the one who hopes good things. Again, if we intend to show that the good person is *eudaimôn* [commonly: 'happy'], we will substitute *eudaimôn* with its etymological account: for it seems that what is signified by *eudaimôn* is a person who is doing well with respect to her *daimôn*.[307] Now, if the *daimôn* of each is the soul, based on what Xenocrates thinks,[308] then *eudaimôn* would be the one who is doing well with respect to his soul; and the excellent man is the one who is doing well with respect to the soul; therefore, the excellent man is *eudaimôn*. Again, if we want to show that there is no *prohairesis* [commonly: 'choice'; etym. 'pre-choice'] in what is irrational, we will take the account of *prohairesis*: this is 'a choice before something else'. But choosing something before something else is in the subjects in which deliberation resides too: for the preliminary discernment of something from something else occurs with rationality; and no irrational being deliberates; so

20   that no [irrational being] *prohaireitai* ['pre-chooses'] either. And again, if we want to show that the moderate man is not encratic, we will substitute 'encratic' with 'self-controlling' (for this is what the word means); and having shown that where something controls there is also something that is controlled, and what is controlled is controlled in that it opposes resistance and fights, and where one part of the soul controls and one part is controlled there is no agreement, while the moderate man has the parts of his soul in agreement with each other, we would have shown what was submitted. The same account applies to the case of the acratic and the licentious. In this way it is possible to show that a friend is not 'well-minded' (*eunous*), if 'well-minded' is the one who thinks correctly

177,1   and thinks what is true or good; but it is not generally true that a friend thinks correctly.

The *topos* is persuasive, reputable and dialectical, but what is said is not sound in all cases: for it is not the case that *euthalassos* [commonly: 'good sailor'; 'lying well by the sea'] is the one who has a good see, nor that *eukheir* [commonly: 'quick'] is the one who has pretty hands (rather than the boxer), nor that 'magnanimous' (*megalophukhos*) is the one who has a big soul. For this reason, the excellent man is not *eudaimôn* either.[309]

112b1 And since of things some are from necessity, whereas others are for the most part and others as it happens.

This *topos* takes its starting point from the difference between things. And in this respect it goes beyond the first *topos* which was presented and which requires 'checking whether what belongs [to the subject] in another way has been given   10 as an accident'.[310] For in the present case this has been somewhat replaced, i.e. what belongs as a genus or as a proprium or as a definition [has been replaced] with 'what belongs from necessity' (for each of them is taken in this way), whereas the accident [has been replaced] with what [belongs] 'for the most part' or 'as it happens': for such is what can belong or not belong, in terms of which the accident was defined.[311] Furthermore, if some accidents, too, are inseparable, these, too, would be the same as things that belong from necessity; for this reason he does not posit an opposition between what is from necessity and the accident. For he does not use the accident or any of the other [kinds of predicates], but rather resorts to what belongs necessarily and what does not belong necessarily as to another division.[312]

For we are presented with the fact that,[313] of things that are, some are of necessity, e.g. that the human being is an animal (what belongs to all and always,   20 this is from necessity: similarly, it is also necessary that god is imperishable), some are contingently.[314] And of these contingent things, some are for the most part, e.g. that human beings have five fingers and that they turn white when they get old; some are less frequent, as the opposites of these, e.g that human beings have four or six fingers (for these things are in this way as well), or that human beings do not turn white when they get old; whereas some others are equally distributed, e.g. that human beings are citizens or not, that they are abroad or not, that they bathe or not. Given, then, that this kind of difference is present among things that are, if someone says that what belongs to something in a certain way belongs to it in another way , swapping their modes of belonging, he   178,1 gives a starting point for a refutative attack. For if someone says that it is contingent that god is imperishable or that the human being is an animal or rational, this person would say that what cannot not be is contingent: for it is impossible that the god is not imperishable or that the human being is not an animal. But the one who says that it is contingent that it is an animal, this person would be saying that it is also possible that it is not an animal, since this is what is contingent. Furthermore, he would be saying that what belongs always does not belong always, for what belongs from necessity belongs always and to all. But even if one set by definition that he calls 'for the most part' what is from necessity, the mistake would be the same, because it is also possible that what is for the

10   most part is not (for this reason what is for the most part is not necessary), as if someone said that a demonstration is true for the most part. The argument would be similar if someone said, vice versa, that what is for the most part is from necessity. For if someone said that the human being has five fingers from necessity, he would be saying that what is contingent is necessary. For it is possible that someone does not have five fingers. But the one who says that every human being has five fingers of necessity says that it is not possible that there be someone who does not have five fingers. But even with respect to 'the contrary of what is for the most part'[315] (and this is what is for the lesser part: for what is for the most part is opposed to what is for the lesser part in the same way as much is opposed to less): if someone says that what is for the lesser part is of necessity

20   or for the most part, he would be refuted either in that he says that what, for the most part, is not such that it is impossible that it is not or in that he posits that it is for the most part, e.g. if someone said that of necessity it rains in the period of the Dog or that for the most part human beings have six fingers. And similarly, if someone says that some of the things that come to be by chance come to be of necessity or for the most part. For the one who says that what obtains of necessity obtains for the most part says that what belongs to all does not belong to all (for as the one who says that the human being has five fingers contingently, denies that every human being has five fingers, so also the one who says that the human being is rational or has respiration contingently, this person would deny that every human being is of such a kind and that this is always the case; for the

179,1   necessary is universal, while the contingent is not of this sort); and similarly if, vice versa, one says that what is for the most part is of necessity. Furthermore, that mistake, of the one who says that what is for the lesser part is of necessity, is even more evident.

It is, then, possible that someone does this by swapping and adding explicitly the modes of belonging, in which case the refutation would become utterly evident. But even if the other one does not add explicitly any qualification, but says, absolutely and without adding the mode of the belonging, that the thing belongs, it is possible for the interlocutor to divert towards that which can be refuted, i.e. towards what is said indeterminately as if it were said in this specific way.

10   With respect to the contingent, then, the *topos* is unpersuasive and patently sophistic: for the one who says that the one who claims without qualification that the human being is an animal has said that it is contingent that it is an animal, will evidently appear to move a false charge. [The *topos*] would turn out to be

dialectical only with reference to those cases in which someone says that what belongs contingently belongs without qualification, e.g. if someone said without qualification that the old person turns white or that every human being has five fingers. For since the necessary belongs without qualification, it seems that what is said to belong without qualification is said as if it belonged necessarily. For the one who is wise strictly speaking is also wise without qualification; and who is so not in this way, is [wise] with qualification, e.g. the carpenter is wise [in a qualified way]: for in all cases what is said strictly speaking is said absolutely and without qualification. But what belongs necessarily belongs strictly speaking. Certainly, the one who says that what belongs contingently belongs absolutely and without   20
qualification would be plausibly corrected as if he were saying that what does not belong in this way belongs necessarily. And this is what he himself clarifies through what he says: for the *topos* has to be used with those who claim that what belongs contingently belongs absolutely and without qualification. For the one who says, absolutely, that disinherited sons are mean would seem to say that they are of this sort of necessity and universally; but this is not so: for it is possible that someone be disinherited without being of this sort; people say, for example, that Themistocles was disinherited, and yet he was not mean.

One might investigate, if what can belong or not belong is an accident, while what belongs necessarily is either a genus or a proprium or a definition or some of the things that fall under these, how the [*topos*]³¹⁶ showing that what is given   30
as belonging of necessity does not belong of necessity would still be ordered   180,1
under the *topoi* relating to the problems from the accident. For this [*topos*] would either show that [what is given] does not belong as a genus or that it does not belong as a proprium or that it does not belong as a definition – but the things that remove the genus belong in the *topoi* relating to the genus, and similarly in the case of the proprium and of the definition. Or perhaps, since it removes [what is posited] not as a genus or a proprium or a definition, but [by establishing] more generally that it is not necessary, it would not be ordered under any of those: for some accident, too, is necessary. Furthermore, it does not remove the necessary through some general method, but by resorting to evidence ready at hand; and by removing this it establishes the accident, so that for this   10
reason it would be ordered under [the *topoi*] about the accident, since it establishes the accident. On this ground he did not convert [the formulation] in the case of the first *topos*³¹⁷ – for he did not say 'if he has given as belonging in any other way what belongs [to the subject] as an accident': for in that converted formulation the *topos* would turn out to be from the genus or from the proprium or from the definition, since the accident would turn out to be given according

to some of these. In the present *topos*, instead, he gave the converted formulation, because in it he resorts to the necessary (which can also be in the accident) and not to the genus or the proprium or the definition.

112b21 Furthermore, if he posited something as an accident of itself, as if it were [something] different.

20   The *topos* is from the polyonyms,[318] and this is what is said through it: since it is not possible that something belong to itself as its own accident (for an accident is in a subject and is different from that to which it belongs as an accident, and it is possible that it belong or do not belong,[319] whereas neither will something be the subject of itself and be something other than itself nor is it possible that something belong or do not belong to itself) – if, then, someone (misled to think, in cases of polyonymy, that things have a difference corresponding to the difference of the names) said that one of them belongs incidentally to the other, e.g. that the sword belongs incidentally to the dagger or the human being to the mortal or the cloak to the mantel or rejoicing to taking pleasure or enjoying oneself to rejoicing – this person would be refuted as saying that one thing

181,1 belongs to itself as an accident: for pleasure, rejoicing, enjoyment, and joy are the same both according to the subject and according to what is signified.[320] And Prodicus[321] tried to associate to each of these words a proper signification in the same way in which the Stoics tried this too, claiming that rejoicing is a rational elevation, pleasure an irrational elevation, joy the pleasure that occurs through the ears, and enjoyment the pleasure that comes through discourses: but this is what name-givers do who, however, do not say anything sound. Saying that pleasure is rejoicing, then, is not a mistake, precisely as it is not a mistake to say that the unit is indivisible or that the point is partless: for it is not a mistake to say that rejoicing is rejoicing or that the unit is a unit. But saying that one of these two belongs incidentally to the other is absurd and false.[322]

<Chapter 7>

10   *112b27 And since the contraries can be combined with each other in six ways, but give place to a contrariety [only] when combined in four ways.*

The *topos* is from the combination[323] of the contraries. The main point in what is said: since the mutual combination of two pairs of contraries[324] produces six pairs of combinations, and, of these, two pairs do not have a contrariety to each other, whereas the remaining four do, it is required that, by making a move from the pairs which present a contrariety, when something is posited in such a way that each of the two terms in the posited problem is contrary to something, checking the combinations that are contrary to the combination in the problem, we try to show that some of them is true. For, once it is shown that one is true, the problem would be removed, since it is impossible that the contraries be true at the same time. And such is the outline of the *topos*.

What is said would become clear if, by setting out the contrarieties and the pairs that come about according to their combinations, we could show how they turn out to be six in total, how come that four out of six are those that present a contrariety, and which ones these are. Let the two pairs of contraries be, the one, just and unjust, and, the other, good and bad; and let them be combined with each other in all ways in which they can be combined, preserving the condition that each pair contains one term of those in each contrariety. In this way the pairs of composite combinations will not be more than six. 'For either each'[325] of the terms of one contrariety 'will be combined with each term' of those of the other, and, combined in this way, there will be two pairs of combinations: for either the good will be combined with the just and the bad with the unjust (and this one pair will be 'the just [is] good / the unjust [is] bad', where the subject in each combination is, in one case, the just and, in the other case, the unjust, whereas the predicate is, in one case, the good and, in the other, the bad). Or it can be that, vice versa, the bad will be combined with the just and the good with the unjust, so that the pair will be 'the just [is] bad / the unjust [is] good'. Or, on the other hand, it can be that each of the predicates will in turn combine with a different subject, e.g. once the good and once the bad with the just, and the other two pairs will result in turn – one 'the just [is] good / the just [is] bad', the other 'the unjust [is] bad / the unjust [is] good'. The remaining two pairs result when, vice versa, we combine each subject separately once with one predicate and once with the other, e.g. once the good with the just and once the bad with the just, and again once the bad with the unjust and once the good with the unjust: so one will be 'the just [is] good / the unjust [is] good', the other 'the just [is] bad / the unjust [is] bad'. The pairs and combinations that come about from combining two contrarieties in the way described above are these and this many.

The first pair is the one having each [term of one contrariety] about one [different term of the other contrariety], i.e. 'the just [is] good / the [unjust] is bad'. The second one obtains in a similar way, but has each [term of the first contrariety] said about the other [term of the other contrariety than in the first pair], i.e. 'the just [is] bad / the unjust [is] good'. The third one is the one having both predicates predicated in turn of only one of the subjects, i.e. 'the just is good / the just is bad'. Similarly, the fourth one, too, predicates both predicates in turn of only one of the subjects, i.e. 'the unjust is good / the unjust is bad'. The fifth is the one having the same thing[326] predicated separately of each subject, i.e. 'the just is good / the unjust is good'. Similarly, the sixth, too, has the same thing

30   predicated of each subject, i.e. 'the just is bad / the unjust is bad'. And it is not

183,1 possible to find any further combination beyond these by preserving the condition that the combination have two terms, one from each contrariety.

Of these six pairs, then, the two which were mentioned first, in which every contrary is combined, do not yield any contrariety. For neither is the combination 'the just is good' contrary to the one 'the unjust is bad' (they are both true and they both 'belong to the same character';[327] for thinking that the just is good and that the unjust is bad is typical of the same character: for they are both noble claims). Nor is the one saying 'the just is bad' contrary to the one saying 'the unjust is good' (for, again, these too are similarly false and 'to be avoided and

10 belong to the same character',[328] for thinking that the just is bad and the unjust is good is typical of the same character). Therefore, they are not in conflict with each other, but rather follow each other:[329] the contraries, instead, remove each other.[330] Having said that both combinations mentioned as second are to be avoided and belong to the same character, and having added that 'what is to be avoided' is not contrary 'to what is to be avoided',[331] given that it was posited in the *Ethics*[332] that there is some vice corresponding to each ethical virtue, and that [vice consists] in one way in an excess and in another way in a defect, <which are not only contrary to virtue>[333] but also to each other, he added 'unless one is according to excess and the other according to defect'.[334] How is it, then, that, there, such things are said to be contrary to each other and to virtue, and that in those writings it was also said that [they are not contrary] to virtue and to each other in a similar way and in the same respect, whereas now he says that they are not contrary to each other, since both things mentioned before, which are to be

20 avoided, are not to be avoided based on excess or defect but without qualification? And he showed that the second pair does not present any contrariety without saying anything about the first one because in the case of the first one the fact that they obtain at the same time was enough: for it is in no way possible that the contraries be the case together and be true at the same time, whereas nothing prevents the contraries from being false together (for contraries do not divide true and false in the same way in which contradiction does).[335] Since, then, the second pair, which consists of two combinations that are both to be avoided,

consists of combinations that are both false – which is not impossible in the case of the contraries – for this reason, in order to show that they are not contrary, he resorted to the argument that what is to be avoided is not contrary to what is to be avoided, with the exception of those cases in which the one is an excess and the other a defect about the same thing. Furthermore, it is evident and universally   30
true that a good is not contrary to a good, whereas it is not universally true that   184,1
what is to be avoided is not contrary to what is to be avoided.

And he says that the remaining four combinations yield a contrariety. For the combination saying that just things are good is contrary to the one saying that just things are bad, from which combinations the third pair was constituted. As indicative of the fact that the combinations in these pairs are contrary, he resorts to the fact that they come about from contrary characters and contrary permanent dispositions: for the one who claims that the just is good and the one who claims that the just is bad are contrary with respect to their character. Using this criterion for the contraries[336] he will likely find that several things are contrary to one. And discerning the contraries through contrariety in character is reputable and dialectical, but it is not true: for also saying that the just is good   10
and that adultery is good derive from contrary characters; and yet that the just is good and that adultery is good are not contrary to each other; but they would be contraries, if adultery were the contrary of the just. For the argument is about things that stand to each other in this way.[337]

And also the fourth pair seems to be composed of contraries, i.e. the [combination] saying that the unjust is good and the one saying that the unjust is bad; for these, too, stem from contrary dispositions. And the fifth is of this sort, too, one [combination] saying that the just is good and the other one saying that the unjust is good: for these are contraries and from contrary dispositions. The sixth, too, is a similar case – one [combination] saying that the just is bad and the other that the unjust is bad: for these are contrary to the aforementioned [combinations].

Having shown these [pairs][338] and having said 'for in each pair one member   20
is choiceworthy and the other one to be avoided, and the one belongs to the fair character, the other to the base one',[339] he added: 'it is therefore clear from what has been said that several things turn out to be contrary to the same',[340] taking this as following from the things that have been posited. For no matter what praiseworthy or true combination we take, all those that are blameworthy or false in all pairs will be contrary to this – and they will not be found to be more than two. And similarly, no matter what blameworthy or false combination we take, all those that are praiseworthy or true in all pairs will be contrary to

this – and these, too, are not more than two. And praiseworthy, i.e. true, in the

30 first pair is supposing that the just is good, blameworthy that the just is bad, so
that this will be contrary to that; but also in the second pair,[341] which has the

185,1 unjust as subject in both combinations, the combination saying that the unjust is
good is blameworthy; therefore this, too, will be contrary to the one saying that
the just is good. And in the two remaining pairs, the blameworthy combinations
are the same as those already mentioned: in one of them (the fifth) the one
saying that the unjust is good is blameworthy, which was the blameworthy
combination also in the fourth [pair], whereas in the sixth [pair] the one saying
that the just is bad is blameworthy, which is the same as the blameworthy
combination in the third pair. Therefore, two [combinations] are contrary to the
one saying that the just is good: the one saying that the just is bad and the one
saying that the unjust is good. But also the combinations contrary to the

10 blameworthy one in the third pair will be two: the one in this same pair saying
that the just is good and the one in the fourth pair saying that the unjust is
bad. The praiseworthy combinations in the fifth and sixth pair are, again, the
same as the two aforementioned ones. Similarly, it will be shown that for each
praiseworthy or blameworthy combination in the remaining three pairs the
contrary combinations are two.

Given, then, that the combinations that are contrary to each combination
made of contraries and encompassing a contrariety are two (the first two pairs
were also from contraries, but did not encompass a contrariety), he says that 'one
should take whatever contrary would be useful with respect to the thesis'.[342] This

20 is said briefly and, for this reason, unclearly, but it is something like this: the *topos*
about the contraries is useful for destructive purposes, but not, in general, for
constructive ones; in the case of contraries without intermediates it is also useful
for constructive purposes when the argument is carried out with reference to the
things that receive them, as was already said before.[343] But since there are also
some contraries that have intermediates, in which the removal of one does not
establish the other and it is only the case that the position of the one removes the
other (for if it is white, it is not black, but it is not the case that, if it is not white,
then it is already black: for it is also possible that it be some of the intermediates)
– for this reason, as I said, the aforementioned *topos* is more useful for destructive
purposes. For it is impossible that the contraries obtain at the same time.[344]
When, then, some problem is composed out of contraries[345] and several things

30 are contrary to it, in demolishing it we have to consider what its contraries are
and, of these, the one which, thanks to its evidence, is more useful to posit [the

186,1 thesis]; by producing this and showing that it is true, it is possible to remove what was posited, which is contrary to this, as not true. For example, if someone says that justice is bad, since two claims are contrary to this (i.e. that justice is good and that injustice is bad), if it is more evident that injustice is bad, since it is a vice and a disease of the soul and what corrupts in one respect the communion of the state and, in another respect, any dealings, and since it is contrary to and against nature for the human beings (for human beings naturally tend to share) – if, then, this is more evident in virtue of these considerations than [the claim] that justice is good, one has to remove that[346] having shown this[347] and having posited it as being contrary to [the claim] that justice is bad. In the case of contraries without intermediates we will also establish what is submitted once we have shown that its contrary does not belong to the subject which can receive it, in whatever sense of contrary we are capable to show this more easily[348]. And this would be the case if both contrarieties from which the combination of contraries is constituted are without intermediates: for, in this case, also the other compounds[349] will be without intermediates. For the one who showed that health is not bad has already shown that health is good, if good and bad are without intermediates in a similar way as health and disease are. In fact, he said 'both for the one who is removing and for the one who is establishing'[350] thinking that the *topos* is also useful for constructive purposes. And one has to consider the higher degree in the predicate terms, e.g. whether being good belongs to justice to a higher degree and more evidently than being bad to injustice.[351] The same considerations apply also if we take some other contraries, e.g. pleasure and pain and good and bad, and combine these. And similarly if we take friends and enemies and doing good and doing evil – which he himself used.[352]

The *topos*, then, is this. However, one would ask how in this context[353] he accepted that several things are contrary to one given that he is happy with [the claim] that [only] one thing is contrary to one.[354] Perhaps when the one thing is simple, then it is necessary that only one thing be contrary to it, whereas when it is not simple, nothing prevents several things from being contrary to it, not in the same respect but each of the considered contraries being contrary to the one thing in a different respect: for it is impossible that several things be contrary to the same in the same respect. And even if something which is one in number and has several potencies has something contrary to each potency in it, it is not the case that, since what is taken is one in number, for this reason several things are contrary to one. For nothing prevents the thing which is one in number from being both cold and white, as the snow, and from having as contraries the warm and the black; but it is not the case that on this ground several things turn out to be contrary to one, because it is not the case that both of them, i.e. the warm and the black, are contrary to the snow in the same respect. And the same happens in the case of the combination of contraries: for 'pleasure is bad' and 'pain is good' are not contrary to 'pleasure is good' in the same respect; rather, the first [combination is contrary to it] because the contrary [of the predicate] is predicated of the same thing, whereas the second [is contrary to it] because the same is predicated of the contrary. For the things that are compounded together are two and each of them has its own contrary. Therefore it is not the case that he contradicts himself here, in the same way in which he does not contradict himself in the *Ethics*, as we have shown also in the notes about it.[355]

10   *113a20 Furthermore, if there is something contrary to the accident.*

If someone said that something belongs to something as an accident, we have to check – he says – whether there is anything contrary to the accident. This *topos* is the same as the one transmitted before it in some [exemplars] and differs from it in linguistic formulation only, in the way in which it is Aristotle's custom to express the same *topos* in different words: for which reason the *topos* before this one is omitted in some [exemplars].[356]

And this *topos*, too, is destructive from the contraries. For since it is impossible that the contraries belong to and are accidents of something at the same time, he says that, if someone says that something belongs incidentally to something, we have to check whether there is anything contrary to what is said to belong incidentally and whether this belongs to the thing to which they say that its

20   contrary belongs. For once it is shown that this belongs to it, what was posited as being an accident of it will have been demolished. For if someone said that injustice is useful for the one who is characterised by it, since damaging is the contrary of useful, and injustice is a disease of the soul, if we take that every disease is damaging for the one who has it, we would have that injustice, too, [is damaging for the one who has it]. And if it is damaging, then it is not useful: 'for it is impossible that the contraries belong to the same thing at the same time'.[357] Similarly, if we show that what is said to be healthy is ill, we would have removed that it is healthy. And also if someone posited that pleasure is good, once it is shown that it is bad, [the claim] that it is good would have been removed: [otherwise] the contraries would obtain at the same time about it.

And this *topos* would differ from the one mentioned a little earlier ('to the

188,1   things to which it is necessary that only one of them belong [...]')[358] because that one was said with reference to contraries without intermediates and, for this reason, it was also constructive and not only destructive, whereas this one is said with reference to contraries that have intermediates and, for this reason, it is only destructive.

113a24 If something of such a sort, i.e. such that, if this is the case, then necessarily the contraries belong [to the same thing], is said of something.

To the previous *topos* he adds this one, which is also about the contraries and destructive. And the *topos* is: it is required that one enquires into whether someone has predicated something of something else as belonging to it [in such a way that] it follows from it that the contraries belong at the same time to the same underlying thing. For if what is posited to belong to something is of this   10
sort, then it would be removed and it would be shown that this is impossible since it is impossible that the contraries belong at the same time to something. He himself resorts, then, to the example of Ideas: for 'if someone says that Ideas are in us'[359] as if Ideas were our forms,[360] it follows from this that he says that Ideas are at the same time immobile and moved, and that they are at the same time intelligible and not intelligible but perceptible. For insofar as they say that Ideas are intelligible and immobile, these [features] will belong to them. But insofar as they say that they are in us, 'given that we move',[361] they will move together with us and, furthermore, they will be perceptible: for we come to know the shape of each thing through sight, and if this very shape is the Idea, then [the Idea] would be perceptible.

And by resorting to this *topos* it is also possible to remove [the claim] that 'I   20
lie' is a proposition. For if it is a proposition, it will be true and false at the same time, as is shown; but this is impossible, for these are contraries; therefore, 'I lie' is not a proposition. For if it were conceded that it is a proposition, then that every proposition is either true or false would be removed – for, if this were the case, then also that proposition would be either true or false. But no matter what is assumed as being the case, its contrary follows too: for if 'I lie' is assumed as being true, it seems to follow that the subject is saying what is false (for in this way he would tell the truth by saying that he is lying); on the other hand, if it is assumed that it is false, then he seems to be telling the truth (for he would lie when he says that he is lying for this reason, i.e. because he is telling the truth).[362] Nor would 'every presentation[363] is true' be a proposition: for it would be true and   189,1
false at the same time – true because this is also a presentation, false because it says that every presentation is true, and this is impossible. And that the contraries obtain at the same time follows also from saying that everything is mixed in everything. But also if someone says that being is one and infinite it follows that

being is one and many: for the infinite belongs to quantity, and quantity is an accident; therefore, it[364] will be both substance and quantity.[365] And also that the same thing is at the same time in motion and at rest follows from positing that all things are in motion: for the very claim that everything is in motion, inasmuch as it is true and stable, will be immobile, whereas inasmuch as it is itself one of all the things it will move too.

And through saying 'for we come to know the form in each thing through the perception of sight'[366] he made clear in what sense he said that Ideas are in us, i.e. as the form and shape of each.

Through this *topos* such [claims] will be removed too: 'Dion knows that he is dead' (for being dead and being alive follow from this);[367] and similarly to this also 'this [day] is not day'[368] too.

113a33 And again, if it is posited that [something] which has a contrary is an accident

This *topos* is like this: since it seems that the same thing is receptive of the contraries, if someone says that something belongs incidentally to something, it is required that we investigate whether there is any contrary of the thing which is said to belong incidentally and, if there is, to see whether the subject is receptive of this too. For if it is receptive of it, then it would be established that it is also receptive of this – but not that the latter is already in it in all cases[369], as he himself will say[370] too. If, on the other hand, it is not receptive of this, then it would not be receptive of what is posited to belong incidentally; and if it is not receptive of it, it would not have that either.

And the *topos* has to be used in those cases in which it is not the case that one of the contraries is natural to a subject, as the white is to the snow.[371] For example, if someone says that hatred follows upon anger, according to this person hatred will be in the same thing in which it is clear that anger is. And anger is 'in the spirited [part of the soul]';[372] therefore, hatred was posited in this, too. Since, then, love is contrary to hatred, the spirited [part of the soul] will be receptive of love as well. If, then, this is not the case (for loving and love are 'in the desiderative part'),[373] hatred will not be in the spirited part either; and if this is so, that hatred follows upon anger would be removed, if indeed anger is in the spirited part and hatred has been shown to be in the desiderative part. And again, if someone said that ignorance is in the desiderative part, it would follow that the desiderative part is receptive of cognition[374] too; if so, it is also receptive of knowledge. So, if it is not this part but rather the dianoetic part that is receptive of knowledge, then the desiderative part would not be receptive of ignorance either. By resorting to this *topos* it is possible to show that none of the ethical virtues is knowledge: for what is receptive of knowledge is also receptive of ignorance. So that if the rational part is receptive of ignorance, this – and not the affective part, in which ethical virtues reside – will be receptive of knowledge too. And one could also show through this *topos* that god is not receptive of life, since he is not receptive of death: for he is life itself, but not receptive of life. Or perhaps he is not receptive of it for this reason, namely because being alive is natural to him as the white is to the snow.

The *topos*, then, is useful for destructive purposes without qualification. But establishing that something belongs [to something] through it is not possible. However, one could establish that something is receptive of what is said to belong to it: for if it is receptive of its contrary, it is also receptive of it. In this way one would establish that matter is not privation, but rather receptive of privation, since it is also receptive of form, which is contrary to privation.[375] If, then, it is shown that the contrary belongs to the subject, it would be shown straightaway that what was posited as belonging to it does not belong to it; nonetheless, it would be established that [the subject] is receptive of it. And if it is only shown that the subject is receptive of the contrary of what is said to belong to it, it is possible that this belongs to it too; if, however, this is one of the contraries without intermediates, then it would also belong [to the subject] in general.

<Chapter 8>

113b15 And since the oppositions are four, one has to check from[376] the contradictions[377] inversely.

The *topos* is from the consequences based on the oppositions. For opposites are opposed to each other in four ways: either as affirmation and negation, or as contraries, or as possession and privation, or as relatives.[378] And there is a certain characteristic consequence according to each opposition, and he sketches how we can establish or demolish something by making a move from this consequence. And the consequence is not of the same type in all oppositions. Rather, the consequence occurring in the case of contradiction is inverse: for example, if the fine is pleasant, what is not pleasant is not fine.[379] But one ought not to say that what is not fine is not pleasant: for the [proposition] taking the predicate of the affirmation in the negative form and predicating the subject of the affirmation also in the negative form of what is taken in this way converts with the affirmation saying 'the fine is pleasant', which is true. For the [proposition] saying 'what is not pleasant is not fine' follows upon and converts with the aforementioned affirmation. But this is not the case with the [proposition] 'what is not fine is not pleasant': for, if this were so, then the consequence would be direct – i.e. if what is taken in the negative form starts from the same [term] from which the affirmation started. Rather, the [proposition] 'what is not pleasant is not fine' is what converts with the aforementioned affirmation. And in general one should take the consequence by taking the opposite of the consequent (if it is in a hypothetical) or of the predicate (if it is in a predicative proposition) and attach it, as what follows, to the opposite of the antecedent (if the proposition is hypothetical) or to the opposite of the subject (if the

20   proposition is predicative).[380] For if the aforementioned affirmation is true, such a negation will be true too, and if the negation is true, necessarily also the corresponding affirmation, converted in the aforementioned way, is true. Similarly, if either of them is false, the other is false too. For if it is false to say that the fine is pleasant, it is also false to say that what is not pleasant is not fine; and if the [proposition] 'the human being is an animal' is true, then also the one saying 'what is not an animal is not a human being'[381] is true. And again, if the [proposition] 'what is not a human being is not Socrates' is true, then also the affirmation saying that Socrates is a human being turns out to be true.

That 'the consequence is inverse'[382] in the case of contradiction must 'be taken' – he says – 'from induction'.[383] For 'if the human being is an animal, then what is

30   not an animal is not a human being';[384] and if a conception is a disposition, what
192,1   is not a disposition is not conception. For this reason, if what has come to be has a principle, then what does not have a principle has not come to be – but not as Melissos believed, that what has not come to be does not have a principle: for this is false. For many non-generated things have principles.[385] And if what is without parts is without extension, then what is not without extension is not without parts.

Sometimes, however, a direct consequence holds true as well, as in the case of propria and definitions. For if the human being is capable of laughing, what is not a human being is not capable of laughing; and if the colour white is capable of dilating sight, the colour that is not white is not capable of dilating sight. This kind of conversion, however, does not apply in general, but only with respect to some specific matter,[386] whereas the aforementioned one is valid in general: for it holds true not only with respect to propria and definitions, but also with respect

10   to genera, differences and accidents. And this sort of conversion is the one that is

called 'with opposition'.[387] And such is the consequence in the opposition of contradiction. And we will use it in this way both for destructive and for constructive purposes. If we are demolishing an affirmative by showing that the negative does not belong to the negative, we will do this: for if this is not the case, neither will the affirmative taken according to the conversion belong to the affirmative. For if it is not true that what is not good is not pleasure, neither is it true that pleasure is good; but the former is not true (the pleasures of the immoderate are pleasures without being good); therefore, pleasure is not good. In the same way, we will remove atomic lines.[388] For if what is indivisible by 20 nature is without parts, what is not without parts is not indivisible by nature; so that there would not be atomic lines, since there are no lines that are without parts: for only points are without parts – and lines are not points. If we are establishing the affirmative, once we have shown that the negative belongs to the negative we would have shown its affirmative converse too. For if what is not an animal is not a human being, then the human being is an animal; and if what is not good is not choiceworthy, then what is choiceworthy is good; and if what is not beneficial is not good, what is good is beneficial; so that, since health is choiceworthy, it is also good, and since it is good, it is also beneficial. And if what is not proper to us is not desirable, what is desirable is proper to us; but the divine is desirable for us; therefore, it is proper to us too.

In the same way in which one can both demolish and establish an affirmation 30 from a negation, one can also both establish and demolish a negation from an affirmation. For the establishment of one of them is also the establishment what 193,1 follows upon it, and similarly for the demolition. And such is the consequence of the opposites according to contradiction, and such are the demolitions and the establishments based on them. And he does not consider what follows upon the contradiction, as it may seem from the verbal formulation,[389] but what follows from either of the propositions from which the contradiction is made, as has been shown and as he says himself through the words: 'it is clear, then, that the consequence based on a contradiction is inverse with respect to both'.[390]

And in the case of the contraries the consequence is of this sort: if one contrary [belongs] to one contrary, then also the other contrary belongs to the other contrary. And this in two ways: for it can be either a direct or an inverse 10 [consequence]; in most cases it is direct, but there are cases in which it is inverse. The consequence of the contraries is direct when, given two contrarieties, the members of one contrariety follow upon the [corresponding] members of the other contrariety.[391] For example, courage and cowardice are contraries, as are virtue and vice; and virtue follows upon courage, whereas vice follows upon cowardice, which is contrary to courage; and being choiceworthy follows upon courage, whereas being worth avoiding follows upon cowardice; for being choiceworthy and being worth avoiding, being contraries, follow each upon one of those. And again, if the pleasant follows upon the fine and the troublesome follows upon the base, the consequence is direct. Also, if being imperishable follows upon being ungenerated and being perishable follows upon being

20   generated, in this case, too, the consequence is direct: for the ungenerated is contrary to the generated, and the imperishable is contrary to the perishable, and the latter two follow, as consequents, upon those two as antecedents. And since being dilating follows upon the white, being contracting follows upon the black: and being dilating and being contracting are contraries in the same way in which white and black are. And such is the direct consequence of the contraries.

An inverse [consequence] is, instead, if, given two contrarieties, it is not the case that both members of one contrariety follow each upon one of the members of the other contrariety, but one member of the first contrariety follows upon one member of the second contrariety, whereas, vice versa, the remaining member of the second contrariety follows upon the [remaining] member of the [first] contrariety, whose other member followed [upon the other member of the second contrariety]. For example, health and illness are contraries, and so are good physical condition and bad physical condition in their turn. And health

30   follows upon good physical condition (for everybody who is in a good physical condition is healthy), but it is not the case that illness (which is contrary to health) follows upon the bad physical condition (which was contrary to the good

194,1 physical condition); it is rather the other way round: bad physical condition follows upon illness (for anybody who is ill is in a bad physical condition, but not everybody who is in a bad physical condition is ill; in fact, there are some who are healthy and still in a bad physical condition). The consequence seems to be inverse also in the case of vice and virtue, and happiness and unhappiness: for unhappiness seems to follow upon vice, but it does not seem to be the case that happiness follows upon virtue; rather the other way round: virtue follows upon happiness (for the one who is happy has virtue from necessity, while, the one who has virtue is not happy in all cases). For as for the unskilled the lack of craft is sufficient for making mistakes in their activities once the matter is there, whereas for the skilled the craft is not enough for doing things correctly, but they

10   also need determinate tools, it seems that the situation is the same in the case of virtue and vice. And the consequences of the contraries are of these kinds. And that they are such – he says[392] – must be taken through induction as in the case of those based on contradiction.

And if we want to establish or demolish [a claim], the attacks from these consequences follow in this way: if we are establishing something, if the contrary follows upon the contrary, then also the contrary will follow upon the contrary, 'either directly or inversely';[393] if we are demolishing, once we show that one of the contraries does not follow upon one [in the other pair] of contraries in any way, we would have shown that the other contrary does not follow upon the other either. For example, in the case of good, bad, white and black, if the aim is to show that the black does not follow upon the bad, once we have shown that the white does not follow upon the good nor does the good follow upon the   20 white, we will have shown that the black does not follow upon the bad either. In the same way we will show that lack of self-control is not a vice by arguing that neither does virtue follow upon self-control nor does self-control follow upon virtue. And in few cases – he says[394] – the consequence of the contraries is inverse. He said 'similarly in the other [cases]'[395] meaning '[in the case of the other] virtues and vices': for as in the case of courage and cowardice, so also in the case of justice and injustice, moderation and immoderation, and all virtues and their contrary vices the consequence is direct.

Further, the consequence in the case of the opposites according to privation and possession is direct, and never inverse – as is the case with the contraries   30 instead. Examples of opposition according to possession and privation are sight and blindness, perception and lack of perception: if perception follows upon sight, lack of perception follows upon blindness. And again, hearing and being   195,1 deaf are opposite to each other as possession and privation; and comprehending and being unable to comprehend [are opposite] to each other in a similar way and, if comprehending follows upon hearing, so does being unable to comprehend follow upon being deaf. And again, order and disorder, form and privation: if form follows upon order, then privation follows upon disorder. But also life and death are opposite according to possession and privation, as well as perception and lack of perception; and if perceiving follows upon being alive, not perceiving follows upon being dead. So, we will establish and demolish either by showing that the one follows upon the other (for the remaining member of the first pair will then follow upon the remaining member of the second pair) or by arguing that the one does not follow upon the other.[396] For if knowledge does not follow   10 upon the living, neither does ignorance follow upon the dead: for one can ignore something even while being alive.

In the case of opposites according to privation and possession we have to make sure that one of the member of one of the two oppositions does not follow upon both of two opposites: for if this is the case, it will not be the case anymore that one member [of one pair] will follow upon one member [of the other pair] in the same way in which the other member [of the first pair] follows upon the other member [of the second pair]: for not only one, but both of them will follow upon it, as is the case with sight and blindness and life and death. For life follows upon both sight and blindness; for this reason death does not follow upon either. And similarly life follows upon being asleep and being awake, as well as upon all perceptions and their corresponding privations. So, one follows upon the other only then, i.e. when only one – and not both – follows upon the other: for it is

20   not possible that privation follows upon that upon which possession follows.

The consequence is similar with respect to the opposites according to what is relative, too: for the consequence is direct. Father and son, ruling and being ruled are opposite to each other as relatives; and if ruling follows upon the father, being ruled follows upon the son. And again, ruling and ruled, and acting well and being acted upon well; if, then, acting well follows upon what rules, also being acted upon well follows upon what is ruled. And again, the triple and the multiple, the third part and the fraction: as the multiple follows upon the triple, so the fraction follows upon the third.[397] But also knowledge is relative to the

30   knowable, and conception to the conceivable: and since conception follows upon knowledge, also the conceivable follows upon the knowable.[398] And similarly the double is relative to the half, and what exceeds is relative to what is exceeded: and

196,1   since what exceeds follows upon the double, what is exceeded follows upon the half. The consequences of these things too, then, are like this.

And the attacks moving from these [*topoi*] are clear, both in establishing and in demolishing. For if one of the opposites follows upon one of the corresponding opposites either according to possession and privation (about which we have talked before) or according to what is relative, also the remaining one will follow upon the other one. And if it is not the case that one member of a pair follows upon one member of the other pair, neither will the remaining member of the first pair follow upon the remaining member of the second pair – provided that the condition[399] specified for possessions and privations is satisfied.[400] For it is not the case that, since being dead does not follow upon being asleep, then being alive also does not follow upon being awake: for being alive follows upon both.

10   And having said these things, he mentions an objection which one can move against the attack from the relatives: for perception and perceptible, knowledge and knowable are both opposites as relatives, and the knowable follows upon the perceptible, but it is no longer the case that knowledge follows upon perception. And although he mentions the objection, he says that it is not correct.[401] For it is not conceded that the knowable follows upon the perceptible: for there is

perception of individual animals, but there is no knowledge of them, if knowledge is of the universals. And if there is no knowledge of them, which are perceptible, they would not be knowable. And he adds that the given example is rather useful with respect to the contrary.[402] What he means is this: one could rather establish that what is perceptible is not knowable from the claim that perception is not knowledge, which is opposite to 'what is perceptible is knowable', which was   20 taken to demolish the *topos*: for in this passage he called 'contrary'[403] not the contrary strictly speaking, but the opposite.

<Chapter 9>

114a26 And again in the case of coordinates and inflections.

The *topos* is from the coordinates. This one, too, is useful both for constructive and for destructive purposes, being from consequence too. For the consequence is that, as something is shown to be the case with respect to one of the coordinates, the same will hold with respect to the others too. And what things are coordinates and what inflections, and that inflections, too, are counted among the coordinates (for inflections are coordinates, whereas coordinates are not inflections) – he himself has illustrated these things clearly through the examples. For the   30 things that derive their name[404] from something, as the just [thing] and the just [man][405] from justice, are coordinates of each other and of justice itself, from which they are named. And the just [thing] and the just [man] are determinate things,[406] respectively: one thing which has come to be from justice and one   197,1 thing that has justice. And similarly for courage, courageous [thing], courageous [man]: these, again, are coordinates of each other, being determinate things – one is a disposition and the others are its paronyms: of the others, one is what has come about according to that disposition, and one what has that disposition. And one would call 'coordinates' these things, i.e. those that, being some determinate things, derive their name from something [and are coordinates] of each other and of that from which they derive their name; e.g. grammar, grammatical, grammarian; medicine, medical, medic; music, musical, musician. And this applies not only to the things that are named after medicine or music or some other disposition for having come about according to it as coordinates of the disposition, as the grammatical and the musical. Rather, it applies in general to all cases displaying a similar linguistic structure, being   10 called in this way by being productive of or by preserving the thing after which they are named. These things, too, are coordinates of the latter: for things are also said to be healthy and wholesome – some because they are productive of health and of good physical condition, some because they preserve health or good physical condition. These things too, then, are coordinate to the things they are 'productive of or preserving',[407] after which they are also named. And he speaks as if it is customary to call 'coordinate' the things of this sort and which derive their name from some things in this way; for this reason he added also: 'such things are usually called "coordinates".'[408] And he says that 'inflections' are called the things with this morphological structure: 'justly', 'courageously', 'musically' – these are inflections (the one of 'just', the other of 'courageous', and the last one of

20   'musical';[409] or one of 'justice', one of 'courage', and one of 'music': for their inflections, too, are said in the same way in which paronyms are said from them). And coordinates would differ from inflections in that those are determinate things, whereas inflections are not indicative of underlying things but of the mode of a certain activity or disposition: for such are the things that are medically, musically and healthily. And he says that both inflections and the corresponding coordinates are with reference to the dispositions from which also the aforementioned coordinates get their names: the inflection 'courageously' with reference to courage, 'justly' with reference to justice, and 'musically' with reference to music. And similarly for the other cases, as if the just [thing], the just [man], and justly were coordinates of justice, whereas the courageous [thing], the courageous [man], and courageously were coordinates of courage. So they

30   are all coordinates to all, whereas they are not inflections in a similar way: for it is not the case that as 'justly' is an inflection of 'justice', so also 'justice' is an inflection of 'justly'.[410]

198,1   And coordinates and inflections are of this sort. And the *topos* is from them: if it is under investigation about something whether something (e.g. being choiceworthy or praiseworthy or something else, e.g. good or to be avoided or something of this sort) is an accident of it, it is required that, by passing over[411] to some of its coordinates, one show that what is under investigation belongs to it. For once it has been shown that what is under investigation belongs to one of the coordinates, it would be shown that it belongs to this too – for what belongs to one belongs to the others as well. For example, if what is under investigation is whether being praiseworthy belongs to justice, if someone shows that being praiseworthy belongs to one of its coordinates, what is submitted will have been shown too: for what is shown to hold for one member of the series of

10   coordination,[412] the same will hold for the rest too. For example, if the just is equal, then also justice is equality and the just man is an equal man and what is

justly is equally; and if being courageously or justly admits of higher and lower degrees, then also courage and justice will admit of higher and lower degrees; whereas if those do not admit of higher and lower degrees, neither will these. Similarly, if it is possible to perceive to a higher or lower degree, then perception will admit of higher and lower degree. And the same applies to pleasure, too. And dying justly is dying praiseworthily, since what is just is praiseworthy; and [it is done] praiseworthily because the action, which is an appropriate judgement,[413] is praiseworthy – where being praiseworthy is said with reference to the judgement through which the person dies, and not with reference to the person who dies.[414] In this way one could show that the wise man is not rich as they say: for if richness consists in the acquisition of wisdom, then wisdom would turn out to be richness, which it is not. So that it is also not the case that the wise man, in so   20 far as he is wise, is rich. Furthermore, if the wise man is rich, then [doing something] wisely will be [doing something] richly. And it is clear that the shift will be to what is better known in the series of coordination and to what can be more easily shown. For the disposition is, by nature, first among its paronyms and it is because something belongs incidentally to it that it also belongs incidentally to them.[415] But in the context of the discussion what is better known to us becomes first, even if it is posterior by nature. And if we want to demolish something, e.g. that what is just is not without advantages, as some people believe, once we show that this does not belong to one of the coordinates, e.g. to justice (for it is a virtue and no virtue is without advantages to the one whose virtue it is), we would have shown also that what is just is not of this sort. And having said, after the other coordinates of justice, that also the inflection [indicating] the   30 just way[416] will be praiseworthy, he added how being praiseworthy will apply to the just way: 'for justly will be said to be praiseworthily according to the same   199,1 inflection from the praiseworthy, precisely in the same way in which justly is said from justice'.[417] For justice will be said to be praiseworthy, and the just thing a praiseworthy thing, and the just man a praiseworthy man, and the just way a praiseworthy way: for as 'justly' is an inflection of justice, so 'praiseworthily', too, is an inflection of the praiseworthy.[418]

114b6 And one should not only consider the very thing that is said, but also the contrary with respect to the contrary.

Having shown the resources for an attack from the coordinates, he adds to the aforementioned *topos* also the *topos* from the contraries of each of the coordinates. And injustice is contrary to justice, the unjust [man] to the just   10

[man], the unjust [thing] to the just [thing], and the unjust way to the just way. One, then – he says –, has to carry out the attack from the contraries of what is submitted too, and not only from the coordinates, by checking whether the contrary [belongs to] the contrary. For if one is enquiring into whether the good is pleasant, one has to see whether the contrary of the pleasant, which is the painful, follows upon the contrary of the good (and this is the bad). And, if it follows, then one has to show that also the pleasant follows upon the good; if, instead, it does not follow (for there are also some bad things that are pleasant), then the pleasant would not follow upon the good in all cases. And also, if one is enquiring into whether justice is knowledge, one has to check whether injustice is ignorance: for if this is the case, then that is also the case, whereas if this is not

20   the case, then that is also not the case. And again, since the unjust way is the contrary of the just way, if one is enquiring into whether 'knowingly and skilfully'[419] follows upon justly, one has to check whether unknowingly and unskillfully follow upon unjustly: for if they follow upon this, then also [those will follow upon] that, whereas if these do not follow upon this – as it seems – neither will those follow upon justly. For it seems that what comes about unjustly comes about rather skilfully than unskillfully: for what comes about unjustly often comes about voluntarily and from deliberation, and these features derive from skill.

And the ground for such an argument is that, as was already said above, if one contrary follows upon one contrary, then necessarily also the other contrary follows upon the other contrary, either directly or inversely, as he spelled out in the consequences of the contraries.[420] For this reason he himself added that

30   'this *topos* was mentioned before, in the consequences of the contraries':[421] for
200,1 the same thing was said there and shown and required based on this *topos*. And the *topos* from the contraries belongs to the same family[422] as the one from the coordinates in so far as, by taking the contrary in the same nominative form or inflection[423] [as the terms of the desired conclusion], we show through it what is submitted too.[424] For example, if one is enquiring into whether what is [done] justly is also [done] praiseworthily, taking what is [done] unjustly we will enquire into whether it is [done] blameworthily; and if we are not considering what is [done] justly but rather the just thing, then we will not consider what is [done] unjustly but what is unjust, taking the contraries according to the same series of coordination according to which the submitted [terms], into which we are enquiring, have been taken: for if the inflection of one contrary belongs to the inflection of one contrary, then also the inflection of the other contrary will belong to the inflection of the other contrary.

114b16 Furthermore both the one who is demolishing and the one who is   10
establishing [should check] with reference to generations and corruptions and
productive things and corruptive things.

Having mentioned both constructive and destructive *topoi* from the
consequents[425] in the case of the opposites and from the coordinates, he sketches
some further resources for attacks which (similarly to the previous ones) are
from consequence and are useful both for constructive and for destructive
purposes. This one[426] is from the generations and corruptions and again from
productive and corruptive things, each of which would be a *topos* in its own
right.[427] 'For the things whose generations are good are good themselves',[428] and
vice versa: 'if the things' that come to be are good, 'then also the corresponding
generations'[429] are good. For example, if the generation of health (and this is the   20
moderate regime) is a good thing, then health, whose generation consists in this
sort of regime, is also a good thing; and if health is a good thing, then the
moderate regime is a good thing in turn. And since virtue is a good thing, its
generation is a good thing too: and this is the conduct, starting from one's
childhood, according to the habits that lead to virtue; and since this conduct,
which is the generation of virtue, is a good thing, then also what comes to be, i.e.
virtue, is a good thing. In a certain way this *topos*, too, is from the coordinates,
except that coordinates are said to be e.g. [what is] conducive to health, healthy,
healthily, whereas recovering health is not a coordinate of health.[430] In this way
you could show that, since education is a good thing, also being educated is
good: for this is the generation of education.   201,1

Alternatively, in this context he calls 'generation' not that through which
something comes to be, but the very coming to be:[431] for if health's coming
to be is a good thing, then health is a good thing, too; and if health is a good
thing, also health's coming to be is a good thing. The same account applies to
virtue as well.

'In the case of corruptions',[432] however, the situation is no longer the same as
in the case of generations; rather, the consequence is inverse: for 'the things
whose corruptions are good, these are bad',[433] whereas things whose corruption
is a bad thing, these are good. For example, if the corruption of a disease is good,
then the disease is bad; for the corruption of diseases consists in the moderate
regime, which is good; and if the corruption of health is bad, health is good: for
the licentious regime, which is bad, is corruptive of health. Alternatively, in these
cases, too, we do not have to take things that are corruptive (for the productive   10
things are those of which he will speak), but the very passing away.[434]

And what applies in the case of generations and corruptions also applies in the case of productive and corruptive things respectively: for the things whose productive and preserving things are good are good too. For example, since things that produce health are good, health is a good thing too. And, vice versa, since health is a good thing, things that produce health are good too. 'On the other hand, the things whose corruptive things are good, these are bad,'[435] and things whose corruptive things are bad, these are good: for what is corruptive of a disease is good, since the disease is bad, and what is corruptive of health is bad, because health is good.

One would also investigate the case of productive things, whether, in the same
20   way in which things whose productive factors are good are good too, so also things whose productive factors are bad, these are bad too, and furthermore, if the latter are good, whether their productive factors are good too. For if this is so, it will seem that what the Stoics say is well said: what comes to be through a bad thing is not good; and richness comes to be also through the trade of a brothel-keeper, which is bad; therefore richness is not good.[436] Or the *topos* is reputable, but not true: for nothing prevents something good from coming to be from something bad, as health comes to be through cauterizations and surgery, which are bad. Perhaps he himself will seem to say this and to make a distinction: for when he says 'the same account applies to the cases of productive and corruptive things,'[437] he adds in what sense and with respect to what he said this: 'for the things whose productive factors' were[438] 'good, these too are good, whereas the
30   things whose corruptive factors are good, these are bad.'[439] But he did not add further 'the productive factors of things whose outcomes are good are good', nor 'the outcomes of things whose productive factors are bad are bad'. For in the
202,1 same way in which, in all cases, if the premises are true, a true conclusion is reached, but not in all cases a true [conclusion derives] from true [premises] (for it is also possible that a true [conclusion is reached] from false premises) – in the same way, then, also what comes to be from good things is good, but it is not the case that, in general, if a thing is good, its productive factors are good. For it is also possible that a good thing comes to be from a bad one. Therefore, he spoke as if up to this point the features of productive and corruptive things conform to what was said for the cases of generations and corruptions, but you would find that there is a difference between a generation and a productive thing, because a generation would be said with reference to the thing itself but not with reference to its productive factors. For example, if virtue's coming to be is good, then virtue is good too, and if virtue is good, then its coming to be is good too; and vice
10   versa, if virtue's passing away is bad, then virtue is good, and if virtue is good,

then its coming to be is good and its passing away is bad. And if a disease's passing away is good, then the disease is bad. The examples of generations provided a little earlier[440] are not cases of generation or of corruption, but rather cases of productive factors, with respect to which only that claim is true, i.e. that if the productive factors are good, then the outcomes are good, and if the corruptive factors are good, then they are bad. However, the vice versa does not hold because it is possible that some good things come to be from bad things too, as health from cauterizations and surgery and from a starvation-diet, or richness from the trade of the brothel-keeper.

<Chapter 10>

114b25 And again with respect to similar things, whether they are in a similar way.

The *topos* that he recalls now is also from consequence, i.e. from the [consequence] in the case of things that are the same by analogy and in the case of similarity. 20 For example, since knowledge and knowable stand to each other in the same relation as opinion and opinable, if knowledge of several things is one, it would be shown that the same applies to opinion too: for this is the consequence. And if this holds in the case of opinion, it would be shown that the same applies to the case of knowledge in turn. In this way, if one takes that sight stands to seeing in the same way in which the sense of hearing stands to hearing, he will show that, since having sight is not sufficient for seeing (for light and distance are needed too), it is also not the case that having hearing is sufficient for hearing. Similarly, if having hearing is not sufficient for hearing, having sight would not be enough for seeing either; and if the one is sufficient, then the other is sufficient too. For the *topos* is both constructive and destructive. And since the art of house-building stands to the house in the same relation as the art of ship-building stands to the ship, if the presence of the art of house-building is sufficient for the production of a house, then also the presence of the art of ship-building would be sufficient for the production of a ship; if, on the other hand, the presence of the one is not sufficient for the production of the corresponding products, neither would the presence of the other be sufficient for the production of the corresponding products. 203,1

And – he says[441] – one should resort to this *topos* both with reference to things that are truly similar and with reference to things that seem to be similar. With

respect to things that are truly similar, what is shown will also be true; with respect to the things that seem to be similar, what is shown will not be true, but will appear to be so. To begin with, it is not true that knowledge stands to what is
10 knowable in all respects in the same way in which opinion stands to to what is opinable, if in truth knowledge is immutable with respect to what is knowable, whereas opinion is not of this sort. But it is also not the case that sight stands to seeing in the same way in which touch stands to touching: for the former receives its proper perceptible through a certain medium and when this is illuminated, whereas touch does not work in this way.

There seems to be a similarity also with respect to the morphology of words: for it seems that *horan* ['seeing'] is similar to *boan* ['shouting'], *ponein* ['suffering'] to *poiein* ['doing'], and *huphainen* ['weaving'] to *hugiainein* ['being healthy'].[442] And if someone required that, since *boan* [shouting] is doing, then also *horan* [seeing] is doing, and since *ponein* [suffering] is being affected, then also *poiein* [doing] is being affected, and since *huphanein* [weaving] is being active, then also *hugiainein* [being healthy] is being active, one will lead an attack from a seeming similarity. For the similarity among the aforementioned terms does not
20 obtain with respect to the thing, but only with respect to the linguistic expression. For this reason the use of this *topos* with reference to such cases is superficial and sophistic.

114b31 And [one should] check whether things are similar with respect to the one and with respect to the many: for sometimes there is a discrepancy.

This *topos*, too, is from consequence. And it is like this: if one thing of a certain kind [relates] to one thing, then several such things will [relate correspondingly] to several things; for this is the consequence. For example, if teaching one person is benefitting one person, then also teaching many will be benefiting many; or, if the latter is not the case, then the former is not the case either. And again, if remembering something occurs together with imagining it, also remembering
204,1 many things would occur together with imagining many. And if one human being is a rational being, then many are rational beings. And if knowing is thinking, also knowing many things at the same time will be thinking many things at the same time; and if it is impossible to think many things at the same time, then knowing would not be thinking. And that thinking many things at the same time does not follow upon knowing many things at the same time is clear from the fact that it is possible to know many things at the same time, but it is impossible to think many things at the same time: for everybody who thinks

thinks of something one. For thinking is an activity and a journey of the soul: thinking many things at the same time is as impossible as uttering many discourses at the same time; for thought is a certain discourse of the soul talking 10 to herself. Or perhaps it is not necessary that, if it is not possible that the one who knows many things at the same time also thinks many things at the same time, then it is also not the case that knowing is thinking. And this is also what he seems to say: for by adding 'for sometimes there is a discrepancy',[443] he added the qualification 'for example, if knowing is thinking, then also knowing many things is thinking many things: but this is not true'.[444] Alternatively, he said 'for sometimes there is a discrepancy' not to discredit the *topos*,[445] but to make clear in what cases the *topos* is useful for destructive purposes. For in the cases in which it looks like something holds for one but it is no longer possible that the same holds for many, in these cases we will demolish also what appears to be the case for one by starting from the many, as it happens for [the claim] that the one who knows thinks. For this, which seems to be the case,[446] is in contrast with the 20 [claim that] it is not possible that the one who knows many things at the same time also thinks many things at the same time; for this reason that, too, would not be true. Alternatively, ['sometimes there is a discrepancy' means that] it is not necessary that, if one is knowledgeable, then also many are knowledgeable, and that if one is dark, it is not necessary that many be dark, and if one has six fingers, it is not [necessary] that many do. Or perhaps the place would go through with respect to things that are naturally and according to nature.[447]

114b37 Furthermore, also from the more and less.

He presents us both constructive and destructive *topoi* from the more and less and, furthermore, from the similar degree. And these *topoi* have their utility in comparisons: for more and less and similar degree occur in them. And he first recalls the *topoi* from the more and the less; then, he adds to these also those 205,1 from the similar degree.

He says that the *topoi* from the more are four,[448] and similarly for the *topoi* from the less, each of which is useful both for destructive and for constructive purposes. The four *topoi*, as he says, are if one takes the comparison according to the more and less with reference to one thing about one thing or with reference to one thing about two[449] or with reference to two about one[450] or with reference to two about two.[451]

And the first one he mentions is of one about one. It is like this: if one is investigating about some things whether the one belongs to the other, if both of them receive the more and the less, it is required that one check whether the more belongs to the more. <For if the more belongs to the more>,[452] then also what is without qualification will belong to what is without qualification. If, instead, the more does not belong to the more, then neither will what is without qualification belong to what is without qualification. For example, if one is enquiring into whether the good belongs to pleasure or not, since both receive the more and the less, one has to check whether more good belongs to more pleasure: for if more pleasure is more good, then also pleasure would be good; if, on the other hand, more pleasure is not more good than less pleasure is, then pleasure would not be good either.[453] And again, if one is investigating whether being unjust is bad, one has to enquire into whether being unjust to a higher degree is bad to a higher degree than being unjust to a lesser degree: for if we show that this is the case, then we would have shown that being unjust is bad; whereas if it were shown that being unjust to a higher degree is not bad to a higher degree, then being unjust would not be bad to start with.[454] And it seems to some people that being a tyrant, which is being unjust to a higher degree, is not bad. And again, if being in pain to a higher degree is bad to a higher degree, then also being in pain is bad; and if being in poverty to a higher degree is bad to a higher degree, than being in poverty, too, [is bad]; and if being laborious to a higher degree is good to a higher degree, then also being laborious is such.

The *topoi* starting from the more are destructive, whereas those starting from the less are constructive: for, in having shown that the more[455] does not belong, both what is without qualification and the less are demolished too; on the other hand, in having shown that the less belongs, what is without qualification and the more are established too. And one has to secure whether the increase of the predicate belongs to the increase of the subject by taking this through induction. For example, the pleasure deriving from sex is pleasure to a higher degree; but also the pleasure deriving from eating and drinking is [so]: for they seem to be more intense. And what is more intense is of this sort to a higher degree. If, then, these pleasures are not good to a higher degree because the corresponding desires are not good either, pleasure would not be good either.

And the *topos* would seem to be reputable rather than true: for the excesses of many things, in addition to not being good, are bad, whereas the things themselves are good. For example, doing gymnastics in the right amount, which is good (for it produces health) has an excess which is bad: for excessive gymnastics corrupts health. And the excess of richness is not good, while richness is a good. Or a higher degree in the amount of richness is not a bad thing if

someone uses it as a tool for good things; and such a [greater amount of richness]⁴⁵⁶ is good. However, if gymnastics is defined in terms of being productive of health or good physical condition, the exercises which do not 10
produce the latter are not gymnastics, since they do not fall under the definition of gymnastics: for in these⁴⁵⁷ the higher degree preserves the proper nature to a higher degree.

*115a5*⁴⁵⁸ *Another* topos: *if one thing is said about two.*

The second *topos* he presents from the more is the one which says 'one thing about two'. It is like this: if one is investigating about some one thing which seems to belong to several things whether it belongs to some of them or not, one has to investigate whether it does not belong to the thing among them to which it seems to belong more; for if it does not belong to the thing to which it seems to belong more, then it would not belong to what is submitted either; whereas if it is shown to belong to the thing to which it seems to belong less, then it would also belong to what is submitted. For the thing that does not belong to that to which it seems to belong more would not belong to that to which it seems to 20
belong less, whereas the thing which belongs to that to which it seems to belong less would also belong to that to which it seems to belong more. For example, if one is investigating whether the good belongs to richness, and the former appears to belong to health more, but it is shown that it does not belong [to health] (either because it is possible that health is put by someone to a bad use or because the one who has it does not do anything good with it), then [the good] would not belong to richness either. And if it were shown that the good belongs to doing gymnastics, which seems to be less good than richness, because it produces health, then it would be also shown that it belongs to richness. For in these cases one thing, i.e. the good, is said about two things, i.e. health and 207,1
richness or doing gymnastics and richness. And again, if pleasure is good to a higher degree than lack of pain is, and pleasure is not good, then lack of pain would not be good either. Or if lack of pain, which seems to be good to a lesser degree than pleasure, is good, then pleasure would be good too. And if wisdom, which is more of an end than pleasure, is not an end, then pleasure would not be an end either. And if the Spartans, who are more of a match in battle than the other Greeks, are not a match in battle, then the other Greeks will not be a match either. And if it is plausible that old people are moderate to a higher degree than young people, and yet they are not moderate, then young people would be not moderate either. However, [this]⁴⁵⁹ does not show that in these cases something 10

does not belong to the thing to which it belongs to a lesser degree or that it belongs to the thing to which it belongs to a higher degree.[460]

115a8 And again, if two things are said about one.

The third *topos* is, in a certain sense, the converse of the second: for, in the second, one thing was said about two, whereas in this one two things are said about one. For when some two things seem to belong to the same thing, if the thing that seems to belong to it to a higher degree does not belong to it, then the one that seems to belong to it to a lesser degree would not belong to it either, whereas if the thing which seems to belong to a lesser degree belongs, then also what seems to belong to a higher degree would belong. For example, if being useful, which seems to belong to learning more than being pleasant, does not belong to it, then being pleasant would not belong to it either; or if this, then that one too. And if

20 the bold man, who seems to be more courageous than wise, is not courageous, then he would not be wise either. And again, if the fair man, who seems to be less just than philanthropic, is just, then he would be philanthropic too.[461] And if being unjust, which is more advantageous than fine, is not advantageous, then it would not be fine either.

115a11 Furthermore, if two are said about two.

The fourth *topos* is if the things that belong are two and the things to which they belong are two and are such that, of these, the one seems to belong to the

208,1 one to a higher degree, whereas the other seems to belong to the other to a lesser degree. For in these cases, too, if it is shown that the thing which seems to belong to something to a higher degree does not belong to it, then the thing which seems to belong to something to a lesser degree would not belong to the latter either; whereas if it is shown that the thing that seems to belong to the its own subject to a lesser degree belongs to it, then also the thing which seems to belong to its own subject to a higher degree would belong to it. For example, if pleasure is good to a lesser degree than toil is bad, and pleasure is good, then also toil would be bad; and if the profligate person seems to be generous to a higher degree than the stingy one seems to be moderate, and the profligate is not generous, then the stingy person would not be moderate either. And if the fair person seems to be just to a lesser degree than the unfair[462] one

10 seems to be unjust, and the fair one is just, then the unfair person would be unjust.

115a15 Furthermore from belonging or seeming [to belong] to a similar degree.[463]

He adds the *topoi* from the similar degree to the four *topoi* from the more and less: for these, too, deal with things that present a comparison and are comparable. And he says that these *topoi*, too, are three, in analogy to the last three aforementioned *topoi* from the more and the less: for there is no *topos* of those from the similar degree which is analogous to the first one of those from the more, through which it was shown that one thing belongs to one thing because the increase belongs to its increase. For in the *topoi* from the similar degree one has to show the similar through the similar, but what is shown through what belongs to a higher or to a lesser degree cannot be shown through what belongs   20 to a similar degree: for what belongs to a thing to a higher or to a lesser degree would not belong to it to a similar degree too. If, then, something seems to belong to a similar degree to two things, if it does not belong to the one it will not belong to the other either, whereas if it belongs to one of them, it would be shown to belong to the remaining one too. For if fame and richness seem to be good to a similar degree, and fame is not good, then richness would not be good either; or, if fame is good, then richness would be shown to be good too. And if one ought to obey the law and his father to a similar degree, if he must obey the law, then he must obey the father too. Or again, if two things seem to belong to a similar degree to one thing, if the one belongs [to it], the other would belong   209,1 [to it] too; or if the one does not belong, the other would not belong either. For example, if the good and the beneficial belong to justice to a similar degree, and the beneficial does not belong to it, then the good would not belong to it either; or, if the one belongs [to it], then the other belongs too. And if both being bold when one ought to and experiencing fear when one ought to belong to the courageous man to a similar degree, if experiencing fear when one ought to does not belong to him, then being bold when one ought to would not belong to him either; or if this, then that one too. Furthermore, if two things seem to belong to two things to a similar degree, one each, if one of the two does not belong to the corresponding one of the two, then the remaining one would not belong to the remaining one either; whereas if one of the things that seem to belong to some things to a similar degree belongs to the one, then the other would belong to the   10 other too. For example, if boldness seems to belong to the courageous man to a similar degree as weakness [seems to belong] to the coward man, if boldness does not belong to the courageous, then weakness would not belong to the coward either; or if weakness belongs to the latter, then boldness, too, belongs to the former. And if the courageous man deals with fears and confidence to a similar degree as the moderate one deals with pleasures and pains, and the courageous man deals with fears and confidence, then also the moderate one would deal with pleasures and pains. And if the just man is a friend of the gods to a similar degree as the unjust is an enemy of the gods, if the one, then the other too; if not the one, then not the other either. And if pleasure is good to a similar degree as toil is bad, and toil is bad, then also pleasure is good.

<Chapter 11>

115a26 Furthermore from addition, if one thing added to the other makes [the latter] good or white.

He presents two *topoi* from the addition of one thing to another that are only constructive. And the first one of them is like this: if something when added to something else makes the latter such and such, without this having been so before, then the former thing is such and such already prior [to the addition].[464] For example, if something, when added to something else which is not white has made it white, then the thing that has been added is white already prior [to the addition]; and if something, when added to something else which is not sweet-smelling, has made it sweet-smelling, then it is itself sweet-smelling; and if something, when added to something which is not sweet, has made it sweet, then the added thing is sweet already prior [to the addition]. And similarly, if a certain figure, when added to some other figure, makes it triangular, then the added figure itself will be a triangle.[465] And if virtue, when added to someone, makes them excellent, then it is itself of such a sort.

   And it is clear that one has to resort to this *topos* with reference to things that are said to be such and such by nature and not by some law and convention. For if an ounce is added to eleven ounces it makes a pound, which [the eleven ounces] were not before; however, it is not the case that, on this ground, the ounce is itself a pound. For pound and ounce are according to convention – ounces and pounds differ from each other among different people. Alternatively, the ounce is not a pound for this reason, i.e. that both it and the things to which it is added, i.e. the eleven ounces, contribute to the constitution of the whole pound. But <this>[466] does not contribute to the eleven ounces' growing heavier: for they have their weight from themselves, whereas the increase in weight derives from what is added. For this reason, since the whole grows heavier with the addition of one ounce, it is necessary that that ounce, too, be heavy, as

210,1

10

the second *topos* shows.[467] In this way Plato, too, showed that the soul is life: if the soul is life, then it could not receive the contrary, and in this way it would be immortal.[468]

The objection to the *topos* is that many drugs, when added to some things, seem to make the whole curative or poisonous, while none of them taken in isolation is of this sort. Or in these cases, too, one can say that, if the cause 20 resides only in what is added, then it, too, would be such and such, whereas if such and such a quality is the result of the mixture and fusion of all ingredients, which all contribute to it, then nothing would be said against the *topos*. For the *topos* says that, if something which is not such and such becomes such and such through the addition of something without any contribution of the substrate to the acquisition of such a property (for this has to be understood), then it is required that what is added was such and such even before – but it does not say that if something becomes such and such from the mixture of some things, then also each of the components of the mixture is such and such: for wine, when mixed with honey, makes the whole *oinomeli*,[469] which it was not before this. But that the last added ingredient is not the only cause of this change in the whole is clear from the fact that, even if, by modifying [the order in which we add the ingredients], we put this in first and, subtracting some other of the ingredients 211,1 which were in the substrate until now, we added it at a later stage, the resulting whole would be similar.

And the first *topos* of those from addition is like this. The second one is this: if something, when added to something else, makes the latter such and such to a higher degree, then it will be such and such itself. And it is clear that this *topos*, too, is useful in things that admit of the more and the less. For if what was added to something sweet has made it sweeter, then it would be sweet itself, and if whiter, the it would be white; if more choiceworthy, then it would be choiceworthy itself; and if heavier, then it will be heavy too, as we said for the case of the ounce.[470] In this way, one could show that each of the things called 'indifferent' 10 and 'preferred' by the more recent [philosophers][471] is choiceworthy and good: for each of them, when added to virtue, makes the whole more choiceworthy for the excellent man. For a life according to virtue is more choiceworthy if it comes with health and with resources and with good reputation. For things to be chosen or to be avoided are discerned through the choice and avoidance of the excellent man.

Having said that if what is added to something makes the latter such and such to a higher degree <etc.>,[472] he added: 'and similarly in the other cases as well',[473] because this applies not only to quality, but also to quantity. For if what is added [to something] makes it bigger, then it [falls] itself within magnitude, and if more numerous, it [falls] itself within plurality. Alternatively, when he says 'if something is added to what is already there and makes it such and such to a

20   higher degree',[474] as if referring to something one and determinate, he added 'and similarly in the other cases as well', in order to clarify that the *topos* does not proceed with reference to this thing only (i.e. the thing which becomes such and such to a higher degree), but also with reference to other things in which this is the case.

The aforementioned *topoi* are useful only for constructive purposes and not for destructive ones. For it is not the case that, if something, when added to something else, does not make the latter white or sweet or whiter or sweeter, then, on this ground, it is also not white or sweet itself. For a little amount of honey mixed with absinthe does not make the latter sweet, nonetheless it is not the case that, on this ground, it is not sweet either. Nor is it the case that, since richness, when added to vice, does not make the whole choiceworthy, it is not choiceworthy on this ground. But it is also not the case that, since sweet wine,

30   when mixed with honey, does not make the latter sweeter, then on this ground it is not sweet. He said: 'the *topos* is not useful in all cases, but in those in which

212,1 there happens to occur an increase in degree'[475] because not all things receive the more and the less. For example, a substance is not more or less than another substance; for this reason the *topos* is not useful for this case: for nothing, when added to a substance, will make it more of a substance. Furthermore 'an increase in degree happens to occur' in those things which are already such and such prior to the addition, e.g. sweet things which will be sweeter, warm things which will be warmer. And since quality receives the more, the *topos* would be useful with reference to things that fall under quality.[476] However, even 'the good, when added to the bad, does not necessarily makes the whole good'.[477]

10   He said this since it is possible that on occasion a great good, when added to a small bad, makes the whole choiceworthy, e.g. if virtue is added to poverty: for virtue is choiceworthy even if it is with poverty. And also the fine deriving from courage, when added to death, which is bad, makes the whole choiceworthy: for this reason some death is glorious. However, it is not the case that any good, when added to a bad, makes the whole good: certainly, richness, when added to illness, does not make the whole choiceworthy. And it would have been more appropriate if this had been added to the previous *topos* in which it was required that 'if one thing, when added to another, makes it good or white while it was not good or white before, then what is added'[478] turns out to be good or white.

115b3 And again, if something is said to a higher or a lesser degree, then it also obtains without qualification.

This *topos*, too, applies to the things that admit of the more and the less and is   20
useful for the corresponding comparison. And, similarly to the previous ones, it
is constructive only, while it is no longer destructive: for what is more or less
something than something else is also this without qualification not in the sense
that it is such and such by its own nature, but rather in the sense that the feature
according to which it is more or less than something else belongs to it. For
example, if this determinate thing is more or less sweet than something else, it is
also sweet without qualification: for if it were not sweet at all, it would not be said
to be more or less sweet than something else. For nothing which does not
participate in something is said to have that more or less than something else: for
example, if it does not participate in the white, it is not more or less white than
something else, if we use 'less' strictly speaking.[479] But what does not participate
in anything else cannot be more or less than anything else with respect to this.   30
The thing which is more and less than something else, this thing also participates   213,1
in that without qualification.[480] Therefore, when we investigate whether
something belongs to something else among the things that admit the more and
the less, we have to investigate whether what is submitted is more or less than
something else with respect to that property about which we investigate whether
it belongs to it. For if any of these cases[481] is shown, it would be shown that it
belongs to it without qualification as well. For example, if [it is shown that] virtue
is more choiceworthy than health, then virtue is choiceworthy; and if a cloak is
less white than snow, it is also white.

It seems that the *topos* admits of an objection: for earth is said to be lighter
than earth, but being light does not belong to it without qualification. Or 'lighter'
is not said of earth strictly speaking, but rather instead of 'less heavy'. Nor is
poverty choiceworthy without qualification, although it is said to be more   10
choiceworthy than illness. Or in these cases too 'choiceworthy' is not said strictly
speaking, but rather in the sense of 'to be avoided to a lesser degree'.

So, as he said, the *topos* is useful for constructive purposes, but no longer for
destructive ones. For it is not true that, if something does not admit of the more
and the less, then it is not so without qualification either, nor that if it is so without
qualification, then it is so more or less than something else as well. For example,
neither substance nor some of the quantities admit the more and the less, as it is
shown in the *Categories*:[482] for this reason it is not necessary that something is not a
human being if it is neither more nor less of a human being [than something else].

115b11 And one has to examine in the same way also what concerns some particular respect and time and place.

20 Having given a constructive *topos* from the more and the less (for the thing which is something more or less than something else, this thing is so without qualification as well), he adds a *topos* with reference to some particular respect, a *topos* from time, and a *topos* from place, as if these bore a certain similarity to the previous *topos*. For in the same way in which what belongs to something to a higher degree also belongs to it without qualification, also what belongs to something in some particular respect or at some time or place seems to belong to it without qualification too. For example, the animal which has sight in some respect also has sight without qualification; and similarly for the animal which hears in some respect or smells in some respect or tastes. And also each of the generated bodies, being at some time, is without qualification as well; and if the hippocentaur or Scylla were somewhere, then they would be without qualification as well.[483] And what heals in summer also heals without qualification, and what

30 heals in Greece also heals without qualification, and the body which is somewhere

214,1 is also without qualification. With reference to these examples, then, the *topoi* are consistent, but they are not true in all cases: for this reason we have to use them as persuasive but not as compelling.[484] Their persuasiveness for constructive purposes is what he used: for if it is impossible that something belongs to something else in general, i.e. without qualification, then it is also not possible that this thing belongs to it in some respect or at some time or place, [if this is so, then] it seems plausible that also what belongs to something in some respect or at some time or place, this thing also belongs [to it] without qualification. However, this is not true: for what follows from the conversion is not that it belongs without qualification, but that it can belong – which is true. For it is clear that what belongs to something in some respect can also belong to it; and similarly

10 for time and place. So that it will be true that what belongs in some respect can also belong without qualification. And he makes it clear himself that it is not true that it belongs without qualification: for example, the Ethiopian is white in some respect (i.e. with respect to his teeth), but it is not true that he is also white without qualification. For this is said without qualification (as he himself says in challenging the *topos*), namely that which is true when said without addition; what needs an addition in order to be true, instead, is not without qualification. For this reason the Ethiopian is not white without qualification, because the claim 'the Ethiopian is white' is not true without addition, whereas, if the reference to a particular respect is added, it is true. And some people, who are not excellent

without qualification, are excellent in some respect: for example, those who are naturally generous or orderly are on the whole naturally orderly or naturally   20
generous, but not so without qualification. For it is possible that, being naturally born with a good disposition towards these features, they are bad for having been nurtured in a bad way: for the one who is excellent without qualification has to be wise and nobody becomes wise by nature, as is shown in the *Ethics*.[485] As for the linguistic formulation, 'naturally'[486] is added superfluously to 'are not without qualification': for 'they are not excellent without qualification' is enough. And again, with respect to time, 'it is possible that some perishable thing does not perish at some time',[487] but it is not possible without qualification that something perishable does not perish.[488] And it is possible that some lunged animal does not breathe at some time, but it is not possible without qualification that it does not breathe. And with respect to place, 'it is advantageous to follow this regime at some places, e.g. in unwholesome places',[489] but not without qualification; and it   30
is possible that at some place there is only one human being, e.g. it is possible that there is one single human being in a theatre, but it is not possible that there is   215,1
only one human being without qualification. In virtue of these objections he spoke about these *topoi* in this way: 'And one has to investigate in the same way also with reference to some particular respect and time and place',[490] meaning that it is useful to investigate these *topoi*, whether they have to be used or not. And resorting to some examples himself, one as signifying place and another as signifying time, he corrects [what he said by saying that] they do not really signify those things. For he said that 'killing one's father'[491] is fine 'among the Triballi'[492] to signify a place, but he corrected this in the sense that this does not signify a place but rather those for which [something is the case]: for at that place there dwell the Triballi and this is fine for them. Furthermore, he said 'taking medicines   10
is useful for those who are ill'[493] as to signify a certain time (i.e. when they are ill), but he corrected this in the sense that this does not signify a certain time but rather a certain disposition: for these things are always healthy for those who are in this disposition, and not only at some time. And it is not the case that what is fine for someone is also fine without qualification and that what is so for those in a certain disposition is also so for everybody.

115b29 [Fine] without qualification is what you will say to be fine without any addition.

Having presented the objections to the aforementioned *topoi* (those who are excellent in some respect are not such without qualification; something which is

20   not perishing at some time is not imperishable without qualification; and at some place, i.e. at unwholesome places, it is useful to resort to such and such a regime, but this is not so without qualification')[494] and having shown that none of these is or is said without qualification, he made clear what it is to be without qualification, providing evidence that the aforementioned objections were spelled out correctly. For what can be said to be truly without any addition, this is of this sort without qualification. And he used the fine and the bad as examples for what is said: for what is fine without addition, this is fine without qualification, and what changes in its own right without addition, this changes without qualification. But what requires an addition in order for change to be predicated

216,1   truly of it, this does not change without qualification: for the thing of which it is true that it changes incidentally and of which it is not possible to predicate truly that it changes without addition, this thing does not change without qualification. And indeed with reference to the aforementioned cases, the things which are said with addition (of some respect or place or time) and to which we can attach 'without qualification' once we have subtracted the addition, these things would be said truly also without qualification. For example, seeing with respect to [one's] eyes is true, but seeing is also predicated truly of the one who sees with respect to his eyes without addition. It is, however, no longer the case that if 'naturally generous' is predicated truly, then also 'generous without qualification'

10   [is predicated truly] in general without addition. And similarly in the other cases.

Notes

1 Alexander's commentary on the first book of Aristotle's *Topics* is available in English translation in this series: Van Opujsen (2001). An Italian translation with introduction and notes can be found in Abbamonte (1996). On the proem see also La Croce (1978–1979).

2 I translate *paradosis* in this way and I translate the corresponding verb *paradidônai* with 'to present'. The noun and verb can be used to indicate the treatment or exposition of a subject of study, but more literally they signify the 'transmission' and the act of 'handing something down' (cf. LSJ *s.v.*).

3 Literally: 'place'. See Note on the translation, p. 33 on the reasons why I leave this technical expression untranslated throughout.

4 Literally: 'he made clear what is the complete in it'.

5 'In general' or 'in common'(*koinôs*) presumably means: without reference to the distinction corresponding to the different types of predicates.

6 About the distinction between problem and premise see Arist., *Top.* 1.4, 101b15–16 and b28–36; cf. Alex., *in Top.* 34,7–41,16 (see, in particular, 36,18–19 about *lêmma* as the dialectical premise which becomes part of a dialectical syllogism); Alex., *in An. Pr.* 9,25–14,23.

7 Arist., *Top.* 1.5, 102a6–17; 7.2.

8 On *thesis* see n. 38.

9 'Dialectical arguments' translates *dialektikôn logôn* at 126,4.

10 Alex., *in Top.* 5,21 ff. See Introduction, pp. 24–30 for some discussion of Theophrastus's definition.

11 More explicitly: 'if a contrary *x* belongs to a contrary *y*, then also the contrary of *x* belongs to the contrary of *y*.'

12 *Protasis*: this can also be translated as 'premise'. There is a general issue as to whether *topoi* should be regarded as premises of attacks; cf. Introduction, pp. 24–30. Given the problematic status of *topoi* as premises (rather than as principles of some other kind) of dialectical deductions, I opt for the more neutral translation 'proposition'.

13 The idea seems to be that a premise is 'appropriate' (*prosekhê* at 126,22; cf. *oikeian kai prosekhê* at 126,26) to the problem if its terms match the level of generality of the desired conclusion. See Introduction, pp. 25–7.

14 It is hard to tell what Alexander means exactly when he says that something is 'potentially and indeterminately contained' in something else, but some aspects of

this relation can be gathered through the examples. Alexander is clearly talking about a relation between propositions, even if the examples he gives suggest that the relation between the *topos* (i.e. the general proposition) and the more specific ones is not spelled out through quantification on the same general terms (as in the relation between a universal and a corresponding particular proposition in the *Analytics*), but rather in terms of propositions in which terms of different generality occur (e.g. 'the contrary belongs to the contrary' in the general proposition corresponds to 'the bad harms' i.e. harming belongs to the bad, where 'bad' and 'to harm' are each a member of a specific pair of contraries). In this sense one could perhaps say that the terms appearing in the specific propositions are 'potentially and indeterminately contained' in the corresponding terms of the general proposition. 'Indeterminately' (*aoristôs*) here probably refers back to the account of *topos* given a little earlier (126,15): a *topos* is determinate as to its universal outline, e.g. it is about the contraries, but it is not determined in it whether it is about these or these specific contraries. The examples that Alexander gives now suggest that the *topos* is a general proposition for which one can find indefinitely many specific instances. The specific instances of the *topos* will be propositions whose terms are at the same level of generality as those of the desired conclusion. These propositions will work as appropriate premises to establish it. As for the potential containment, the locution 'are potentially [. . .] contained' (*dunamei [. . .] periekhetai*) is unusual, but there are a few interesting occurrences. One possibly related occurrence in Alexander is Alex., *in An. Pr.* 179,15. One further occurrence (not in Alexander) is the formulation of the fourth account of true conditional in Sextus Empiricus, *Pyrr. Hyp.* 2.112, according to which a conditional is true if the consequent is 'potentially contained' in the antecedent. It is hard to tell whether and how these occurrences are related to each other (among other reasons, because we do not know anything about the origin of the fourth account in Sextus), but the phrase is unusual enough to suggest a common conceptual framework in the background. In absence of further evidence this remains highly speculative, but perhaps the reference to Theophrastus in the account of *topos* in Alexander's commentary could give us a clue, especially given that we know that Theophrastus dealt with conditionals.

15 This is certainly not the most natural translation of the *topos*, but it is what is needed if the *topos* has to be 'of one [property] about two [subjects]' (see Arist., *Top.* 2.9, 114b6–14 for such labels) and if it has to fit the examples provided below. The natural translation ('If the thing that seems to belong to something to a higher degree does not belong to it, [127,1] neither will the thing that seems to belong in a lesser degree belong to it') strongly suggests that the *topos* is about two properties and one subject ('of two about one': cf. Arist., *Top.* 2.9, 114b8–10).

16 The Greek is *oikeios*; there does not seem to be a difference between a 'pertinent' and an 'appropriate' (*prosekhês*) premise (cf. n. 13).

17 Throughout the *Topics* Aristotle oscillates between a exclusive and a inclusive conception of the sort of predication conveyed by the accident. According to the exclusive conception, the accident is a specific kind of predicate (one that can belong or not belong to its subject; or one that does not belong in the essence of the subject and cannot be predicated instead of the subject, i.e. one that has a different extension from the subject). On this conception, if a predicate is shown to be an accident, it is excluded that that predicate is a proprium, a genus, a difference or a definition of the subject. This conception of the accident can be found for example in *Top.* 1.8, 103b12–19; cf. 1.5, 102b4–14; 2.2, 109a34–b12. According to the inclusive conception, accidental predication turns out to be unqualified predication, i.e. predication in which the precise modality of belonging of the predicate to the subject is left unqualified. In this sense, the inclusive conception of the accident in the *Topics* anticipates the notion of unqualified belonging (*huparkhein*) of the *Analytics*. The inclusive conception can be found e.g. in *Top.* 1.6, 102b31–3; 2.2, 109b13–29; 6.1, 139a26–b3. I take it that in this passage Alexander is resorting to the inclusive conception of the accident (in terms of unqualified belonging) in order to justify the place of the books about the accident before those about the other types of predicates and I translate accordingly. On the order and structure of the *Topics* see also n. 18. At least two further different translations are possible for the text in the parenthesis: (1) 'for [the property of] belonging belongs to everything', which simply does not seem to be true if one endorses (as Alexander seems to do) the idea of the *Categories* that at least primary substances do not belong to anything (in the sense that they are neither said of anything nor inhere in anything); (2) 'for [the property of] being the case belongs to everything', which however would require taking the two occurrences of the verb *huparkhein* in two different senses: one should take *to huparkhon* in the sense of 'being the case', 'obtaining' (corresponding to an absolute use of the verb *huparkhein*) and *huparkhei*, together with the immediately preceding dative *pasin*, in the sense of 'belonging to' something (according to the relational use of the verb). Apart from requiring a switch in the use of the same verb within the same (short) sentence, it is not immediately clear how the point made in (2) would be directly relevant to Alexander's argument.

18 It is likely that the order and structure of the *Topics* and, more radically, the extent to which the treatment of *topoi* is systematic, were regarded as problematic already by Aristotle's fellow Peripatetics and immediate successors if not by Aristotle himself. Alexander himself, for example, reports (and criticizes) Theophrastus's attempts at rearranging the materials. For a survey of the evidence and some discussion see Castelli (2013).

19 Arist., *Top.* 1.5, 102b1–2.

20 For this account of priority cf. Arist., *Metaph.* 5.11, 1019a2–4; *Cat.* 12, 14a29–35.

21 The verb used here (*antikatêgoreisthai*) and the way in which Aristotle spells out this procedure in *Top.* 1.5, 102a19–22 suggest that the idea is that the predicate can be

predicated of all and only the things of which the subject can be predicated. With reference to this account of 'being predicated instead', it might be worth reminding that typically both subject and predicate in dialectical propositions are general terms. The procedure Aristotle refers to in 1.5 is different from the procedure of 'converting' (*antistrephein*) the terms of a proposition (see e.g. *An. Pr.* 1.1, 25a6 ff.) where he talks about swapping subject and predicate. For some discussion see Brunschwig (2009: 122).

22 'Go beyond [...] and reach out to [...]' is the translation of the phrase *peritteuousin para* + accusative *en* + dative. The language is unusual, but the sense is clear: the *topoi* about the other types of predicates go beyond establishing the unqualified belonging of a predicate to a subject in that they are supposed to establish a specific way in which the predicate belongs to the subject.

23 There is a textual problem at 128,25. Wallies prints *allêlois* with a crux (*panta katholou ta problêmata † allêlois dunatai lambanesthai*, which would yield the impossible translation: 'it is possible to take all problems as universal † to each other'), but in the apparatus he suggests *alêthôs* as his conjecture (*panta katholou ta problêmata <alêthôs> dunatai lambanesthai*), which yields the translation I give. The point of the remark would then be that the only case in which the particular formulation of a problem can be taken as true with respect to some individual only is the case in which the problem is about an accident. All cases in which the predicate of the problem signifies a genus, a definition or a proprium of the subject, even if the particular (saying e.g. that animal belongs to some human being) is true, it will not be true because it is only true of some individual human being (e.g. Socrates or Callias) that he or she is an animal; rather, the corresponding universal proposition ('animal belongs to all human beings') will be true too. In this sense, in all problems concerning types of predicates other than the accident one can assume that the universal proposition expressing the predication of a genus, a definition or a proprium is true.

24 'Of the same species' translates *homoeidôn* at 128,26. I opt for this translation rather than for a more generic one (e.g. 'of the same kind') because Alexander seems to think that a species (*eidos*) is the typical subject (a universal subject) of the propositions in which the predicate expresses an accident, a genus, a proprium or a definition, although there can be problems in which the predicate is the *eidos* (such problems will belong together with the problems about the genus since the type of predicate that the species is with respect to the individuals falling under it is the same as the type of predicate that the genus is with respect to its species): see Alex., *in Top.* 39,2–10.

25 Arist., *Top.* 2.1, 109a1 ff.

26 Alexander argues for the priority, in the order of presentation, accorded to *topoi* establishing a universal conclusion and, in particular, to those establishing a negative universal conclusion based on two sorts of considerations. First, universal

propositions entail the corresponding particulars (the universal affirmative entails the particular affirmative and the negative universal entails the negative particular). Accordingly, being able to argue for a universal claim turns out to be useful independently of whether the claim we intend to establish is universal or particular. Second, the most common task for the dialectician is that of demolishing a claim; since claims are usually put forth in the affirmative form, the dialectician will typically try to establish the contradictory or the contrary of an affirmative, i.e. the corresponding negative particular or universal. For the relations of implication and oppositions between propositions see Arist., *Int.* 7, 17b16–18a12.

27 For the distinction between dialectical premises in interrogative form and premises taken as parts of a syllogism cf. Alex., *in An. Pr.* 13,20–14,16; Arist., *An. Pr.* 1.1, 24a22–8; see also n. 6. On Alexander's views about dialectical premises in interrogative form and dialectical questions see also Alex., *in Top.* 40,13–41,10; 68,23–70,11; 294,16–19; Ammonius, *in Int.* 202,3–203,20 (where Ammonius mentions a dispute between Alexander and Iamblichus about the nature of the dialectical question and oddly ascribes to Alexander a view that Alexander explicitly rejects in *in Top.* 40,13–41,10).

28 Arist., *Int.* 7, 17b3–12.

29 I take it that the dative 'to some' alludes to the formulation of a predicative proposition in terms of the predicate's belonging to the subject. Cf. below 130,22–3 '[…] the one who shows that it belongs to some […]'.

30 Arist., *Top.* 3.6, 119a31; Alex., *in Top.*, 279,11 ff.

31 Literally: 'concluding that [something] belongs [or: obtains] universally'.

32 One characteristic feature of the argumentative procedures described in the *Topics* is that several *topoi* require that, in order to establish the desired conclusion, one manages to show or produce an argument for a claim p which is distinct from the conclusion q and such that, once p has been shown, q has been shown too. The precise relation between p and q varies for the different *topoi*. The general idea seems to be that q follows from p, where this relation of 'following from' cannot be cast in syllogistic form. In the present case, Alexander spells out the relations of implication between universal and particular of the same quality (i.e. affirmative or negative respectively): the universal implies the particular of the same quality but not the other way round. There are other cases, however, in which the relation between p and q (e.g. in *topoi* from the coordinates and inflections or in *topoi* from the opposites) are more difficult to spell out. One can see, however, how some theory of implication and of conditionals might have been involved in the analysis of arguments based on *topoi*: cf. n. 14 on Theophrastus and a puzzling account of a true conditional in Sextus.

33 i.e. both for universal and particular problems.

34 Alex., *in Top.* 129,8–13.

35 Alexander alludes here to one of the goals of the treatise and, more generally, of dialectic, which is that of being a sort of argumentative gymnastics in which the soul is trained to argue against or to support a certain thesis, independently of its truth, without falling into contradiction. For dialectic as *gumnasia* cf. Arist., *Top.* 1.2, 101a27–30; 8.5, 159a25–37; 11, 161a25 ff.; 14, 163a29 ff.; Alex., *in Top.*, 27,8 ff. Cf. also Plato, *Parm.* 135C ff.

36 'In arguments' translates *en tois logois* at 131,10. A possible alternative translation is 'in discussions'.

37 The Greek text could also mean: 'Eudemus's work *On the Analytics* bears the same title'. In other words, the Greek text is compatible with two possibilities: either Alexander is referring to one work with two titles or he is referring to two works with the same title. The first option seems more likely and the reference would be to Eudemus's book on the Analytics (cf. Philoponus, *in Cat.*, Busse 7,20–2). I am grateful to Katerina Ierodiakonou for her comments on this point. I am not sure, however, that the other possibility (i.e. of two books, one by Aristotle himself and one by Eudemus) can be excluded: Philoponus (*in Cat.*, Busse 7,16 ff.) mentions the existence of works by Theophrastus, Phanias and Eudemus with the same titles as Aristotle's writings as one issue for establishing the authenticity of Aristotle's works and we know of at least one other case, i.e. the famous case of the *Eudemian Ethics*, of one work whose ascription to Aristotle has been disputed (among other reasons) because of the title. On various aspects of Eudemus's activity see Bodnár and Fortenbaugh (2002) and, more specifically, on Eudemus's logic with reference to Aristotle's and Theophrastus's works see Huby (2002).

38 This is presumably a comment about Aristotle's use of *theseis* in *Top.* 2.1, 109a9. In *Top.* 1.11, 104b19–34 *thesis* designates more specifically a paradoxical tenet held by some well-known philosopher: e.g. Antisthenes' claim that it is not possible to contradict, or Heraclitus's claim that all things are in motion are *theseis* in this specific sense. At 104b34–105a2 in the same chapter, however, Aristotle refers to the widespread practice of calling every dialectical problem a *thesis*.

39 For the different kinds of conversions cf. Alex., *in An. Pr.* 29,7–29.

40 English grammar requires the insertion of the indeterminate article, which may suggest that the subject of the proposition Aristotle is talking about are individuals. The formulation in Greek (which does not have indeterminate articles) does not carry (even if it does not exclude) such implications. In fact, typically both subject and predicate in the *Topics* are general terms (common nouns or adjectives).

41 Presumably Alexander alludes to the distinction between predicates that are propria of a subject 'without qualification', and predicates that are propria only with respect to something: for the distinction see Arist., *Top.* 1.5, 102a24–8; 5.1, 128b16–21.

42 Namely in the case of the accident.

43 For the insertion of the indeterminate articles see n. 40.

44 'To belong incidentally' translates the verb *sumbebêkenai* (where *sumbebêkos* is the accident).

45 i.e. in the comments about 108b34ff (129, 16–25).

46 *anaskeuê* ('demolition') and *elenkhos* ('refutation') and the corresponding verbs are not interchangeable. Strictly speaking, an *elenkhos* is a deductive argument having as its conclusion the contradictory of the claim that is refuted (*SE* 5, 167a22–7), whereas in order to have an *anaskeuê* it is enough if the conclusion is semantically incompatible with the claim defended by the interlocutor (see e.g. 140,6–10) or the latter is formally inadequate. An additional difference in the use of the verbs *elenkhein* and *anaskeuazein* is that *elenkhein* is used with reference to a person (the interlocutor can be refuted: 133,28–9; 136,2; 137,26) or to a claim (a claim or a problem can be refuted: 134,20), whereas *anaskeuazein* is only used with reference to what is submitted.

47 It is not clear what 'their' (*autôn* at 134,1) refers to. Based on the considerations spelled out in n. 46, it could refer either to the interlocutors that undertake the defence of the claim that is 'laid out' at the beginning or to the things that are submitted at the beginning. The interlocutors are certainly those who are supposed to acknowledge and agree upon the mistakes on which the refutation will be based. The problem is that there is no plural noun indicating the interlocutors in the preceding lines to which the plural genitive at 134,1 can be referred (at 133,28 the defender of the claim is in the singular). I therefore assume that 'their' refers to the problems mentioned at 133,31. For a similar use of the terminology of refutation (*elenkhos*, *elenkhein*) taking a problem (rather than an interlocutor) as what is refuted cf. 134,20.

48 Presumably: the problems at 134,2 (cf. *en autois* at 134,4).

49 See n. 48.

50 'Defends' translates *paristamenos* (literally 'that stands by') at 134,5–6.

51 '[…] the underlying nature, whatever it is, […]' translates *tên […] hupokeimenên phusin hêtis pote estin* at 134,11. The phrase refers to whatever it is that one might be talking about. The phrase *ho pote on esti* is used by Aristotle in crucial passages, e.g. in his accounts of time in *Phys.* 4.11–14 and of blood in *PA* 2.3; for a thorough discussion of the syntax of the phrase and its use in Aristotle's natural philosophy see Lederman (2014). It does not seem to me that in this context Alexander attaches any particular philosophical implications to the use of the phrase *hetis pote estin*, but perhaps one could find here a trace of a crystallised usage to indicate a subject or substrate whose precise nature is left unspecified (cf. Arist., *Phys.* 4.11, 219b18–19).

52 'Beautiful' translates *kalon* at 134,14; 'fine' would be an alternative translation (which I have adopted in other contexts: see e.g.134,10), but the account of *kallos* ('beauty') at 134,18–19 makes clear that Alexander is here talking about the physical characteristic of a beautiful body.

53 These are the so-called *paradoxa stoicorum* (cf. Cicero's work with this title) and what Alexander presents here is a piece of standard criticism against the Stoics: cf. Gal., *Inst. Log.* IV 6. Cf. also n. 91.

54 Namely Aristotle.

55 Arist., *Top.* 2.1, 109a31–2.

56 These are not necessarily arguments in which the mistake is exposed: cf. 135,23–7. About the two different *elenkhoi* for the two different mistakes cf. 136,8–11.

57 Note that this *topos* is clearly based on the exclusive conception of the accident as a predicate that can belong or not belong to its subject and which neither can be predicated instead of nor belongs in the definition of the subject. Most of the following *topoi* rather rely on the inclusive conception of accidental predication as unqualified belonging (for the distinction see n. 17).

58 More explicitly: if the contrary of x belongs to the contrary of y, then also x belongs to y.

59 For the issues involved in translating *protasis* as 'proposition' rather than 'premise' see n. 12. 'Proposition' seems right here both because Alexander underplays the distinction between *topos* and precept (which is certainly not a premise) and because he suggests that the actual premises of dialectical arguments are more specific than the *topos* from which they are found. The distinction between precept and *topos* as Alexander describes it seems twofold: the precept is more general than the *topos* in the same way in which a *topos* is more general than the premises which are taken by making a move from it; the precept is an injunction and not a declarative sentence, whereas the *topos* is a declarative sentence.

60 I take this to mean: 'since the *topos* is already included in the precept'. Alternatively, one could translate more neutrally 'since these things, then, are not external to the account', i.e. 'since these considerations are not extrinsic to the discussion'.

61 Arist., *Top.* 2.1, 109a27 ff.

62 *Sumbebêkenai*, which I translate as 'to belong incidentally', is the perfect infinitive of *sumbainô*, 'come together', of which *sumbebêkos* (the standard term for 'accident') is the perfect participle.

63 Arist., *Top.* 1.8.

64 Namely the difference between what belongs to the subject as a genus and what belongs to it as an accident.

65 *Cat.* 5, 2a27 ff.

66 This may not be the best translation of *grammatikos*, but 'grammarian' has the advantage of being a paronymous of 'grammar' as the Greek *grammatikos* is of *grammatikê*. For some discussion of two technical meanings of *grammatikê* see Sextus, *Adv. Math.* 1.44–56.

67 cf. Alex., *in Top.* 53,2–10 about the reasons for classifying problems in which unqualified being is predicated of a subject under problems concerning the accident rather than under problems concerning the genus.

68 See the examples of propria in Arist., *Top.* 5.1, 128b17–20: 'naturally tame animal' is a proprium of human being; 'immortal living being' is a proprium of god.

69 'those of which they are paronyms', namely 'to laugh' and 'to have knowledge'.

70 i.e. those things whose paronyms are predicated of *x* are accidents of *x*.

71 Arist., *Top.* 1.4, 101b18–19.

72 'Is an accident and belongs' translates the *sumbebêkenai kai huparkhein* at 138,6. I am not sure whether Alexander is interested in keeping a distinction between ascribing a predicate to a subject as an accident and ascribing a predicate to a subject without qualification (cf. n. 17 on the two understanding of the accident in the *Topics*). For this reason, I opt for this literal if somewhat redundant translation rather than for a simpler 'belongs as an accident', which is a possible translation taking *sumbebêkenai kai huparkhein* as a hendiadys.

73 'The indivisible things' translates *ta atoma* at 138,17. *Atomon* was used above (e.g. 128,26–8) to refer to individuals, but in this context it refers to the last indivisible species which can be reached through a process of division of the universals that are the subject or the predicate of the universal claim which has to be established or demolished through the division. See Alexander's remark at 138,24.

74 Alexander refers *verbatim* to the second and revised account of the relatives in *Cat.* 7, 8a31–2, which Aristotle gives in order to avoid the problem that some substances (more specifically: secondary substances) may turn out to be relatives according to the first account of the relatives given at the beginning of the chapter in *Cat.* 7, 6a36–7 (according to the first account, relatives are those things that are said to be precisely what they are of or with reference to something else).

75 For the different definitions of love, cf. 144,1 ff.

76 At 139,32 I depart from Wallies, who inserts *ou* before *khrê*: 'one should <u>not</u> suffer etc.'. Both through his own activity as an arbiter (cf. Arist., *Ath. Resp.* 5, 1–3) and through his legislation, which included a specific law forcing all citizens to take side and join one party in case of strife (Arist., *Ath. Resp.* 8, 5), Solon supports the view that the wise man <u>should</u> take part in politics and in strife. The two possible interpretations of the negative clause 'not to take part in strife' are then fully spelled out at 139,33–140,3. On the rejection of Wallies' *ou* see also Roselli (2002: 141–2).

77 *sunagôn* at 140,2 makes little sense. It could perhaps be translated with 'reconciling'. I follow the emendation proposed by Roselli (2002: 142–3) of *sunagôn* into *sunalgôn*, mainly based on Plutarch, *Sol.* 20 but also supported by other texts. Roselli also suggests to emend *metekhei* at 139,32 into *metekhein*; the correction makes sense and I translate accordingly. The translation of Wallies' text would be: 'Similarly, "does not participate in strife" can have [...]'. Roselli (2002) provides more generally an illuminating discussion of this difficult passage in Alexander's commentary.

78 'In the same situation' translates *en tois autois*. The Greek is difficult (see also n. 76 and 77), but the thought seems to be that the wise man will be more effective in putting an

end to a strife if he takes side with one party and shares in the situation of those who are at strife rather than if he detaches himself from the political situation and assumes a neutral stand. Solon's law against neutrality in case of *stasis* was much discussed in antiquity as somewhat paradoxical. For some context see, once again, Roselli (2002).

79 Arist., *Top.* 2.2, 109b23–4.

80 Arist., *Top.* 2.2, 109b24–5.

81 What falls under the universal subject and 'is not in this way' is something which does not respond to the claim expressed in the affirmative universal, i.e. a counterexample.

82 As in the former case, in order to demolish a negative universal one can find a counterexample, i.e. a case of something that falls under the universal subject and to which the predicate (which was posited not to belong to any of the things falling under the subject) belongs.

83 Arist., *Top.* 2.2, 109b13–14.

84 Alexander is commenting on Arist., *Top.* 2.2, 109b26.

85 A *topos* is universally destructive if it is useful to demolish both particular and universal claims; the current *topos* is useful to demolish only universal claims. For the distinction cf. Alex., *in Top.* 130,3 ff.

86 Arist., *Top.* 2.2, 109b33.

87 Arist., *Top.* 2.2, 109b34.

88 This reduction of a topical argument to syllogistic form is not an isolated episode in Alexander's commentary. See introduction pp. 4–24 for some assessment of the historical and philosophical relevance of such attempts.

89 Arist., *Top.* 1.5, 102a5–17.

90 'active' translates *energôn*.

91 That the wise man is rich is one of the so-called Stoic paradoxes. Cf. n. 53.

92 There is no explicit subject for the verb 'require' (*axioi* at 142,28), but the following lines suggest that the subject is Aristotle himself, who 'has already said' (see 142,32 and 143,1) the same things in the first book.

93 Namely the difference between the defined terms.

94 'With respect to health' (*pros hugieian* in Arist., *Top.* 1.15, 107b9) is deleted in Brunschwig's edition of Aristotle's text.

95 At 107b11 Ross prints *toiouton*. Brunschwig prints *tosouton* as in Alexander's text.

96 cf. Arist., *Top.* 1.15, 107b6–12.

97 I take it that in this context 'the given things' are the subject ('what produces health') and the predicate ('a sign of health') of the submitted problem.

98 For the definition of change cf. Arist., *Phys.* 3.1, 201b31–2.

99 'What is set before us' translates *to prokeimenon hêmin* at 143,29. I think this is an unusual way to refer to the problem which has been submitted for dialectical investigation (cf. *to prokeimenon*, 'what is submitted', at 143,32).

100 SVF, 3.180.

101 Plato, *Phaedr.* 249D ff.; for the different definitions of love cf. above 139,22 ff.

102 cf. examples below at 144,20 ff.

103 'Breath' translates *pneuma* at 144,15.

104 cf. Arist., *DA* 2.1, 412a27, b5.

105 Plato, *Phaedr.* 245C.

106 I translate 'premise' because Alexander's illustration of this procedure at 145,22 ff. suggests that its first step consists in formulating an interrogative proposition in the form of a dialectical premise as described in *Top.* 1.4, 101b28–36. As mentioned before (see e.g. 129, 16–25 and n. 27), it is only a corresponding declarative sentence that is actually used with the function of a premise in a deductive argument.

107 Arist., *Top.* 2.2, 109b13–14.

108 'Mode' translates *tropos* at 145,17; cf. the commentary on Arist., *Top.* 2.5, 111b32, where Aristotle speaks of a 'sophistic *tropos*' (but see below on some peculiarities in the manuscript tradition). Both here and there the *tropos* seems to indicate a certain way of proceeding in leading an attack, but it is hard to tell whether the vocabulary of *tropos* can be regarded as technical. In the Sceptic tradition the terminology of *tropoi* becomes standard to indicate standard modes of argumentation, while the tradition of Peripatetic dialectic seems to preserve the use of *topoi*. I discuss the possible relation between Peripatetic dialectic and scepticism in Castelli, 'Peripatetic dialectic, scepticism, *topoi* and *tropoi*' (in preparation). Note, however, that in the manuscript tradition of the *Top.* and *SE* there is some oscillation between the two expressions: see e.g. *SE* 4, 166b20; 6, 169a18; 7, 169a37; 11, 172b5; 12, 172b25 and the very *Top.* 2.5, 111b32.

109 i.e. a starting point: cf. 145,4–5.

110 *Top.* 2.2, 110a15–16.

111 *ibid.* 110a18–19.

112 *ibid.* 110a19–20.

113 Literally: 'but rather something else'. This formulation is ambiguous in that it can either mean that the person who makes the mistakes calls 'healthy' something else (i.e. not what is productive of health), or that he calls this thing (i.e. what is productive of health) 'something else', i.e. not 'healthy' but with a different name. Given the general sense of the *topos*, I take it that the second construction of the sentence gives the right sense.

114 i.e. the Stoics.

115 Arist., *Top.* 2.2, 110a19.

116 'Or' (*ē*) is neither in Ross's nor in Brunschwig's text at 110a20 but is clearly part of a quotation introduced by *to* in Alexander's text at 147,27. See, however, Alexander's own remarks about 'or' a few lines later.

117 'Equivalent' translates *ison* at 147,27.

118　At 147,27 the manuscripts only have *estin*, whereas *esti tôi ê* is Wallies' conjecture. I translate Wallies' text. The text of the manuscripts would yield the translation: 'which is equivalent: 'in whatever way [. . .]'.'

119　Arist., *Top.* 1.15.

120　Namely 'appropriate'.

121　'We have to' translates *khrê* at 148,26 (which, if one wanted to keep the order of the Greek text, would be right after the semicolon: 'And again, if it is posited that it is appropriate for the excellent man to get involved in politics: [. . .]').

122　i.e. what is advantageous and what is necessary.

123　i.e. 'that it is not appropriate for the excellent man to get involved in politics'; cf. 139,30 ff.

124　'The latter', namely what was posited in the problem.

125　In the *Protrepticus* Aristotle would have argued that both if one ought to do philosophy and if one ought not to do philosophy one ought to do philosophy, the point of the argument presumably being that asking the very question whether one ought to do philosophy or not is doing philosophy. Alexander is not the only one to refer to this argument in the *Protrepticus*; for the other *testimonia* on this point see Ross (1963, *Protr.* 2), Hutchinson-Johnson (2017: 4 ff.). Alexander refers to the same argument again at 151,24–5 with one important difference in formulation: at 149,11–12 Alexander formulates the problem in terms of whether *khrê philosophein*, whereas at 151,24–5 he uses the formulation *ei philosophêteon*. Later testimonies phrase the argument as in 151,24–5. While both the original structure of Aristotle's argument and Alexander's rephrasing of it are problematic (see Castagnoli 2012: 51–9), it is worth noticing that the presence in Alexander of both formulations does not allow us to draw any inference concerning Aristotle's original phrasing of the argument. In particular, Castagnoli (2012: 55 n. 89) doubts whether Aristotle's argument had *philosophêteon* rather than *khrê philosophein* partly based on the evidence in Alexander at 149,11–12. But 151,24–5 shows that the alternative formulation can be found in Alexander too. I am grateful to an anonymous reader for drawing my attention to the importance of the presence of the two different formulations in Alexander.

126　I translate Wallies' text, which includes a conjecture at 149,17, where Wallies writes *alla ê ek tinos ê ek tinôn* instead of *alla ê hekaterou ê ek tinôn* ('but rather either *of each* or from some'), which does not make much sense and where *ê hekaterou* can be easily explained away as a mistake (see the immediately preceding *ê hekaterou* at the beginning of 149,17).

127　'Explicit' translates *phanera*, which can also be translated with 'clear', 'evident'. I opt for 'explicit' because I take it that Alexander intends to draw a contrast between the present case (in which we have the resources to argue for a claim with reference to all senses of one ambiguous expression appearing in it) and the case considered above, in which the ambiguity escapes notice and we proceed by drawing a distinction 'for ourselves', which we then use for our purposes without revealing the ambiguity.

128 Arist., *Top.* 2.3, 110a25–6.

129 'Reply' translates *apantêsis*; cf. Arist., *Metaph.* 4.5, 1009a20; *SE* 17, 176a23.

130 i.e. it is clear that the proponent of the initial claim was not talking about the picture.

131 'In general' taking *to* at 150,2 in *to katholou deiknunai* with *deiknunai* (and not with *katholou*); cf. 149,33. Alexander's point seems to be that the use of 'establishing' in this context does not carry any implications as to whether what is posited is posited through an affirmative or a negative proposition, whereas it is usually the case that what is posited is posited through an affirmative formulation.

132 <*kai to katholou apophatikon*> at 150,7–8 is a reasonable conjecture by Wallies, where the manuscript tradition splits between manuscripts that retain *to kathoulou kataphatikon* and those that retain *to kathoulou apophatikon*.

133 See n. 26 for the relations of implication obtaining between propositions of different quality and quantity.

134 Arist., *Top.* 2.3, 110a33.

135 Arist., *Top.* 1.18, 108b8, 12–19.

136 Arist., *An. Pr.* 1.23, 41a40.

137 Literally 'it does not convert', i.e. it is not the case that all deductions from a hypothesis are from agreement. For example, *reductio ad absurdum* is usually taken to be from a hypothesis but not from agreement (for some discussion of evidence in Aristotle about this distinction see Crivelli 2011). For Alexander's classification of arguments from a hypothesis see Introduction, pp. 5–16.

138 Arist., *Top.* 1.18, 108b13–14.

139 'Establish by convention' translates *suntithesthai*. The verb could be translated more generally as 'to establish through agreement', but it has the same root as *sunthêkê*, 'convention', which appears explicitly at 151,13–14.

140 i.e. a soul of a certain kind.

141 Arist., *Top.* 2.3, 110b5.

142 'Applicable' translates *epharmozontos*. The way in which Alexander spells out Aristotle's contrast between arguing for a universal conclusion from agreement and arguing from a universal conclusion in the way in which the geometer does is clearly reminiscent of Aristotle's theory of scientific demonstration in *An. Post.* For the use of *epharmozein* to indicate the way in which a proof 'fits' its intended object cf. Arist., *An. Post.* 1.7, 75b4.

143 *Top.* 2.3, 110b8.

144 See n. 125.

145 Literally: 'with reference to some of the things signified'. Similarly below.

146 i.e. neither the affirmative nor the negative.

147 Arist., *Top.* 2.3, 110b14.

148 The Greek at 152, 8 is *logos*, i.e. complex linguistic expression as opposed to a single word.

149 Wallies inserts at this point a parenthesis, which is then closed at 153,11. It is true that the sentence and the train of thought which are interrupted here are only taken up again at 153,11, but in the translation I have eliminated the two-page long parenthesis and broken up the period accordingly.

150 cf. Arist., *Top.* 2.3, 110b21–5.

151 i.e. to the things of which the science is principally.

152 See n. 67 on being as an accident.

153 Arist., *Top.* 2.3, 110b22–3.

154 *ibid.* 110b23–4.

155 The Greek is ambiguous in that it can mean either that the geometer will know incidentally that the equilateral triangle has its angles equal to two right angles or that he will know that having its angles equal to two right angles belongs incidentally to the equilateral triangle. Given the way in which the *topos* is construed, I take it that the first paraphrase gives the right sense.

156 'The same science is of many things' at 152,17–18.

157 Literally 'according to some of the things signified'. Similarly elsewhere.

158 I translate 'which are of some interest' the Greek phrase *tôn ekhontôn tina zêtêsin* at 153,30. The Greek could also mean 'which require some investigation', or, perhaps, 'which involve some controversy' (cf. *zêtêsis* in LSJ *s.v.* 4: 'judicial enquiry', pl. 'controversies'). As for the latter option, cf. *Top.* 1.11, 104b3–17 about dialectical problems as being about controversial issues. These different interpretations are not mutually exclusive.

159 As it was illustrated above, medicine is of health principally and of good complexion incidentally.

160 Arist., *Top.* 2.3, 110b28.

161 It is difficult to find a translation of the Greek that preserves the ambiguity of the Greek construction. The Greek sentence is ambiguous in that it can mean (a) 'I know everybody who, having more pebbles, won', or (b) 'I know that everybody who got more pebbles won'. I have not been able to come up with an English construction that mirrors the Greek construction, but the translation I propose is ambiguous in a way that makes sense of Alexander's comments.

162 On this title of Theophrastus see Huby (2007), p. 10 (20ab), and p. 172 (133).

163 i.e. collectively.

164 i.e. distributively.

165 Arist., *Top.* 2.3, 110b33.

166 At 154,30 I read *aporein* ('to lack resources') with B instead of *euporein* in Wallies' edition.

167 Wallies puts 'of the end and of the means to the end' (155,5–6) and 'as of what is in its own right and of what is incidentally' (155,6–7) into quotation marks. The

distinction is drawn by Aristotle in *Top.* 2.3, 110b18–25. As on other occasions, it is hard to tell whether Alexander is quoting or simply paraphrasing the text. On this point see the general Note on the translation.

168 Arist., *Top.* 2.3, 110b33–4.

169 Or 'that a science is [productive] of something'. The generalisation at 155,10–11 in any case suggests that Alexander is thinking more generally of claims of the form 'science *x* is . . . of something'.

170 'The object of the argument' translates *to deiknumenon*, literally: 'what is shown'.

171 Wallies seems to take *ôs telous* (155,11), *ôs pros to telos* (155,12), *ôs kata sumbebêkos* (155,13) as direct quotations (presumably of Arist., *Top.* 2.3, 110b35–6; note, however, that at least in modern editions the second and third phrase are *ôs tôn pros to telos* and *ôs tôn kata sumbebêkos* respectively). This does not seem to be necessary since Alexander is simply paraphrasing the text.

172 *Top.* 2.3, 111a1–2.

173 For the example cf. Arist., *Top.* 2.3, 110b38–111a6.

174 Arist., *Top.* 2.3, 110b38.

175 At 156,8 Wallies' text *autos houtôs deiknusi* would yield the translation: 'He himself [*scil.* Aristotle] shows in this way. . .'. Wallies refers to *DA* 2.6 as the place where Aristotle would show what follows, but *DA* 2.6 does not seem to support Wallies' choice. I therefore translate the text of the manuscripts: *auta houtôs deiknuousi*.

176 Arist., *Top.* 2.3, 111a7.

177 'Engaged with many things' is a paraphrastic translation of *polupragmôn* (similarly, 'engagement with many things' translates *polupragmosunê*), whereas 'meddlesome' translates *philopragmôn* (and, similarly, 'meddlesomeness' translates *philopragmosunê*) both in this passage and later at 157,12 ff. The two adjectives (and the corresponding two nouns) have a very similar meaning (as they must have in order for the *topos* to apply) and the difference is spelled out by Alexander: the latter, but not the former, has a pejorative connotation stressing the zeal and the intention to interfere in things that are not one's concern. On *polupragmosunê* see Erhenberg (1947).

178 The example is mentioned in Arist., *Top.* 2.4, 111a9, but the way in which Alexander spells it out in full employs a Stoic conceptual framework.

179 Wallies signals a lacuna at 157,17 after *spoudaiou*. Wallies' proposal that the missing text should be something like *anankaia, oud' an pasa hupolêpsis tou spoudaiou* seems likely and the words 'is necessary, then not every conception of the excellent man' translate this text.

180 Although the *topos* is about substituting linguistic expressions, the use of the articles and the variations in expression suggest that Alexander is describing the *topos* in terms of turning something into something else, i.e. in terms of bringing about a sort of misrepresentation of reality through a certain use of language.

181 cf. Aeschines, *Contra Ctesiphon*, 83.

182 Thuc., *Hist.* III 39.2.

183 Literally: 'is full of such use'.

184 Plato, *Gorg.* 491E.

185 Arist., *Top.* 2.4, 111a15–16.

186 i.e. we should use the genus.

187 I translate 'disposition' rather than 'a disposition' because the *topos* is about disposition as a genus (and not about something that is a disposition).

188 cf. Arist., *Top.* 2.4, 111a21–2.

189 Arist., *Top.* 2.4, 111a21.

190 The subject here could be either the *topos* or the discussant who resorts to the corresponding *topos*.

191 The participial formulations with the masculine ('the one moving', etc.) are compatible with taking the subject to be the *topos* or an interlocutor applying the *topos*. However, 'the first' at 159,5 and '*topos*' at 160,4 make it clear that the subject is the *topos* throughout.

192 Arist., *Top.* 2.4, 111a25–6.

193 The things 'that belong in the substance' of the genus are presumably the features that figure in the definition (i.e. the account of the essence or of the substance) of the genus. The genus is synonymous with its species (see *Cat.* 1, 1a6–12: both the name and the definition of the genus apply to its species; for example, both the name 'animal' and the definition of the genus Animal apply to each of its species – cat, dog, human being, etc.). The fact that the definition of the genus applies to its species indicates that whatever spells out what the genus is also spells out what each of the species is.

194 'Cover up' translates *sumplêrounta* at 159,6.

195 The relation between genera and contraries is a particularly complex issue in Aristotle's logic and metaphysics. For an overview of the problems see Castelli (2018, Introduction, part 2 and chapter 9).

196 This relation of 'being in' is not to be confused with the relation of 'being in a subject' in *Cat.* 2 (see in particular 2, 1a24–5): in *Cat.* 2, the items that are in something else are accidents which inhere in a subject (which is, ultimately, a substance); in our passage the relation of 'being in' is a relation of extensional containment: what is contained in the species is also contained in the genus (which has a greater extension than the species), but not the other way round.

197 For some comments on the relevance of the analysis of the present *topos* with reference to Alexander's views about the relation between *Topics* and *Analytics* see Introduction, pp. 20–1.

198 As before (see nn. 190, 191) the Greek is compatible with taking the subject of this and the following sentence to be one of the two *topoi* (one of which would be true

and one of which would be false) or the interlocutor arguing in a certain way (which would then be right or wrong, respectively). For the reasons explained above, I take it that the subjects are *topoi* throughout.

199 The formulation is very compressed, and it is not fully clear what the point of the sentence is. Since it is introduced by *gar* at 160,16, I take it that 'for if it belongs [...] which is precisely the genus' is supposed to explain what was said immediately before (i.e. that what does not belong to what is more extended does not belong to what is less extended either), without spelling out the whole thought. I take the explanation to be the following: assume (against the assumption that what does not belong to what is more extended does not belong to what is less extended either) that something belongs to the species *x* of genus *y* without belong to *y*; since *x* is necessarily included in *y*, the same will belong to *y*, against the assumption that it does not belong to *y*.

200 Namely, it is possible that it be in what is more extended.

201 'To the animal' at 160,25 is Wallies' addition, but it must be understood in any case.

202 Alexander considers and dismisses a possible objection to the claim that what belongs to (or 'is in', according to the terminology above) the species also belongs to (or 'is in') the genus. 'Falling under the genus' belongs to the species of the genus (more specifically: it belongs to each species of the genus) but does not belong to the genus. Alexander replies that 'falling under the genus' will also belong to the genus insofar as it belongs to some part(s) of it, provided that in order for claims of the form '*x* is in *y*' or '*x* belongs to *y*' to be true it is not necessary that *x* be in the whole of *y*. On this point cf. the remarks at 159,27 ff. Alexander suggests in this way that this case would not be very different from the case of the opposites that belong to the genus in that one of them belongs to some of the species or individuals that fall under the genus and the other belongs to other species or individuals.

203 The idea is that the genus does not exist as something separate or independent from its species. Cf. 161,27 ff.

204 Alexander's point is that the genus is predicated of something only insofar as some of its species is also predicated of it. The exception is the case in which the subject of which the genus is predicated is the result of an immediate division of the genus; in this case, the subject is a species of the genus such that there is no intermediate species of the genus between the genus and the subject.

205 i.e. the winged animal.

206 i.e. in the case in which the subject is a proximate species of the genus which is predicated.

207 e.g. 'the dog is coloured': 'coloured' is a predicate which is a paronym of the genus colour.

208 *Top.* 2.4, 111a36–8.

209 *ibid.* 111a38–b1.

210 Literally: 'by being had by it'.

211 'In existence' translates *en hupostasei* at 161,29.

212 Throughout the passage Alexander seems to use *huparkhein* ('to belong', the generic
    verb to indicate that a predicate belongs to a subject without specifying the
    modality of such a belonging) and *sumbebêkenai* (the verb cognate to *sumbebêkos*,
    'accident', which I have systematically translated with 'belong incidentally') as
    interchangeable. Similarly elsewhere. On the inclusive understanding of accidental
    predication as unqualified predication as opposed to the exclusive understanding
    of accidental predication as opposed to the other three types of predications
    Aristotle distinguishes in the *Topics* see n. 17.

213 *Top.* 2.2, 109a34–b12. The two formulations are, e.g., 'colour belongs incidentally to
    the dog' and 'the dog is coloured'.

214 *Top.* 2.4, 111b4–5.

215 cf. n. 213.

216 *Top.* 2.4, 111b5.

217 For this classification and the terminology (especially the use of *meiôsis* instead of
    phthisis to indicate decrease), cf. Arist., *Cat.* 14. Aristotle does not say that change is
    a *genos* (in fact, he explicitly says that the types of change are distinguished
    according to the categories: see e.g. *Phys.* 3.1, 200b33–201a3; 5.1, 225b5–9), but he
    does refer to the *eidê* of change (*Cat.* 14, 15a13), which, however, need not be taken
    in the technical sense of 'species' of a genus. In *Phys.* 5.1 Aristotle restricts the use of
    kinêsis (as opposed to the more generic *metabolê*) to those types of change which
    are from a substrate to a substrate (5.3, 225b1–3), i.e. changes in quality, quantity
    and place. According to this classification, generation and corruption are types of
    metabolê but not of *kinêsis*. It is presumably with this restricted notion of *kinêsis* in
    mind that Alexander stresses that in the passage he is commenting upon *kinêsis* is
    used in its broader and more generic sense (in which it occurs e.g. in *Phys.* 3.1 as
    well as elsewhere), which covers all types of change.

218 Wallies prints a *crux* after the parenthesis at 162,12. Some integration, possibly
    along the line of the one suggested in the translation '<check whether>' is required.
    See also Wallies apparatus *ad loc.*

219 Numbers cannot undergo a change in quantity without undergoing a change in
    substance (i.e. without passing away) since, by definition, each number is a definite
    discrete quantity.

220 If one uses the *topos* to demolish a definition, then the problem becomes a problem
    about the definition, whereas in this context (i.e. in *Top.* 2) it is introduced as a
    topos about the accident.

221 *EN* 3.1, 1109b35–1110a1.

222 *EN* 3.2, 1110b32 ff.

223 Arist., *Top.* 2.2, 109b30–1 (with omissions).

224 *Top.* 2.4, 111b14.

225 There is no explicit subject for the verb 'requires' (*axioi* at 164,3). Other occurrences of the verb show that the subject can either be a *topos* (see e.g. 177,9) or a person. I take the subject to be the *topos* since nothing in the vicinity of the passage suggests that Alexander is talking about a person; alternatively, one could take the subject to be the author of the *topos*, i.e. Aristotle himself (cf. 142,28). Similar considerations apply to 164,11.

226 Anst., *Top.* 2.4, 111b12.

227 Literally: 'nor lack', i.e. neither lacks anything with respect to the other.

228 This view can be ascribed to the Cyrenaics: see DL 2.86.

229 cf. *EN* 7.13, 1152b13.

230 cf. Plato., *Crat.* 419C.

231 cf. Arist., *EN* 7.13, 1153a14.

232 cf. Arist., *EN* 10.4, 1174b31–3.

233 Arist., *Top.* 2.4, 111b12.

234 Alexander's analysis of this *topos* clearly displays his integration, within a unified system of Peripatetic logic, of a theory of hypothetical syllogisms based on Stoic logic and terminology. See Introduction pp. 4–24 for a more comprehensive account of Alexander's views on this point. For an analysis of Alexander's resort to the Stoic indemonstrables see Bobzien (2014).

235 This description of the argumentative procedure emphasises the characteristic structure of arguments from a hypothesis that something is shown 'together with' something else, where one typically produces a syllogistic argument only for the latter, while the former (i.e. the desired conclusion) is established through the hypothesis. Cf. Introduction pp. 5–6, 32; n. 240.

236 Plato, *Phaedo* 69E–72E.

237 Plato, *Meno* 87C.

238 Note that the last inferential step (from 'the man who has virtues has knowledge' to 'virtue is knowledge') is not a syllogistic inference but rather an inference from the coordinates. Throughout the *Topics* this sort of inference is regarded as fundamentally unproblematic. The basic idea seems to be that if someone is ready to concede the claim 'the one who has the virtues has knowledge', he will also be ready to concede 'virtue is knowledge', which seems equally reputable: cf. Arist., *Top.* 2.9, 114a38–b3; 3.6, 119a36–b16, especially 119a38–b1 and b15–16.

239 Literally: 'is a knower'.

240 Note the syllogistic structure of the arguments in support of the claim which has to be established in order to establish the desired claim through the consequence. In Alexander's reconstruction, the overall argumentation will include a hypothetical component as well as a categorical syllogism. For some discussion of this feature of Alexander's analysis of the arguments in the *Top.* see Introduction, pp. 4–24.

241 Alex., *in An. Pr.* 260,18 ff.

242 Plato, *Resp.* 348C ff.

243 i.e. based on the mutual agreement or harmonious disposition of the parts of the soul.

244 Alexander considers the possibility that the argument he has just outlined would be an argument concerning the definition (i.e. an argument aiming at either establishing or refuting a definition) rather than an argument concerning the accident, as all arguments in *Top.* 2 are supposed to be.

245 'Consequents' translates *tôn akolouthountôn* at 167,5 (literally: 'the things that follow'), whereas 'consequence' in 'from consequence' translates the abstract noun *akolouthia* (167,4).

246 'Equivalent' translates *ep'isês* at 167,8. In this context the phrase seems to mean that the two propositions are equally true or always true together. In other contexts, the phrase can indicate that a proposition is as often true as it is false or, with reference to terms, that they are co-extensive (for further comments and references see Müller and Gould 1999: 175 *s.v.*). If Alexander thinks of the items that follow upon each other as terms rather than as propositions (as the following examples, 'growing' and 'the things that are nurtured' may suggest), then 'co-extensive' would be a possible translation.

247 The translation reflects the Greek construction of the sentence. The construction is interesting in that it shows that for Alexander (and, presumably, for Peripatetic logicians starting with Aristotle more generally) it is not at all obvious that relations of consequence obtain between terms or propositions rather than between things or states of affairs. For a thorough analysis of the texts in which this feature emerges and of the philosophical consequences for the logical analysis of conditionals, see Bobzien (2000). Cf n. 388.

248 'Diverting' translates *metapherein* at 167,25. About the vocabulary of diversion and replacement, see the Note on the Translation, p. 32.

249 Arist., *Top.* 2.5, 111b33–4.

250 *ibid.*, 111b32.

251 'Is established at the same time' translates *sunkatasteuazetai*. Cf. 129,1–5.

252 cf. Arist., *Top.* 2.5, 111b33.

253 *Top.* 2.5, 111b34.

254 Namely the one he asked for as a premise to establish the desired conclusion.

255 Alexander emphasizes that the questioner in this case has more than one argument to show the substituted claim that everything according to nature is good. Note, in the second argument, the use of the general premise that if the contrary belongs to the contrary, then also the contrary belongs to the contrary and of the premise 'what is against nature is bad' in order to establish the second premise of the syllogism 'what is according to nature is good'. Unlike the first argument, which is

clearly intended as a syllogism in first figure in which the two premises are (1) 'what is according to nature is proper to each thing', and (2) 'what is proper to each thing is good', the second argument establishes the same conclusion through the use of the *topos* in a way which cannot be reduced to a syllogistic figure in any obvious way. What Alexander thinks about this sort of argument is not clear, but he seems to think that general *topoi* may figure as premises in deductive arguments (see Introduction pp. 24–30).

256 i.e. that every pleasure is good.

257 i.e. for the claim that everything that is according to nature is good.

258 *An. Pr.* 2.25, 69a20–36. The situation described in *An. Pr.* is that of a syllogism in which one premise is not evident and yet more plausible than the conclusion or such that it can be proved by resorting to few middle terms. Alexander's idea seems to be that in this situation one can proceed to establish one of the premises which is needed to establish the desired conclusion, provided that producing an argument for the premise is an easier task than arguing for the desired conclusion.

259 *poiêsamenos* (masculine nominative) is the first of two readings that Alexander discusses; the second one, *poiêsamenou* (masculine genitive, accepted by Ross and Brunschwig) is discussed at 170,10 ff. On the first reading the participle in the nominative refers to the subject who 'undertakes the removal', whereas on the second reading the interlocutor who undertakes the removal of a claim and the one who carries out the induction must be different.

260 Arist., *Top.* 2.5, 111b38–112a2.

261 i.e. the interlocutor can simply deny the premise which is asked in order to establish the desired conclusion.

262 Alexander keeps referring to the argumentative situation and to the example used to illustrate the general procedure described in the immediately preceding section of the commentary: one intends to establish the problem that every pleasure is good; in order to do this, he takes the premise that everything that is according to nature is good; the interlocutor, however, does not concede this premise. The discussion then turns to establishing or demolishing the premise that everything that is according to nature is good, which becomes the new 'submitted claim'.

263 *Top.* 2.5, 112a1: *dia tou keimenou*.

264 The questioner wants to get the premise 'everything that is according to nature is good'. The answerer can either simply reject it or show by induction that it is false. If the questioner then tries to remove what was established through induction by the answerer he switches the target of the argument, but the shift is necessary in that the removal of what was established by induction is necessary in order for the questioner to get the premise he needs ('everything that is according to nature is good') in order to establish what he originally wanted to argue for ('every pleasure is good'). Note the complexity of the argumentative exchange Alexander is describing:

the questioner *a* wants to establish that every pleasure is good. In order to do this, he asks for the premise that everything that is according to nature is good. The answerer *b*, however, does not concede this premise – either simply or by carrying out an induction to the effect that not everything that is according to nature is good. If *b* has shown through induction that not everything that is according to nature is good, then *a* must remove the conclusion of the inductive argument, e.g. by qualifying the results of the inductive argument as irrelevant to the original argument.

265 'Making use of the proposed [*topos*]' translates *proskhrômenon tôi prokeimenôi. to prokeimenon* is also used by Alexander to indicated the problem at stake or what is submitted, but I do not see in what sense the interlocutor who carries out the induction would make use of the submitted claim (presumably: that no pleasure is good). For this reason, I prefer to take the reference to be to the 'proposed' or 'submitted' *topos*.

266 The inductive argument is supposed to remove the premise that no good is a process of coming to be; the strategy is to show by induction that there are processes of coming to be that are good.

267 i.e. that no good is a process of coming to be.

268 i.e. the premise that no good is a process of coming to be.

269 In the scenario considered so far, the interlocutor who is switching to arguing for a different claim than the original desired conclusion is the questioner, who tries to establish a premise he needs in order to establish the original desired conclusion. But, Alexander adds here, one could also imagine that the interlocutor who is leading away the discussion in order to establish something which is necessary for his purposes is the answerer, where the purpose of the answerer is that of preventing the questioner from drawing a conclusion which contradicts the thesis he – the answerer – is defending. Accordingly, in carrying out an induction to the effect of denying a premise which is necessary for the questioner, the answerer switches to establishing a claim which is necessary for his purposes.

270 Alexander is commenting on *Top.* 2.5, 111b38–112a2.

271 cf. n. 259.

272 In this scenario: the answerer.

273 i.e. the questioner.

274 i.e. that what is according to nature for the human being is good for the human being.

275 'Taking as an additional premise' translates *proslambanôn* at 171,6.

276 The scenario Alexander is envisaging to make sense of Aristotle's text is, again, quite complex. The main idea seems to be this: imagine that the questioner wants to establish *p*. In order to establish *p*, he shows by induction that *q*, from which *p* follows. In the induction he resorts to *r*, which the answerer does not concede. The questioner, however, has plenty of arguments to establish *r*; he therefore turns to establishing *r*, which is necessary to establish (by induction) *q*, which is necessary to establish the original claim *p*. In this scenario, the one who carries out the

induction is the questioner and the one who is trying to overthrow the induction by not conceding r and, therefore, by denying q is the answerer.

277 *Top.* 2.5, 112a5.

278 *ibid.*

279 i.e. that pleasure is according to nature.

280 I am not sure whether the reputable (i.e. 'endoxastic') character of this induction only has to do with the reputable character of the premises which are used in the induction rather than with the reputable character of its logical role (it is used to establish something that seems necessary for the problem at issues but is not really necessary) rather than with the reputable character of its logical structure (it seems to establish something, but it does not). Alexander (and interpreters more generally) tend to regard reputability as a feature of the premises of dialectical arguments, but there might be a general question whether for Aristotle and/or for Alexander reputability can also be a property of inferential steps.

281 Judging from the reconstruction of the argumentative strategy in the immediately following lines this seems to be the claim which is supposed to be established through induction (i.e. 'what is submitted' with respect to the inductive argument). The conclusion of the induction is, however, not really necessary to establish the original claim. From the way in which Alexander describes this scenario, it looks like there occur two shifts: first, in arguing whether pleasure is according to nature, one turns to discussing whether everything that comes to be by nature is for the sake of something, since he has several arguments about this, even if the claim that everything that comes to be by nature is for the sake of something is not necessary to establish the claim that pleasure is according to nature. The second shift occurs in case one tries to establish the claim of the first shift (e.g. that what comes to be by nature is for the sake of something) through induction and one of the premises of the inductive argument (e.g. that breathing is for the sake of something) is not conceded but is one for which one has plenty of arguments. Either way, one tries to obtain a claim which is not necessary for the purposes of the problem at stake and for which he has (directly or indirectly) plenty of resources.

282 The reason why this sort of shift to what seems to be necessary (but is not really necessary) for the sake of the argument is still dialectical (unlike the sophistic move described in the immediately following lines) seems to be that the answerer also regards the shift as necessary. It is not clear what it means that the induction carried out in the scenario envisaged by Alexander is 'reputable'; cf. n. 280.

283 I take it that the verb *parexelenkhein* differs from the simple *elenkhein* ('to refute') precisely in that it emphasizes that the refutation is not really relevant to the main argument and not to the point; in this sense it is rather a 'side-refutation'.

284 The two options ('some things were said incorrectly', which translates *tina sesoloikikota*, or 'against the given information', which translates *par'historian* at

172,13) may allude to the two types of mistakes that Aristotle has distinguished at the beginning of book 2 (109a27ff.), i.e. deviating from the accepted use of language and saying something which is not true.

285 *Top.* 2.4, 111b17–23.
286 *Top.* 2.4, 111b18.
287 Namely the former *topos* in *Top.* 2.4, 111b17–23.
288 Note that modern editions have *eirêkôs* at 112a16, while Alexander (173,4) has *eipôn*.
289 *Top.* 2.5, 112a16.
290 Alexander's paraphrase of Aristotle's text strongly suggests that he does not (or not exclusively) takes 'the things that follow upon what is said' to be propositions following from another proposition. He rather seems to think of a relation between general terms. On this point and, more generally, on the extent to which Aristotle and/or Alexander envisage elements of propositional logic see Introduction pp. 1–16 and cf. nn. 245–7, 388.
291 The Greek construction (*ho eipôn* + the accusative without any article of the words whose translation I put between quotation marks) certainly does not unequivocally suggest that Alexander is talking about mentioning words. I take it that acceptable translations would be 'the one who says that [something is a] human being has also said [that it is an] animal [. . .]' or 'the one who talks about [a] human being has also talked about [an] animal [. . .]'.
292 cf. Aristotle's arguments against the existence of void in *Phys.* 4.11, 215a24–216a21.
293 *Top.* 2.5, 112a21–2.
294 *Top.* 2.5, 112a21.
295 That is: it is often the case that it is easier to remove what was originally posited.
296 Plato, *Gorg.* 480B.
297 About Alexander's analysis of arguments from consequence (*akolouthia*) or conflict (*makhê*) cf. nn. 247, 290, 329, 388.
298 cf. Arist., *Cat.* 10, 11b38–12a2.
299 cf. Arist., *Cael.* 1.5. For some discussion of this example and the implications that it carries for Alexander's assessment of this sort of arguments see Castelli (2015).
300 Contraries range over and are ontologically linked to a certain type of subject; contradictories are not characterized by any similar restriction. Cf. Arist., *Metaph.* 10.3, 1054b18–22; *Cat.* 10, 13b12–35.
301 The structure of the fifth indemonstrable: either *p* or *q*; but not *p*; therefore, *q*.
302 The structure of the fourth indemonstrable: either *p* or *q*; but *p* therefore, not *q*.
303 *Top.* 2.6, 112a33.
304 The examples are for the most part untranslatable since the etymological accounts that Alexander provides do not apply to the English counterparts of the words which are supposed to be replaced. For this reason, I have left the Greek words untranslated whenever this seemed necessary in order to preserve the intelligibility

of the examples. In such cases I provide the etymological rendition and/or the usual meaning of the words in square brackets.

305 Note that the example includes a step from the coordinates (if one has managed to establish that the courageous man is not *eupsukhos* he will have also established that courage is not *eupsukhia*).

306 The similarity in this *topos* is understood in terms of mere morphological and phonetic similarity between linguistic expressions.

307 About *daimones* in the Platonic tradition see Brisson et al. (2018).

308 The reference to Xenocrates is in Aristotle (*Top.* 2.6, 112a36–8).

309 i.e. the good man is not the one who has a good *daimôn*. This is a comment on Xenocrates' account of the *eudaimonia* of the good man in terms of the identification of the soul with the *daimôn* which was mentioned a few lines earlier.

310 *Top.* 2.2, 109a34–5.

311 *Top.* 1.5, 102b6–9.

312 Alexander's point here seems to be that there is no straightforward correspondence between the division accident *vs.* other types of predicates, and the division between what belongs for the most part or as it happens *vs.* what belongs from necessity. The two distinctions yield different non-overlapping classifications of predicates. It is however interesting that Alexander raises the issue of the correspondence between the different types of predicates and modalities. For a recent analysis of the relations between the distinction of the types of predicates in the *Top.* and Aristotle's modal logic see Malink (2013).

313 Literally: 'For we have that'.

314 'Contingent' translates *endekhomenos*. This translation (and correspondingly for related expressions) gives a good sense in most cases. There are, however, some occurrences in the text of the commentary on this very same *topos* where 'possible' seems to be a better translation and I have translated accordingly. The reader should bear this problem in mind throughout. Something is contingent if it is possible that it is not the case.

315 *Top.* 2.6, 112b9.

316 This seems to be the natural interpretation of the masculine.

317 *Top.* 2.2, 109a34–5: '[…] has given as an accident what belongs [to the subject] in any other way'.

318 Polyonyms are (literally) things with many names (i.e. cases of synonymy in our sense of synonyms – and not in Aristotle's sense of *Cat.* 1, 1a6–12).

319 Of these three features of the accident, the first relies on the distinction between being-in and being-said-of of *Cat.* 2, the second captures the idea that things are the same as their essences which is developed, e.g. in *Metaph.* 7.6, and the third picks up the account of the accident in *Top.* 1.5, 102b4 ff.

320 The double qualification 'both according to the subject and according to what is signified' presumably emphasizes the difference from cases of incidental predication

(e.g. the just is musical) in which subject and predicate happen to belong to the same subject (i.e. some particular individual such as Socrates) but, in some sense, do not signify the same. Polyonyms are not merely co-referential, but rather correspond to what we would call synonyms.

321 Prodicus of Ceos, a sophist who flourished in the fifth century BCE and was particularly well known for his subtle distinctions between words with similar meaning. See e.g. Plato, *Hp. Ma.* 282C; *Crat.* 384B; *Prot.* 337A–C, 340A–D.

322 In the conceptual framework of *Top.* 1.7 the mistake consists in expressing what for Aristotle (and, presumably, for Alexander) would be a case of numerical sameness conveyed by as a case of accidental numerical sameness, which is one way to spell out the relation obtaining between subject and predicate when the predicate expresses an accident of the subject.

323 'Combination' translates *sumplokê*. It is possible that with this expression Alexander does not simply intend to refer to any combination of terms coming from two pairs of contraries, but rather to a combination which leads to the composition of propositions in which those terms are the subject and the predicate; by way of contrast, in *Cat.* 2, 1a16–19 Aristotle provides an account of the things that are said without *sumplokê*.

324 The more accurate translation of the Greek *enantiôseôn* at 181,13 would be 'contrarieties' (instead of 'contraries'), which might be misleading in that it may suggest that Alexander is dealing with two pairs of pairs (since each contrariety obtains between two contraries).

325 *Top.* 2.7, 112b31.

326 The masculine *ton auton* at 182,27 and the again at 182,28–9 is somewhat confusing, but the sense of the passage is clear.

327 *Top.* 2.7, 113a3–4.

328 *ibid.*, 113a5.

329 Conflict (*makhê*) and consequence (*akolouthia*) are the two main types of relations obtaining between 'combinations', i.e. between propositions obtained from the terms belonging to the pairs of contraries as specified in the set-up of the *topos*.

330 Contrary propositions cannot both be true at the same time (but they can be both false); see *Int.* 7, 17b20–2. The pairs of propositions analysed above, however, are such that, in each pair, if one is true the other is also true. Accordingly, they cannot be contrary.

331 *Top.* 2.7, 113a5–6

332 *EN* 2.8, 1109b11 ff.

333 The text at 183,14 seems damaged in its transmitted form; the addition is suggested by Wallies in the apparatus.

334 *Top.* 2.7, 113a6–7.

335 According to Aristotle it is necessarily the case that either *p* or not-*p* is true, whereas contrary propositions cannot both be true but can both be false.

Propositions that are opposed as contraries (*enantiôs*) in *Int.* 7, 17b20–2 are universal propositions of opposite quality ('all S are P' and 'no S is P'), but in *Top.* 2.7 the contrariety of propositions has to do with the opposition of contrary subjects and/or contrary predicates (e.g. 'the just is bad' and 'the unjust is good').

336 i.e. establishing which combinations are contrary to each other based on the character from which they stem. See also n. 337.

337 Alexander's point is that stemming from contrary characters is not the only criterion Aristotle uses in order to identify contrary claims in this passage: Alexander has already made clear from the way in which the *topos* is built that each pair of combination must respect the condition that subjects will belong to one of two pairs of contrary terms and predicates to the other of the two pairs of contrary terms.

338 The feminine at 184,20 *tautas* can either refer to *suzugiai* ('pairs') or to *sumplokai* ('combinations'). I opt for 'pairs' because it seems to me that the emphasis in the former passage and in the quotation that immediately follows lies on pairs of claims rather than on the single combinations that enter the pairs, whereas from now on Aristotle (and Alexander) will focus on the relation of opposition obtaining between one single combination and all other combinations in the various pairs.

339 *Top.* 2.7, 113a12–14.

340 *ibid.* 113a14–15.

341 The Greek is *sumplokê*, but what is meant here is clearly that in the second *suzugia* the combination saying that the unjust is good is blameworthy.

342 *Top.* 2.7, 113a18–19.

343 Presumably the reference is to *Top.* 2.6, 112a24–31.

344 The verb *sunhuparkhein* can be translated either absolutely 'to obtain at the same time' or, understanding an implicit dative, 'to belong [to a subject] at the same time'. Both readings are possible, but they may refer to different understandings of what the contraries at issue are. On the first rendition, the sentence is most naturally understood as being about contrary propositions (or states of affairs), whereas on the second rendition contraries are most naturally understood as contrary properties of a subject.

345 This means that both the subject and the predicate of the problem have a contrary.

346 i.e. one has to remove that justice is bad.

347 i.e. by having shown that injustice is bad.

348 This complicated phrasing 'in whatever sense of contrary' translates *kath' hopoteron [. . .] sêmainomenon tou enantiou*. What Alexander wants to say is (I think) that it does not matter which one of the two contraries to the submitted claim we manage to establish.

349 The compounds are presumably the combinations made of a subject and a predicate that have contraries without intermediates.

350 *Top.* 2.7, 112b29–30.

351 This consideration seems out of context. Perhaps it is occasioned by the remark that the *topos* might be useful both for constructive and for destructive purposes in the immediately preceding lines: cf. *Top.* 2.10, 114a37 ff. and especially 115a11–14 about the use of the more and the less both for constructive and for destructive purposes.

352 See Aristotle's examples to illustrate combinations and pairs throughout *Top.* 2.7, 112b32–113a15.

353 See Arist., *Top.* 2.7, 113a14–18.

354 cf. Arist., *Metaph.* 10.4, 1055a19–23.

355 This could be a reference to a (lost) commentary on *EN*, but it could also be a back-reference to the considerations above (183,11 ff.) about whether what is to be avoided is or is not contrary to what is to be avoided.

356 From Alexander's paraphrasis of the *topos* it looks like Alexander is commenting on the second of two very similar *topoi*; Ross and Brunschwig 113a20–3 print the first formulation (i.e. the one Alexander alludes to by saying that it is recorded in some exemplars and omitted in others). For some discussion of the situation of the manuscripts see Brunschwig (1968).

357 *Top.* 2.7, 113a22–3.

358 *Top.* 2.6, 112a24.

359 *Top.* 2.7, 113a25–6.

360 'Idea' translates *idea*, 'form' translates *eidos*, and a few lines below 'shape' translates *morphê*.

361 *Top.* 2.7, 113a29.

362 Alexander is commenting on the well known paradox of the liar.

363 'Presentation' translates *phantasia* at 189,1.

364 i.e. being will turn out to be both substance and quantity, i.e. many.

365 cf. Arist., *Phys.* 1.2, 185a32–b5.

366 *Top.* 2.7, 113a31–2.

367 Since one can only know what is true, if Dion knows that he is dead, Dion is dead; but since in order to know something one has to be alive, if Dion knows that he is dead, Dion is alive.

368 One has to guess what the problem with 'this is not day' is. In his commentary on *An. Pr.* (177,28–182,8) Alexander spells out (in a different context but with reference to similar examples) that the demonstrative pronoun 'this' refers to what is present when it is present. Accordingly, 'this day' means 'the day which is, when it is'; he also mentions several times the conditional 'if it is night, this is not day' (*ouk estin hautê hemera*) (see e.g. *in An. Pr.* 178,5–8; 180,4–5; 181,35–182,8). Perhaps Alexander's point is that if one says 'this is not day' he is saying both that it is day (as the use of *hautê* in the feminine, i.e. 'this [day]', implies) and that it is not day. I am grateful to an anonymous reader for comments on this point.

369 'In all cases' translates *pantôs* at 189,21. Similarly below. Alexander's point will become clear at 190,15 ff.

370 *Top.* 2.7, 113b7–14.

371 Aristotle mentions the case of things that are naturally characterized by one contrary e.g. in *Cat.* 10, 12b35–13a3.

372 *Top.* 2.7, 113a36.

373 *ibid.* 113b2.

374 'Cognition' translates *gnôsis* (190,5), whereas 'knowledge' translates *epistêmê* (190,6).

375 The analysis of the opposition of form and privation as a contrariety is not to be taken for granted. For example, it does not appear in *Cat.* 10, where Aristotle is rather interested in showing that the four types of opposites (relatives, contraries, possession and privation, contradictories) are distinct from each other. The identification is rather the result of theoretical analysis. Alexander is presumably thinking of the way in which Aristotle disentangles privation and matter in *Phys.* 1.

376 The lemma in Wallies' edition of Alexander has *ek* ('from') here, whereas both Ross's and Brunschwig's editions have *epi* ('in the case of', 'with reference to').

377 The literal translation 'contradictions' sounds clumsy, but since Alexander explicitly comments on this formulation at 193,3–5 I opt for the literal translation which fits with Alexander's remarks.

378 The fourfold partition is standard in Aristotle and can be found e.g. in *Cat.* 10.

379 cf. Arist. *Top.* 2.8, 113b22–3.

380 About the analogies between hypothetical and predicative propositions and the consequences that they have for the reduction of fully hypothetical syllogisms to standard syllogisms see Barnes 1983.

381 cf. examples in *Top.* 2.8, 113b17–18.

382 *Top.* 2.8, 113b19.

383 *ibid.* 113b17.

384 *ibid.* 113b17–18.

385 cf. Arist., *Phys.* 1.3, 186a10–16; *SE* 28, 181a27–30.

386 Alexander resorts to the distinction between form and matter of arguments or propositions and premises on various occasions, but he never spells out the distinction, which seems to pick out different aspects on different occasions. For a survey and some discussion see Flannery (1995, chapter 3). In this context Alexander suggests that the distinction of types of predicates concerns the matter of the terms involved in a relation of consequence, whereas (presumably) the analysis of the inversion of the consequence independently of the more specific features of the terms involved concerns the form of the consequence.

387 'The one … opposition' translates: *hê sun antithesei legomenê.* at 192, 11.

388 Note that the analysis of the examples throughout this passage leaves room for ambiguity as to whether Alexander is thinking in terms of establishing or removing propositions or 'things' through the use of consequences and, correspondingly, as to between what sort of items consequences obtain. Cf. n. 247.

389 Alexander seems to be referring to the formulation at 113b15–16 with which the *topos* is introduced: the formulation may suggest that Aristotle is about to analyse what follows from contradictions (rather than from the single contradictories, i.e. *p* or *not-p* respectively). Cf. n. 377.

390 Arist., *Top.* 2.8, 113b24–6.

391 Throughout the passage Alexander seems to think of pairs of contraries as ordered pairs in which the first member of each pair is, in some axiological sense, positive and the second one negative.

392 *Top.* 2.8, 113b29.

393 *ibid.* 113b28.

394 *ibid.* 114a1–3.

395 *ibid.* 113b34.

396 The text printed by Wallies at 195,7–10 would yield the translation: 'So, we will establish and demolish either by showing that the one follows upon the other (for the remaining member of the first pair will then follow upon the remaining member of the second pair), or *we will demolish* by arguing that the one does not follow upon the other', which is clumsy and does not make much sense. I therefore depart from Wallies' text in that I omit *anaskeuasomen* ('we will demolish') at 195,9–10.

397 Aristotle's example: cf. *Top.* 2.9, 114a14–17.

398 cf. *Top.* 2.8, 114a18–19.

399 'Condition' translates *diorismou* at 196,8. See also n. 400.

400 The condition for the occurrence of consequences between members of pairs of opposites according to possession and privation is spelled out at 195,11–20: one has to check that it is not the case that one member of a pair of opposites according to possession and privation (e.g. life, which is opposed to death) follows upon both members of another pair of opposites according to possession and privation (e.g. sight and blindness).

401 *Top.* 2.8, 114a22–3.

402 *ibid.* 114a24: 'Furthermore, what was said is not less useful with respect to the contrary'.

403 *ibid.* 114a24: *enantion.*

404 'The things that derive their names' translate *ta panônomasmena*. Through this terminology Alexander stresses the conceptual link between coordinates and inflections (which play a pivotal role in several *topoi* throughout the *Top.*) and paronymy in *Cat.* 1, 1a12–15. Note that paronymy in *Cat.* 1 is introduced in terms

of 'difference in inflection' (1a13). It is perhaps noteworthy that Ammonius (*in Int.*, 13,19–14,17) ascribes to Alexander the claim that adverbs are *onomata* ('nouns' or 'names', in the context of the distinction between nouns and verbs which rules Aristotle's *De interpretatione*). It is hard to reconstruct the exact thesis of Alexander through Ammonius's criticism, but it seems possible that the view Ammonius criticizes was about the sort of adverbs that are inflections. One point of Ammonius's criticism is that adverbs (unlike names) cannot be the subject or the predicate of any proposition; interestingly enough the account of inflections in Alexander's commentary on the *Topics* makes room for the possibility that inflections replace the subject and the verb of the desired conclusion. This fact might help in making Ammonius's criticism slightly more intelligible.

405 The Greek text only has *to dikaion* (singular neuter) and *ho dikaios* (singular masculine).

406 'Determinate things' translates *pragmata tina*. The point of this remark will become clear at 197,21 ff., where Alexander distinguishes between the coordinates, which indicate some underlying things, and inflections, which indicate the modality of an action or of a disposition.

407 *Top.* 2.9, 114a30.

408 *ibid.* 114a32–3.

409 The use of the masculine nominative introduced by the genitive article suggests that Alexander is mentioning the corresponding adjective; in the immediately following line he speaks of justice, courage and music in such a way that it is not clear whether he is making a point about the relations obtaining between linguistic expressions (as seems to be the case here) or between inflections and things picked out by the corresponding abstract nouns. See also n. 410.

410 A general difficulty in the whole passage clarifying what coordinates and inflections are is that it is not clear whether Alexander primarily thinks of extra-linguistic (extra-mental or mental) items rather than of linguistic expressions, and whether he thinks the same about coordinates and inflections. More specifically, even if one is willing to concede that coordination obtains between extra-linguistic items (e.g. justice, the just thing, the just person), one might still be in doubt whether the same concession should be made about inflections. In fact, unless one is willing to claim that 'justly' strictly speaking designates a way of being or of acting, it may look like the relation between an inflection and what it is an inflection of is primarily a relation obtaining between linguistic expressions. *Ptôsis* is the technical expression to indicate the *casus*, i.e. the different cases in the declension of nouns or adjectives. In Aristotle's passage in the *Top.*, however, it seems to be confined to adverbial expressions (on the relation between the technical grammatical use of the term and Aristotle's use see Primavesi 1994). Bearing in mind that this is a problem and a controversial issue, in the translation I

have mentioned words when Alexander's point can be taken to be primarily a linguistic one, whereas I have opted for alternative solutions otherwise. In such cases I occasionally avoid mentioning words by translating the modal adverbs 'the [...] way' – e.g. 'the just way' instead of 'justly'; 'the courageous way' instead of 'courageously', etc. Any choice here will be arbitrary, at least to a certain extent, and the reader should bear this difficulty in mind throughout. Note, in any case, that Alexander's distinction between 'underlying things' and 'modes' is philosophically interesting and cannot be directly extrapolated from Aristotle's text nor from Aristotle's distinction of the different categories.

411 'Passing over' translates *metabantas* at 198,4. The argumentative procedure through coordinates and inflections is one further case of a 'shift' from what is initially submitted to something else (cf. p. 32). It is part of the theory of coordinates and inflections that what is shown for one of them holds for all of them; therefore, one can show something about what was originally submitted if one manages to show something about its coordinates or inflections (which are, in any case, something else).

412 'Series of coordination' translates *sustoikhia*. A *sustoikhia* is a column in which items are ordered under one primary item. Items can be of different sorts and the order can respond to various criteria. In addition to the case of the coordinates of the *Top.*, Aristotle refers for example to the *sustoikhiai* of contraries ('tables of contraries': see e.g. *Metaph.* 1.5, 986a22 ff.; 4.2, 1004b27) and to the 'columns' of predication (e.g. *An. Post.* 1.15, 79b5–11).

413 'Judgement' translates *krisis*.

414 I take it that Alexander is spelling out the sense in which 'praiseworthily' (which is an inflection) qualifies an action and not an 'underlying thing'. Cf. n. 410.

415 i.e. it is because something belongs incidentally to the disposition that what belongs incidentally to the disposition also belongs incidentally to its coordinates and inflections.

416 See n. 410.

417 *Top.* 2.9, 114b3–5.

418 About the general difficulty of disentangling use and mention throughout the passage see n. 410.

419 *Top.* 2.9, 114b10.

420 *Top.* 2.8, 113b27–114a6.

421 *Top.* 2.9, 114b13–14.

422 'Belongs to the same family' translates *oikeioumenon*. The terminology is unusual and could allude to some systematic arrangement of *topoi*.

423 *Klêsis* ('nominative form') and *ptôsis* ('inflection') indicate in the technical vocabulary of the grammarians the nominative and the oblique case respectively. However, in Aristotle's *Top.* inflections are typically (and, judging from the examples, exclusively) adverbial forms. Alexander's resort to grammatical technical

terminology may be taken as a hint that he thinks of inflections as linguistic expressions. Cf. n. 410.

424 On the argumentative strategy of arguing for something by arguing for something else see p. 32 and n. 411.

425 I preserve in the translation the terminological variation between 'consequents' (*hepomena*), which occurs here, and 'consequence' (*akolouthia*) used elsewhere. Although the same word *hepomenon* is also used by Alexander to indicate the consequent of a conditional proposition, the 'consequents' in this text are often construed as terms, whereas the relation of consequence often indicates a relation obtaining between 'combinations' of terms or propositions (cf. n. 329). It is not clear, however, whether Alexander is fully aware of the distinction and resorts to a corresponding distinction at the terminological level consistently.

426 The feminine nominative *hautê*, 'this one', at 200,16 presumably refers back to *euporian*, 'resource', at 200,14.

427 The remark that the give *topos* could split into a number of *topoi* is perhaps interesting in that it may allude to the idea that a *topos* refers to only one argumentative strategy with one specific 'starting point'. Cf. Introduction, pp. 24–30.

428 *Top.* 2.9, 114b17–18.

429 *ibid.* 114b18–19.

430 One might wonder why Alexander does not regard recovering health (*hugiazesthai*) as a coordinate of health. One reason might be quite simply that Aristotle keeps generation and corruption (and the *topoi* based on them) separate from the coordinates and the corresponding *topoi* (see e.g. *Top.* 2.9, 114a26 and 114b16 respectively). One additional and possibly complementary reason is that *hugiazesthai* is a verb and the lists of coordinates that Aristotle gives do not include verbs. The idea that coordinates are 'things' and not processes might also play some role. In the commentary on *Top.* 4, at 333,1–2, however, Alexander says that building (*to oikodomein*), which is a (process of) generation is a coordinate of having built (*oikodomêkenai*) and similarly for being in action (*energein*) and having been in action (*enêrgêkenai*). This passage may suggest that processes have their own class of coordinates. I am grateful to an anonymous reader for comments on this point and the reference to Alexander's commentary on *Top.* 4.

431 It is hard to pin down the difference between the two interpretations that Alexander is distinguishing. Perhaps the idea is that, on the first interpretation, the generation of *x* is identified with the whole process through which *x* comes to be, whereas on the second interpretation the very coming to be of *x* (at any time, independently of whether it is completed or not) is good as long as *x* is good. Alternatively, on the first reading the generation of *x* is taken as equivalent to the things (whatever they are) that produce *x*, whereas on the second reading the generation of *x* is the very process of coming to be. In support of this second option see 201,9–10; cf. 202,6–7.

432 *Top.* 2.9, 114b20.

433 *ibid.*

434 See n. 431.

435 *Top.* 2.9, 114b24.

436 Wallies prints the whole argument at 201,22–4 in quotation marks. However, nothing suggests that this is meant as a direct quotation rather than as a paraphrase of a Stoic argument.

437 *Top.* 2.9, 114b22–3.

438 'Were' (*ên*) at 201,29 is not in Aristotle's text.

439 *Top.* 2.9, 114b23–4.

440 See 201,19 ff.

441 cf. *Top.* 2.10, 114b27–8.

442 The similarity obtaining between the Greek words Alexander comments upon gets lost in the English translation; for this reason, I transliterate the Greek words and only provide the English translation in square brackets.

443 *Top.* 2.10, 114b32.

444 *ibid.* 114b32–4.

445 Interestingly enough in this passage Alexander suggests that a *topos* can be discredited if one manages to find cases in which it does not apply. This may suggest that a *topos* is supposed to be a *true* general proposition. Cf. Introduction pp. 28–30 for some considerations on the status of *topoi* as principles of deductive arguments.

446 i.e. that the one who knows thinks.

447 It is not clear what this last option is about. I take it that it is occasioned by the last suggested reading of the clause 'for sometimes there is a discrepancy', where Alexander gave as a counterexample to the *topos* that it is not necessarily the case that if one has six fingers, then many have six fingers. The idea would then be that the *topos* applies only to things that are 'naturally and according to nature', in which case what holds for one is likely to hold for many – at least as far as what is according to nature is understood as what is for the most part. For example, since it is natural for human beings to have hands with five fingers, it will be true that one human being has five fingers and that many human beings have five fingers. The restriction of the *topos* would then amount to a restriction of the validity of the inference from one to many with respect to properties that things have 'naturally and according to nature'.

448 *Top.* 2.10, 114b37–8.

449 *ibid.* 115a6

450 *ibid.* 115a8–9

451 *ibid.* 115a11

452 There is a lacuna in the text at 205,9. The addition is suggested by Wallies in the apparatus.

453 cf. *Top.* 2.10, 114b39–115a1.

454 cf. *ibid.* 115a1–2.

455 i.e. what seems to belong more.

456 The predicate (*agathon*) makes it clear that the subject (the singular masculine of 'such', which in itself could also refer to the person and pick up *tis*) is *ploutos*.

457 i.e. in the things that fall under the given definition of gymnastics.

458 In Wallies' edition the reference for the printed lemma is 115a5, but in modern editions the text starts at 115a6.

459 It is not clear what the subject of the sentence is supposed to be; it could be the *topos*, an argument built according to the *topos*, the one who resorts to the *topos* or Aristotle himself. I prefer either of the first two options, but I do not think the other two can be discarded.

460 The *topos* is used to produce two types of arguments: if a property *P* does not belong to the thing *x* to which it seems to belong more than it seems to belong to the subject *y* of the submitted claim, then it does not belong to *y* either; whereas if *P* belongs to *x* to which it seems to belong to a lesser degree than it seems to belong to *y*, then it belongs to *y* too. Alexander's final remark on the *topos* can be taken in different ways. He could be saying that the arguments produced through this *topos* do not establish their desired conclusion by proving it directly, but by arguing for something else, while the desired conclusion is reached in virtue of a hypothesis (note that, if this is Alexander's point, the same point could be made about pretty much all arguments from a hypothesis). Alternatively, the point could be that the *topos* is not about what belongs and what does not belong without qualification to any subject, but rather about what seems to belong to a subject to a higher or lesser degree than to another subject. A third option is that Alexander is drawing a contrast between this *topos* and a *topos* such as the one in Arist., *Top.* 2.11, 115b3 ff. which is used to show that, if something has a property to a higher or a lesser degree, that thing also has that property without qualification.

461 For the choice of the example cf. Arist., *EN* 8.1, 1155a22–8.

462 'Fair' and 'unfair' translate *epieikês* and *anepieikês* respectively.

463 'To a similar degree' translates *homoiôs*, which could also be translated more generically 'in a similar way'. The translation takes into account the fact that it is clear that these *topoi* are the counterpart of those from the more and the less (i.e. from what seems to belong to a higher or to a lesser degree respectively) in the previous section of the chapter.

464 i.e. prior to and, therefore, independently of the addition.

465 The example of the triangle is unfortunate since being triangular does not seem to be a property which can be conferred to things by addition of something triangular in the same way in which being good can be conferred to things by addition of something good. One might wonder whether the whole sentence about the triangle

(210,3–4) was a gloss which at some point crept into the text, but since (as far as I can see) there is no evidence for this, here is a way to make some sense of the text as it stands. Even if Alexander's example does not seem to refer to any well-known theorem, the idea seems to be that, if the result of the addition of a figure A to another figure B is a figure which is a triangle, then the added figure itself must be a triangle. Stated in this form, however, the theorem is not quite accurate, since what can be established is rather that one of the two figures which were added to each other must be a triangle. Alexander's reference to the shape of the figures that are added to each other and of the resulting figure suggests that he is not talking about the addition of areas, but rather about the process of attaching one side of figure A to one side of figure B on the exterior so that the ends of the sides coincide. On this understanding of addition, suppose that you were to add figure A to figure B in such a way that the resultant figure is a triangle. One can think of the problem in terms of the number of vertices of the figures involved: A has n vertices, B has m vertices, and the resultant figure has 3 vertices. In the process of addition as described above, two vertices of A (i.e. the vertices on the side along which A will be attached to B) will be attached to two vertices of B. Three cases are possible: the 4 vertices (2 of A and 2 of B) will become 2, 1 or 0 in the resulting figure (2 if the sum of the two vertices, one of A and one of B, that come together is smaller or greater than 180 degrees; 1 if the sum of one pair of vertices, one of A and one of B, is equal to 180 degrees and the sum of the other pair is smaller or greater than 180 degree; 0 if the sum of both pairs is 180 degree). Suppose that they become:

(1) 2 vertices (2 vertices disappear). Then $n + m - 2 = 3$; so $n + m = 5$. But this is not possible since the resultant figure must be a triangle and so must have only 3 vertices.

(2) 1 vertex (3 vertices disappear). Then $n + m - 3 = 3$; so $n + m = 6$, which means that both A and B are triangles. (To see this draw a triangle with a line from one vertex to the opposite side.)

(3) 0 vertices (all 4 vertices disappear). Then $n + m - 4 = 3$; so $n + m = 7$, which means that one of A and B is a triangle and the other a quadrilateral. (Consider a triangle that is divided by a line from one side to another.)

I am very grateful to Michael Griffin and, especially, to Alan Bowen for their help in spelling out what Alexander may have had in mind.

466 I take that the subject of the sentence is the single ounce; if so, the plural in the Greek text at 210, 12 (*hautai*) does not make much sense.

467 See the next *topos* and, in particular, 211,8–9: if x, when added to y, makes the whole $x+y$ heavier than y, then x is heavy (i.e. has a weight).

468 Plato, *Phaedo* 105C–E.

469 *Oinomeli* was (as the name suggests) a drink made of a mixture of wine and honey.

470 See 210, 7 ff.

471 The reference is to the Stoics and their doctrine of so-called 'indifferents' and 'preferred indifferents'. According to the Stoics there is only one good and choiceworthy thing (the perfection of reason, which is virtue) and, accordingly, only one bad thing (the corruption of reason, which is vice). All other things are strictly speaking indifferent, in the sense that they are in themselves neither good nor bad and neither to be chosen nor to be avoided. Among the indifferents, however, the Stoics distinguished between preferred indifferents and dispreferred indifferents; the former are things that are according to the nature of the human being and such that it is rational to choose them (e.g. health, beauty, wealth, etc.). Dispreferred indifferents are against the nature of the human being and such that it is usually rational to avoid them – but there might be situations in which it will be rational to choose them rather than to avoid them. The argument Alexander refers to aims at establishing that indifferents and, in particular, preferred indifferents are in fact choiceworthy.

472 Wallies puts 'if what [. . .] higher degree' into quotation marks (211,15), but this looks like a paraphrase of Arist., *Top.* 2.11, 115a29–31 rather than a direct quotation. Presumably, the reason to put the sentence into quotation marks is that it is a floating protasis without an apodosis. I prefer to add <etc.> rather than to add quotation marks.

473 *Top.* 2.11, 115a31.

474 *ibid.* 115a29–30.

475 *ibid.* 115a31–3.

476 Alexander's attention to the categorial framework of comparisons is emphasized in the introductory remarks to his commentary on the third book of Aristotle's *Top.* See Alex., *in Top.* 217,13–19; 218,13 ff. See also the remarks above at 211,17–18 about addition within different types of quantity.

477 *Top.* 2.11, 115b1–2.

478 *ibid.* 115a27–8.

479 i.e. not trivially for things that are not white at all (and are, in this sense, less white than anything that is white).

480 The Greek formulation is rather compressed, but the sense becomes clear through the explanation that immediately follows. Imagine that we want to establish that something x has property P and P is such that it admits of degrees. If we manage to establish that x is more P or less P than something else y, then we will have established that x is P.

481 i.e. if it is shown that it has some of the properties with respect to which it receives the more and the less.

482 *Cat.* 5, 3b33–4a9; 6, 6a19–25. See also n. 476.

483 cf. *Phys.* 4.1, 208a29–31.

484 'As compelling' translated *hôs iskhun ekhousi* at 214,3, literally: 'as having force'.

485 Wallies refers to *EN* 6.9, 1142a13–16, but the passage does not seem to convey the point Alexander refers to. The passage in *EN* 6.9 only stresses that, while there can be young people who are excellent at theoretical sciences such as geometry and arithmetic, no young people can have wisdom (*phronêsis*), since the latter requires experience, which is gathered over a long time. I would rather suggest that the reference is to the discussion in *EN* 6.13, 1144b1–1145a6, where Aristotle argues that ethical virtues strictly speaking (unlike natural virtues) require *phronêsis* and vice versa. The contrast between natural virtue (*aretê phusikê*) and virtue strictly speaking (*kuria aretê*) and the emphasis on the fact that only the latter comes with *phronêsis* may provide the background for Alexander's remark here.

486 *Top.* 2.11, 115b16.

487 *ibid.* 115b17–18.

488 cf. Arist., *Cael.* 1.12.

489 *Top.* 2.11, 115b19–20.

490 *ibid.* 115b11–12.

491 *ibid.* 115b23.

492 *ibid.*

493 *ibid.* 115b26–7.

494 cf. *Top.* 2.11, 115b19–20; Wallies puts the last example into quotation marks, but the wording is slightly different from the wording of Aristotle's text Alexander quoted earlier at 214,29–30.

Bibliography

Primary sources (critical editions only)

Alcinous

Whittaker, J. (ed.), (1990), *Alcinous, Enseignement des doctrines de Platon*, Paris: Budé.

Alexander of Aphrodisias

Wallies, M. (ed.), (1883), *Alexandri in Aristotelis Analyticorum Priorum librum I commentarium*, CAG 2.1, Berlin: G. Reimer.

Wallies, M. (ed.), (1891), *Alexandri Aphrodisiensis in Aristotelis Topicorum libros octo commentaria*, CAG 2.2, Berlin: G. Reimer.

Wallies, M. (ed.), (1898), *Alexandri quod fertur in Aristotelis sophisticos elenchos commentarium*, CAG 2.3, Berlin: G. Reimer.

Ammonius

Busse, A. (ed.), (1897), *Ammonius. In Aristotelis de interpretatione commentarius*, CAG 4.5, Berlin: G. Reimer.

Wallies, M. (ed.), (1899), *Ammonius. In Aristotelis analyticorum priorum librum I commentarium*, CAG 4.6, Berlin: G. Reimer.

Aristotle

Brunschwig, J. (ed.), (1967–2007), *Aristote. Topiques*, Tome I & II, Paris: Les Belles Lettres.

Ross, D. (ed.), (1949), *Aristotle's Prior and Posterior Analytics*, Oxford: Oxford Clarendon Press.

Ross, D. (ed.), (1958), *Aristotelis Topica et Sophistici Elenchi*, Oxford: Clarendon Press.

Ross, D. (ed.), (1963), *Aristotelis Fragmenta Selecta*, Oxford: Clarendon Press.

Boethius

Nikitas, D.Z. (ed.), (1969), *Boethius, De topicis differentiis*, in *Boethius, De topicis differentiis kai hoi buzantines metafraseis tou Manouel Holobolou kai Prochorou Kudone*, Athens/Paris/Brussels: Academy of Athens/Vrin/Ousia.

Orbetello, L. (ed.), (1969), *De hypotheticis syllogismis*, Brescia: Paideia.
Orelli, J.C. and Baiter, J.G. (eds.), (1833), *Boethius. In Ciceronis Topica*, in *M. Tulli Ciceronis opera omnia* V 1, Zurich.

Cicero

Reinhardt, T. (ed.), (2003), *Cicero's Topica*, Oxford: Oxford University Press.

Diogenes Laertius

Dorandi, T. (ed.), (2013), *Diogenes Laertius. Lives of Eminent Philosophers*, Cambridge: Cambridge University Press.
Long, H.S. (ed.), (1964), *Diogenes Laertii Vitae Philosophorum*, Oxford: Clarendon Press.
Marcovich, M. (ed.), (1999), *Diogenes Laertius. Vitae philosophorum*, Stuttgart and Leipzig: B.G. Teubner (3 Bände).

Galen

Kalbfleisch, K. (ed.), (1896), *Galen, Institutio Logica*, Leipzig.

Philoponus

Wallies, M. (ed.), (1905), *Ioannis Philoponi in Aristotelis Analytica Priora Commentaria*, CAG 13.2, Berlin: G. Reimer.

Sextus Empiricus

Bury, R.G. (ed.), (1939–49), *Sextus Empiricus* (Loeb Classical Library), 4 volumes, Cambridge, MA: Harvard University Press.
Mutschmann, H. and Mau, J. (eds.), (1912–1962), *Sexti Empirici Opera*, Leipzig: Teubner (4 Bände).

Stoics

v. Arnim, H.F.A. (ed.), (1964), *Stoicorum veterum fragmenta*, Leipzig: Teubner.

Theophrastus and other Peripatetics

Fortenbaugh, W.W.; Huby, P.; Sharples, R.W.; Gutas, D. (eds.), (1993), *Theophrastus of Eresus. Sources for his Life, Writings, Thought and Influence*, Leiden/New York/Köln: Brill.

Wehrli, F. (ed.), (1944–1959; 2. Auflage 1967–1969), *Die Schule des Aristoteles. Texte und Kommentare*, Basel: B. Schwabe & Co.

Secondary literature (including modern commentaries and translations)

Abbamonte, G. (1995), 'Metodi esegetici nel commento *In Aristotelis Topica* di Alessandro di Afrodisia', in I. Giallo (ed.), *Seconda miscellanea filologica* (Università degli Studi di Salerno. Quaderni del Dipartimento di Scienze dell'Antichità 17), Napoli: Arte Tipografica, 249–266.

Abbamonte, G. (1996), *Alessandro di Afrodisia. Il primo libro del commentario di Alessandro di Afrodisia in Aristotelis Topica*. Saggio introduttivo, testo, traduzione e note, PhD thesis, Salerno.

Abbamonte, G. (2013), 'Cicerone, Alessandro di Afrodisia, Boezio: tre modi di leggere i Topici di Aristotele tra I sec. a.C. e VI d.C.', in Y. Lehmann (ed.), *Aristoteles Romanus. La réception de la science aristotélicienne dans l'Empire gréco-romain* (Recherches sur les rhétoriques religieuses 17), Turnhout: Brepols, 341–370.

Adamson, P. (2010), 'The Last Philosophers of Late Antiquity in the Arabic Tradition', *Entre Orient et Occident: la philosophie et la science gréco-romaines dans le monde arabe*, Entretiens sur l'antiquité classique LVII, 1–43.

Algra, K.; Barnes, J.; Mansfeld, J.; Schofield, M. (1999), *The Cambridge History of Hellenistic Philosophy*, Cambridge: Cambridge University Press.

Annas, J., and Barnes, J. (2002), *Sextus Empiricus: Outlines of Scepticism*, Cambridge: Cambridge University Press.

Annas, J., and Barnes, J. (2005), *Sextus Empiricus: Against the Logicians*, Cambridge: Cambridge University Press.

Annas, J., and Barnes, J. (2012), *Sextus Empiricus: Against the Physicists*, Cambridge: Cambridge University Press.

Baldassarri, M. (1985), *La logica stoica. Testimonianze e frammenti*, Testi originali con introduzione e traduzione commentata, Como: Libreria Noseda.

Barnes, J. (1969), 'Aristotle's Theory of Demonstration', *Phronesis* 14, 123–152.

Barnes, J. (1981), 'Proof and the Syllogism', in E. Berti (ed.), *Aristotle on Science: the 'Posterior Analytics*, Padua: Antenore, 17–59.

Barnes, J. (1983), 'Terms and Sentences: Theophrastus on Hypothetical Syllogism', *Proceedings of the British Academy* 69, Oxford: Oxford University Press.

Barnes, J. (1985), 'Theophrastus and Hypothetical Syllogistic', in J. Wiesner (ed.), *Aristoteles: Werk und Wirkung I*, Berlin: W. de Gruyter, 557–76. (repr. in J. Barnes 2012: 413–432)

Barnes, J. (1997), *Logic and the Imperial Stoa*, Leiden/New York/Köln: Brill.

Barnes, J. (1999), 'Aristotle and Stoic Logic', in K. Ierodiakonou (ed.), *Topics in Stoic Philosophy*, Oxford: Oxford Clarendon Press, 23–53. (repr. in J. Barnes 2012: 382–412)

Barnes, J. (2012), *Logical Matters. Essays in Ancient Philosophy II*, Oxford: Oxford University Press.

Barnes, J.; Bobzien, S.; Flannery, K.; Ierodiakonou, K. (1991), *Alexander of Aphrodisias On Aristotle's Prior Analytics 1.1–7*, London: Duckworth.

Blank, D. (1998), *Sextus Empiricus: Against the Grammarians*, Oxford: Clarendon Press.

Blumenthal, H. and Robinson, H. (eds.), (1991), *Aristotle and the Later Traditions*, Oxford: Oxford Clarendon Press.

Blumenthal, H. (1996), *Aristotle and Neoplatonism in Late Antiquity*, London: Duckworth.

Bobzien, S. (1997), 'The Stoics on Hypothesis and Hypothetical Arguments', *Phronesis* 42, 299–312.

Bobzien, S. (2000), 'Wholly Hypothetical Syllogisms', *Phronesis* 45, 87–137.

Bobzien, S. (2002a), 'Pre-Stoic Hypothetical Syllogistic in Galen', in V. Nutton (ed.), *The Unknown Galen, Bulletin of the Institute of Classical Studies*, supplement volume, 57–72.

Bobzien, S. (2002b), 'The Development of Modus Ponens in Antiquity: From Aristotle to the 2nd Century AD', *Phronesis* 47, 359–394.

Bobzien, S. (2014), 'Alexander of Aphrodisias on Aristotle's Theory of the Stoic Indemonstrables', in M. Lee (ed.), *Strategies of Argument: Essays in Ancient Ethics, Epistemology and Logic*, Oxford: Oxford University Press, 199–227.

Bochenski, I.M. (1947), *La Logique de Théophraste*, Fribourg: Librairie de l'Université.

Bochenski, I.M. (1951), *Ancient Formal Logic*, Amsterdam: North Holland.

Bodnár, I. and Fortenbaugh, W. (eds.), (2002), *Eudemus of Rhodes*, Rutgers University Studies in classical humanities 11, New Brunswick: Transaction Publishers.

Brandis, C.A. (1835), 'Über die Reihenfolge der Bücher des Aristotelischen Organons und ihre Griechischen Ausleger'. Abhandlungen der königlichen Akademie der Wissenschaften zu Berlin (aus dem Jahre 1833), 249–299.

Brisson, L. et al. (eds.), (2018), *Neoplatonic Demons and Angels*, Leiden: Brill.

Brunschwig, J. (1968), 'Observations sur les manuscrits parisiens des *Topiques*', in G.E.L. Owen (ed.), *Aristotle on Dialectic*, Oxford: Oxford University Press, 3–21.

Brunschwig, J. (1991), 'On a Book-title by Chrisippus: "on the fact that the ancients admitted dialectic along with demonstrations"', *Oxford Studies in Ancient Philosophy*, 81–95.

Buhl, G. (1978), 'Zur Funktion der Topoi in der aristotelischen Topik', in K. Lorenz (ed.), *Konstruktion vs Positionen. Beiträge zur Diskussion um die konstruktive Wissenschaft*, Bd. 1, Berlin and New York: W. de Gruyter, 169–175.

Castagnoli, L. (2012), 'Self-refutation and Dialectic in Plato and Aristotle', in J. L. Fink (ed.), *Dialectic and Dialogue: The Development of Dialectic from Plato to Aristotle*, Cambridge: Cambridge University Press, 27–61.

Castelli, L.M. (2013), 'Collections of Topoi and the Structure of Aristotle's Topics: Notes on an Ancient Debate (Aristotle, Theophrastus, Alexander and Themistius)', *Philosophia Antiquorum* 7, 65–92.

Castelli, L.M. (2014), 'Alexander of Aphrodisias: Methodological Issues and
Argumentative Strategies between *Ethical Problems* and *Commentary on the Topics*',
in M. Bonelli (ed.), *Le questioni etiche di Alessandro d'Afrodisia,* Bibliopolis, 19–42.

Castelli, L.M. (2015), 'Alexander on Aristotle, *APr I 31,* Division and Syllogistic',
Documenti e studi sulla tradizione filosofica medievale XXVI, 33–54.

Castelli, L.M. (2018), *Aristotle. Metaphysics Iota*, Oxford: Oxford Clarendon Press.

Castelli, L.M. and Rapp, Ch. (in preparation), 'The Logical Branch of Aristotle's
Dialectics. Traces of an Early Progress'.

Clark, M. (1980), *The Place of Syllogistic in Logical Theory*, Nottingham: Nottingham
University Press.

Crivelli, P. (2011), 'Aristotle on Syllogisms from a Hypothesis', in A. Longo (ed.),
Argument from Hypothesis in Ancient Philosophy, Naples, 95–184.

De Pater, W.A. (1965), *Les Topiques d'Aristote et la dialectique platonicienne: la
methodologie de la définition*, Fribourg: Editions St. Paul.

Dillon, J. (1993), *Alcinous: The Handbook of Platonism,* Oxford: Oxford University
Press.

Donini, P.L. (1995), 'Alessandro di Afrodisia e i metodi dell'esegesi filosofica', in C.
Moreschini (ed.), *Esegesi, parafrasi e compilazione in età tardoantica. Atti del terzo
congresso dell'Associazione di studi tardoantichi*, Napoli: M. D'Auria Editore, 107–129.

Ebert, T. and Nortmann, U. (2007), *Aristoteles. Werke in deutscher Übersetzung, Band 3
Teil 1: Analytica Priora – Buch I*, Darmstadt: Wissenschaftliche Buchgesellschaft.

Erhenberg, V. (1947), 'Polypragmosyne: A Study in Greek Politics', *Journal of Hellenic
Studies* 64, 46–76.

Flannery, K. (1995), *Ways into the Logic of Alexander of Aphrodisias*, Leiden: Brill.

Fortenbaugh, W.W. (2003), 'Theophrastus of Eresus: Rhetorical Argument and
Hypothetical Syllogistic', in Id., *Theophrastean Studies*, Stuttgart: Franz Steiner Verlag,
35–50.

Frede, M. (1974), 'Stoic vs. Peripatetic Syllogistic', *Archiv für Geschichte der Philosophie*
56, 1–32.

Gili, L. (2011a), *La sillogistica di Alessandro di Afrodisia*, Hildesheim/Zurich/New York:
Olms.

Gili, L. (2011b), 'Boeto di Sidone e Alessandro di Afrodisia intorno alla sillogistica
aristotelica', *Rheinisches Museum für Philologie* 154, 375–397.

Gohlke, P. (1928), 'Untersuchungen zur Topik des Aristoteles', *Hermes* 63, 457–479.

Gohlke, P. (1936), *Die Entstehung der aristotelischen Logik*, Berlin: Junker und Dünnhaupt.

González Calderón, J.F. (2014), *Historia de la tradición textual del comentario de
Alejandro de Afrodisias a los* Tópicos *de Aristóteles*, PhD Thesis, Getafe.

González Calderón, J.F. (2018), 'Formas de hacer filosofía en época imperial: Alejandro
de Afrodisias y su Comentario a los Tópicos', *ΠΗΓΗ/FONS* 3, 31–49.

Gottschalk, H.B. (1987), 'Aristotelian Philosophy in the Roman World from the Time of
Cicero to the End of the Second Century AD', in W. Haase (ed.), *Aufstieg und
Niedergang der Römischen Welt* II.36.2, Berlin: W. de Gruyter, 1079–1174.

Hadot, P. (1990), 'La logique, partie ou instrument de la philosophie?' in *Simplicius. Commentaire sur les Catègories*, dir. I. Hadot., fasc. 1, Introduction, Leiden, 183–188.

Hambruch, E. (1904), *Logische Regeln und der Platonischen Schule in der Aristotelischen Topik*, Wissenschaftliche Beilage zum Jahresbericht des Askanischen Gymnasiums zu Berlin, Berlin: Weidemann.

Hasnawi, A. (2007), 'Boèce, Averroès, et Abū Al-Barakāt Al-Baġdādī, témoins des écrits de Thémistius sur les Topiques d'Aristote', *Arabic Sciences and Philosophy* 17, 203–265.

Huby, P. (2002), 'Did Aristotle Reply to Eudemus and Theophrastus on Some Logical Issues?', in I. Bodnár and W. Fortenbaugh (eds.), *Eudemus of Rhodes*, Rutgers University Studies in classical humanities 11, New Brunswick: Transaction Publishers, 85–106.

Huby, P. (2007), *Theophrastus of Eresus: Logic*, Leiden/New York/Köln: Brill.

Hugonnard-Roche, H. (2004), 'La constitution de la logique tardo-antique et l'elaboration d'une logique 'materielle' en Syriaque', in V. Celluprica and C. D'Ancona (eds.), *Aristotele e i suoi esegeti neoplatonici*, Napoli: Bibliopolis, 55–83.

Hutchinson, D.S. and Johnson, M.R. (2017), *Aristotle. Protrepticus or Exhortation to Philosophy (citations, fragments, paraphrases, and other evidence* (version 20 Sept. 2017), http://www.protrepticus.info/protr2017x20.pdf

Ierodiakonou, K. (1998), 'Aristotle's Logic: an Instrument, Not a Part of Philosophy', in N. Avgelis and F. Peonidis (eds.), *Aristotle on Logic, Language and Science*, Thessaloniki: Sakkoulas Publications, 33–53.

Kapp, E. (1931), 'Syllogistik', in *Pauly-Wissowa's Real-Encyclopädie der classischen Altertumswissenschaft*, 2nd ser., IV A, cols. 1046–1067; repr. in Id., Ausgewählte Schriften, Berlin 1968, 254–77.

Karabatzaki-Perdiki, H. (1992), Ἡ σχέση της Σωκρατικής και Αριστοτελικής διαλεκτικής κάτω από το φως των σχολίων του Αλεξάνδρου Αφροδισιέως', *Dodoni* 21, 73–82.

La Croce, E. (1978–1979), 'Alexandri Aphrodisiensis, Comentario al tratado de los Tópicos de Aristóteles. Proemio al libro I, traducción & notas', *ethos* 6–7, 227–244.

Lear, J. (1980), *Aristotle and Logical Theory*, Cambridge: Cambridge University Press.

Lederman, H. (2014), '*ho pote on esti* and Coupled Entities: A Form of Explanation in Aristotle's Natural Philosophy', *Oxford Studies in Ancient Philosophy* 46, 109–164.

Lee, T.S. (1984), *Die griechische Tradition der aristotelischen Syllogistik in der Spätantike*, Hypomnemata 79, Göttingen: Vandenhoeck and Ruprecht.

Lejewski, C. (1976), 'On Prosleptic Premisses', *Notre Dame J. Formal Logic* 17, 1–18.

Lejewski, C. (1961), 'On Prosleptic Syllogisms', *Notre Dame J. Formal Logic* 2, 158–176.

Lloyd, A.C. (1956), 'Neoplatonic Logic and Aristotelian Logic', *Phronesis* 1, 58–79, 146–170.

Longo, A. (2011), *Argument from Hypothesis in Ancient Philosophy*, Elenchos LIX, Napoli: Bibliopolis.

Łukasiewicz, J. (1951), *Aristotle's Syllogistic from the Standpoint of Modern Formal Logic*, Oxford: Oxford Clarendon Press.

Lynch, J.P. (1972), *Aristotle's School. A Study of a Greek Educational Institution*, Berkeley: University of California Press.

Maier, H. (1986–1900), *Die Syllogistic des Aristoteles*, Tübingen: H. Laupp.

Malink, M. (2013), *Aristotle's Modal Syllogistic*, Cambridge, MA: Harvard University Press.

McCall, S. (1963), *Aristotle's Modal Syllogistic*, Amsterdam: North-Holland.

Militello, C. (2017), *Dialettica, genere e anima nel commento di Alessandro di Afrodisia al IV libro dei "Topici" di Aristotele*, Introduzione, saggi di commento, traduzione e note (Temi metafisici e problemi del pensiero antico 145), prefazione di M. Bonelli, presentazione di L. Cardullo, Milano: Vita e Pensiero.

Moraux, P. (1973), *Der Aristotelismus bei den Griechen*, Volume 1 (Die Renaissance des Aristotelismus im 1. Jh. v. Chr.), Berlin: W. de Gruyter.

Moraux, P. (1984), *Der Aristotelismus bei den Griechen*, Volume 2 (Der Aristotelismus im I. und II. Jahrhundert n. Chr.), Berlin: W. de Gruyter.

Moraux, P. (2001), *Der Aristotelismus bei den Griechen*, Volume 3 (Alexander von Aphrodisias), in J. Wiesner (ed.), Berlin: W. de Gruyter.

Müller, I. (1969), 'Stoic and Peripatetic Logic', *Journal of Philosophy* 51, 173–87.

Müller, I. with Gould, J. (trans.), (1999), *Alexander of Aphrodisias on Aristotle's Prior Analytics I.8–13 and I,14–22*, 2 vols, London: Duckworth.

Müller, I. (2006), *Alexander of Aphrodisias on Aristotle's Prior Analytics I. 23–31 and I. 32–46*, 2 volumes, London: Duckworth.

Nortmann, U. (1996), *Modale Syllogismen, mögliche Welten, Essentialismus: eine Analyse der aristotelischen Modallogik*, Berlin: W. de Gruyter.

Owen, G.E.L. (ed.) (1968), *Aristotle on Dialectic. The Topics,* Proceedings of the third Symposium Aristotelicum, Cambridge: Cambridge University Press.

Patterson, R. (1995), *Aristotle's Modal Logic: Essence and Entailment in the Organon*, Cambridge: Cambridge University Press.

Patzig, G. (1969) with Barnes, J. (trans.), *Aristotle's Theory of the Syllogism*, Dordrecht: D. Reidel.

Pfeiffer, R. (1968), *A History of Classical Scholarship*, Oxford: Oxford University Press.

Pickard-Cambridge, W.A. (1984), *Topics* (trans.), in J. Barnes (ed.), *The Complete Works of Aristotle*, Princeton: Princeton University Press (revised version originally in D. Ross (ed.) [1928]).

Prantl, C. (1853), *Über die Entwicklung der aristotelischen Logik aus der Platonischen Philosophie*, Munich: Verlag der königlichen Akademie.

Primavesi, O. (1994), '*Casus – Ptōsis*: zum aristotelischen Ursprung eines umstrittenen grammatischen Terminus', *Antike und Abendland* 40, 86–97.

Primavesi, O. (1996), *Die aristotelische Topik*, Munich: C. H. Beck.

Rapp, Ch. (2000), 'Topos und Syllogismos bei Aristoteles' in Th. Schirren and G. Üding (eds.), *Topik und Rhetorik: Ein interdisziplinares Symposium*, Tübingen: Niemeyer, 15–35.

Rapp, Ch. (2002), *Aristoteles Rhetorik. Übersetzt und erläutert*, 2 Halbbände, Berlin: Akademie Verlag.

Rapp, Ch. and Wagner, T. (2013), 'On Some Aristotelian Sources of Modern Argumentation Theory', *Argumentation* 27, 7–30.

Reinhardt, T. (2000), *Das Buch E der Aristotelischen Topik*, Göttingen: Vandenhoeck & Ruprecht.

Repici, L. (1977), *La logica di Teofrasto*, Bologna: Il Mulino.

Rini, A. (2011), *Aristotle's Modal Proofs: Prior Analytics A 8–22 in Predicate Logic*, Dordrecht: Springer.

Roselli, A. (2002), 'Solone in Alex. Aphr. *Comm. in Arist. Top.* II 2 (CAG 2.2, p. 139,26 - 140,3 Wallies)', *Cuadernos de filología clásica* 12, 137–144.

Rubinelli, S. (2009), *Ars Topica. The Classical Technique of Constructing Arguments from Aristotle to Cicero*, Dordrecht: Springer.

Sainati, V. (1968), *Storia dell'Organon aristotelico*, vol. 1, Firenze: Le Monnier.

Sainati, V. (1993), 'Aristotele, dalla Topica all' Analitica', *Theoria* XIII, 1–117.

Schenkeveld, D.M. (1984), 'Stoic and Peripatetic Kinds of Speech Act and the Distinction of Grammatical Moods', *Mnemosyne* 37, 291–351.

Schramm, M. (2004), *Die Prinzipien der Aristotelischen Topik*, Munich and Leipzig: K.G. Saur Verlag.

Sharples, R.W. (1987), 'Alexander of Aphrodisias: Scholasticism and Innovation', in W. Haase (ed.), *Aufstieg und Niedergang der Römischen Welt*, Berlin: W. de Gruyter, 1176–1243.

Shiel, J. (1974), 'Boethius and Eudemus', *Vivarium* XII, 14–16.

Shorey, P. (1889), 'Syllogismoi ex Hypotheseos', *The American Journal of Philology* 10, 460–2.

Slomkowski, P. (1997), *Aristotle's Topics*, Leiden/New York/Köln: Brill.

Smiley, T. (1974), 'What Is a Syllogism?', *Journal of Philosophical Logic* 1, 136–154.

Smith, R. (1997), *Aristotle: Topics Books I and VIII with Excerpts from Related Texts*, Oxford: Oxford Clarendon Press.

Smith, R. (1989), *Aristotle. Prior Analytics*, Indianapolis: Hackett.

Solmsen, F. (1929), *Die Entwicklung der aristotelischen Logik und Rhetorik*, Weidmann: Berlin.

Sorabji, R. (ed.) (1990), *Aristotle Transformed: the Ancient Commentators and Their Influence*, London: Duckworth.

Striker, G. (1979), 'Aristoteles über Syllogismen 'Aufgrund einer Hypothese'', *Hermes* 107, 33–50.

Striker, G. (1994), 'Modal vs. Assertoric Syllogistic', *Ancient Philosophy* (special issue), 39–51.

Striker, G. (2009), *Aristotle's Prior Analytics book I*, Oxford: Oxford Clarendon Press.

Strobach, N. (2001), 'Schlüsse aus Annahmen bei Aristoteles. Eine argumentationstheoretische Deutung des syllogismos ex hypotheseos', *Zeitschrift für philosophische Forschung* 55, 246–257.

Stump, E. (1974), 'Boethius's Works on the Topics', *Vivarium* 12, 77–93.

Stump, E. (1978), *Boethius's De Topicis Differentiis*, Ithaca: Cornell University Press.

Stump, E. (1982), 'Topics: Their Development and Absorption into the Consequences', in
  N. Kretzmann et al., *The Cambridge History of Later Medieval Philosophy*,
  Cambridge: Cambridge University Press, 273–299.

Stump, E. (1988), *Boethius's in Ciceronis Topica. Translated, with notes and introduction*,
  Ithaca: Cornell University Press.

Stump, E. (1989), *Dialectic and its Place in the Development of Medieval Logic*, Ithaca:
  Cornell University Press.

Summerell, O.F. and Zimmer, T. (2007), *Alkinoos: Didaskalikos*, Berlin: W. de Gruyter.

Thom, P. (1981), *The Syllogism (Analytica)*, Munich: Philosophia Verlag.

Thom, P. (1996), *The Logic of Essentialism: An Interpretation of Aristotle's Modal
  Syllogistic*, Dordrecht: Kluwer.

Van Opuhijsen, J.M. (2001), *Alexander of Aphrodisias on Aristotle's Topics 1*, translated
  with notes, London: Duckworth.

Von Fritz, K. (1978), *Schriften zur griechische Logik, I & II*, Stuttgart: Verlag Frommann-
  Holzboog.

Wagner, T. and Rapp, Ch. (2004), *Aristoteles Topik*. Übersetzt und kommentiert,
  Stuttgart: Reclam.

Wallies, M. (1891), *Die griechischen Ausleger der aristotelischen Topik*, Berlin: Gaertner.

Wians, W.R. (ed.), (1996), *Aristotle's Philosophical Development: Problems and Prospects*,
  Lanham: Rowman and Littlefield Publishers, Inc.

Zadro, A. (1974), *Aristotele. I Topici, traduzione, introduzione e commento*, Napoli:
  Loffredo.

Bibliography

English–Greek Glossary

absurd: *atopos*

accident: *sumbebêkos*
    to be an accident: *sumbebêkenai*

account: *logos*

affirmation: *kataphasis*

affirmative: *kataphatikos*

to agree: *homologein*

agreement: *homologia*

amphibolous: *amphibolos*

antecedent: *hêgoumenon*

appropriate: *prosekhês*

argument: *deixis; logos*

assumption: *lêmma*

to assume in addition; to assume as an additional premise: *proslambanein*

attack: *epikheirêma; epikheirêsis*

to belong: *huparkhein*
    to belong at the same time: *sunuparkhein*
    to belong incidentally: *sumbebêkenai*

to change: *metapherein*

to coin new names: *parakharassein*

combination: *sumplokhê*

common: *koinos*

to concede: *sunkhôrein*

to conclude: *perainesthai; sunagein*

conclusion: *sumperasma*

conflict: *makhê*

consequence: *akolouthia*
    direct: *epi ta auta*
    inverse: *anapalin*

consequent: *hepomenon; akolouthon*

constructive: *kataskeuastikos*

to be contingent: *endekhesthai*

contingently: *endekhomenôs*

contradiction: *antiphasis*

contrary: *enantios*

convention: *sunthêkê*

conversion: *antistrophê*

to convert: *antistrephein*

coordinate: *sustoikhon*
    series of coordination: *sustoikhia*

corruption (process of): *phthora*

corruptive: *phthartikos*

counterexample: *antipipton*

credible: *piston*

to deduce: *sullogizein*

deduction: *sullogismos*
    to produce a deduction: *sullogizein*

to defend: *paristasthai; proïstasthai*

definition: *horismos; horos*
    concerning the definition: *horikos*

to demolish: *anaskeuazein*

demolition: *anaskeuê*

destructive: *anaskeuastikos*

determined: *hôrismenos*

to deviate: *parabainein*

dialectic: *dialektikê*

dialectical; dialectician: *dialektikos*

difference: *diaphora*

discourse: *logos*

discussant: *dialegomenos*

discussion: *logos*

disposition: *hexis*

to divert: *metapherein; paragein*

to divide; to carry out a division: *diairein*

division: *diairesis*

to drag: *metagein*

element: *stoikheion*
essence: (*to*) *ti ên einai*
to establish: *kataskeuazein*
    to establish at the same time: *sunkataskeuazein*
establishment: *kataskeuê*
equivalent: *ep'isês*
existence: *hupostasis*
expression: *ekphora*

figure (syllogistic): *skhêma*
to follow upon: *hepesthai; parakolouthein*
form: *eidos*
formula: *logos*
formulation: *logos*

general: *katholou*
generation (process of): *genesis*
genus: *genos*
    concerning the genus; of the sort of the genus: *genikos*
to give: *paradidonai*
given: *prokeimenon; proteinomenon*
to go beyond and reach out to: *peritteuein para+* acc. *en+*dat.

to have a great supply: *euporein*
homonym; homonymous: *homônumon*
hypothesis: *hupothesis*
hypothetical: *hupothetikon*

impossible: *adunatos*
indemonstrable: *anapodeikton*
indeterminate: *aoristos*
indeterminately: *adioristôs*
individual: *atomos*
individually: *kath'hekaston*
indivisible: *atomos*
induction: *epagôgê*
inductive: *epaktikos*
inflection: *ptôsis*
instrument: *organon*
intelligible: *gnôrimos*

interlocutor: *prosdialegomenos*
investigation: *pragmateia*

known: *gnôrimos*
to lead a side-refutation: *parexelenkhein*
to lead an attack: *epikheirein*
to lead away: *apagein*
to lead to a conclusion: *sunagein*
leading away: *apagôgê*
to leave aside: *aphienai*
(the) less, lesser degree: (*to*) *hêtton*

to make a move: *hormaô*
mistake: *amartia* (*amartêma/diamartia*)
mode: *tropos*
(the) more, higher degree: (*to*) *mallon*

name: *onoma*
necessary: *anankaios*
necessity: *anankê*
    from necessity: *ex anankês*
negation: *apophasis*
negative: *apophatikos*

objection: *enstasis*
    to make an objection; to object: *enhistasthai*
objective: *prothesis*
to obtain: *huparkhein*
    to obtain at the same time: *sunuparkhein*
opinion: *doxa*
opposite: *antikeimenon*
opposition: *antithesis*
to order together with: *suntassein*
outline: *perigraphê; perilêpsis*

pair: *suzugia*
particular: *epi merous; kath' hekaston*
to pass over (from sth to sth else): *metabainein*
per se: *kath' hauto*
persuasive: *pithanos*
plausible: *eulogos*

to posit: *tithenai*
possession: *hexis*
potentially: *dunamei*
precept: *parangelma*
preceptive: *parangelmatikos*
predicate: *katêgoroumenon*
to be predicated: *katêgoreisthai*
to be predicated instead: *antikatêgoreisthai*
predicative: *katêgorikos*
premise: *protasis*
to present: *paradidonai*
presentation: *paradosis*
principle: *arkhê*
privation: *sterêsis*
problem: *problêma*
productive: *poiêtikos*
proposed for debate: *proballomenon*
proposition: *protasis*
proprium: *idion*
proximate: *prosekhês*

quality: (*to*) *poion/poiotês*
quantity: (*to*) *poson/posotês*

rational: *eulogos*
refutation: *elenkhos*
to refute: *elenkhein*
relation: *skhesis*
relative(s): (*ta*) *pros ti*
to remove: *anairein*
    to remove at the same time: *sunanairein*
to replace: *metalambanein*
replacement: *metalêpsis; metathesis*
    to make a replacement: *metalambanein*
reply: *apantêsis*
reputable: *endoxos*

reputable opinion: (*to*) *endoxon*
to require: *axioun*

(the) same: (*to*) *tauton*
to secure: *pistousthai*
to set aside (what was submitted): *kataleipein*
to set out: *ektithênai*
shift: *metabasis*
to show: *deiknusthai*
(the) similar degree: (*to*) *homoiôs*
similarity: *homoiotês*
sophistic: *sophistikos*
species: *eidos*
    of the same species: *homoeidês*
to start: *hormaô*
starting point: *aphormê*
statement: *logos*
subject: *hupokeimenon*
submitted: *proballomenon; prokeimenon; proteinomenon*
substance: *ousia*
substrate: *hupokeimenon*

to take: *lambanein*
term: *horos*
thesis: *thesis*
tool: *organon*
topos: topos
to transgress: *parabainein*
transmitted: *pheromenos*

universal: *katholou*
universally: *katholou*
unpersuasive: *apithanos*
(the) what-it-is: (*to*) *ti estin*

word: *onoma*

Greek–English Index

References are to the page and line numbers of the Greek text (indicated in the margins of the translation).

adioristôs, indeterminately 129,25; 179,9.
adunatos, impossible 139,11; 166,22;
    174,14; 178,4.20;181,20; 183,27;
    185,27; 186,28; 187,16.24;
    188,10.21; 189,3; 204,3.6.8;
    214,4.
akolouthia, consequence 165,6.13; 166.13;
    167,4; 172,25; 174,5; 191,3.17;
    192,12; 193.18.20; 194,24; 195,22;
    196,25; 199,28; 200,15; 202,19;
    203,24.
    anapalin, inverse 194,24.
    epi ta auta, direct 193,18.20; 195,22.
akolouthêsis, consequence 190,27;
    191,5.6.13.28; 192,4; 193,2.6.8.11.25;
    194,3.10.12.29; 195,21; 196,2; 199,30;
    201,5.
    anapalin, inverse 191,5.28;
    193,6.10.11.25; 192,2; 194, 30; 201,4.
    epi ta auta, direct 191,12; 192,4;
    193,9.10.11.24; 194,27.30.
amartia (amartêma/diamartia), mistake
    133,29.–31; 134,2.19.21.25.27;
    135,23; 136,3; 158,11; 163,14; 178,9;
    179,3; 181,7.
amphibolos, amphibolous 152,8.10.13;
    153,12.13.29; 155,3.
anairein, to remove 127,23–25 *passim*.
anankaios, necessary 123,3; 126,9; 127,34;
    129,12; 148,27.32; 157,3.4.16; 159,4;
    161,1; 168,6.10–15; 169,1.7.22;
    170,1.5.19.25; 171,9.29.32;
    172,6.7.12; (vs. for the most part or
    contingent) 177,18 ff.
anankê, necessity; necessary 139,11;
    159,3.13.25; 160,1.12.14.16;
    161,12.14.18.26; 174,8.14; 175,4;
    186,25; 187,29; 191,21; 199,27;
    204,10.22; 210,14; 212,8.

ex anankês, from necessity 177,12 ff.
    (vs. for the most part or contingent);
    194,6.
anapodeikton, indemonstrable
    (first) 165,13 ; (second) 166,12;
    (fifth; cf. 175,25: fourth) 175,23.
anaskeuastikos, dcstructive; with
    destructive purposes; useful for
    demolishing 128,1 *passim*.
anaskeuazein, to demolish 130,6 *passim*.
anaskeuê, demolition; demolishing 130,3
    passim.
antikatêgoreisthai, to be predicated instead
    127,34; 128,4; 136,7.
antikeimenon, opposite 129,11; 131,9; 138,
    21.22.26.27; 139,2.12; 148,18; 149,18;
    150,8; 151,4.5.7; 151,33; 153,24;
    154,6; 158,31; 159,1; 159,15–24;
    170,31; 175,23; 177,24; 191,1.15.17;
    195,12 193,2: 194,29; 195,21; 196,
    4.6.11.20.21; 200,12.
antiphasis, contradiction 129,17–20;
    133,25; 138,29.32; 175,2; 183,25;
    191,5.28; 192,12; 193,2.3.5.6;
    194,12.
antipipton, counterexample 138,27.
antistrephrein, to convert 131,25.27;
    132,2.5.8.9.12.25–30; 133,3.8; 136,6;
    149,30; 180,12.13.15; 191,8.11.14.21;
    192,15.24; 207,13.
antistrophê, conversion 131,23.30; 132,7.8;
    133,4; 192,8.11; 214,7.
antithesis, opposition 175,3; 190,27;
    191,3.5; 192,11.12; 194,31; 195,13.
aoristos, indeterminate 126,15.31; 127,4.
apagein, to lead away 170,8.
apagôgê, leading away 169,9.
apantêsis, reply 149,25.
aphienai, to leave aside 164,29; 172,12.

aphormê, starting point 126,11; 145,5;
    146,5.16.28; 148,12; 164,6; 177,8;
    178,1.
apithanos, unpersuasive 179,10.
apophasis, negation 139,6; 175,5–7;
    191,1.20.21; 192,29–30.
apophatikos, negative 129,12; 130,15;
    131,10–12.25; 138,5.11; 139,22;
    140,9.13; 142,3; 149,33; 150,8.9.12–
    14; 151,11; 191,9.10.13; 192,14.23.
aporein, to lack resources 154,30
atomos, indivisible; individual 128,22.26–
    28; 132,24; 133,3; 136,33;
    138,17.23.24.27; 196,14.
atopos, absurd 140,23; 166,20.24; 170,9;
    173,20; 181,9.
axioun, to require 140,22.27; 142,28; 145,3;
    147,8.9; 159,2; 163,24; 164,3.11;
    172,2 *passim.*

deiknusthai, to show 125,13.17.20;
    127,9–16 *passim.*
deixis, argument 130,19 *passim.*
diairein, to divide; to carry out a division
    138,15.20.22.25.26; 139,14.27.30;
    148,15.17.22.26; 149,3; 151,27.31;
    152,4; 154,9; 159,20; 183,24.
diairesis, division 125,21; 128,16.18.30.31;
    138,3.5.10–13.16.23.30; 139,28;
    140,16; 145,10.12.18; 146,4; 149,19;
    150,12; 151,22; 153,31; 154,25;
    177,18.
dialegomenos, discussant 129,10; 131,8;
    170,24.
dialektikê, dialectic 126,8.
dialektikos, dialectical; dialectician
    126.1.4.6.12; 129,13.22;
    131,7.9.12.14.17; 133,28; 168,8;
    170,22; 172,4; 172,15; 174,2; 177,1;
    179,12; 184,10.
diaphora, difference 125,5.16; 135,11;
    136,10; 137,27.28; 142,27.30; 143,16;
    150,10; 159,20; 163,2; 173,6;
    177.8.27; 180,24; 192,10.
doxa, opinion 158,18.19.29; 164,1;
    202,21–24; 203,9.11.
dunamei, potentially 126,31; 173,5.7.

eidos, species; form 136,21; 188,13 *passim.*

ekphora, expression 125,16.
ektithênai, to set out 133,1; 154,28; 157,9;
    174,5.
elenkhein, to refute 133,29; 134,20; 136,2.9;
    137,26; 147,7.10; 178,20; 179,8;
    180,27.
elenkhos, refutation 134,1; 179,5.
enantios, contrary 126,15 ff.; 138,28.30;
    139,4.10; 152,18; 158,10 ff.; 174,7 ff.;
    181,12 ff.; 187,12 ff.; 189,17 ff.; 191,2;
    193,8 ff; 199,9 ff.
endekhesthai, to be possible, be contingent
    (vs. to be necessary or for the most
    part) 177,22 ff.
endekhomenôs, contingently (vs. from
    necessity or for the most part)
    177,21 ff.
(to) endoxon, reputable opinion 125,7.
endoxos, reputable 129,21; 141,25; 143,28;
    150,23; 171,24.30; 173,26; 177,1;
    184,9; 201,24; 206,2.
enhistasthai, to make an objection; to
    object 145,3; 145,16; 148,5;149,22;
    169,11.29; 170,17.31.
enstasis, objection 140,22.24;
    145,2.6.7.14.19–21.24.28;
    146,3.5.11.12; 149,23; 170,8.25;
    171,7; 196,10.13; 210,17; 213,7;
    215,2.18.23.
epagôgê, induction 125,20; 126,3.5;
    169,10.15.19.21.24.33;
    170,2.9.11.14.21.22.28; 171,25.28.30;
    191,28; 194,11; 205,28.
epaktikos, inductive 150,20; 170,23.
ep'isês, equivalent 167,8.
epi merous, particular 128,19 ff.; 129,30.
(to) epi (to) polu, (vs. from necessity or
    contingently) 177,13 ff.
epikheirein, to lead an attack; to attack
    126,20; 131.9 *passim*
epikheirêma/epikheirêsis, attack 126,11.12
    passim
eulogos, rational; that makes sense;
    plausible 163,4; 173,12; 207,10; 214,6.
euporein, to have a great supply; to have
    resources 125,11; 126,6 *passim*

genikos, concerning the genus; of the sort
    of the genus 128,3; 137,28.

207,15 ff.; 207,26 ff.; 211,6; 212,2.4.6; 212.20 ff.

metabainein, to pass over (from sth to sth else) 168,3.17.24; 169,22.30; 174,1; 198,4.

metabasis, shift 168,6.29; 169,8; 172,15.16; 198,22

metagein, to drag 154,20; 167,28.

metalambanein, to replace; to make a replacement 131,32; 144,3 156,21 ff.; 171,2; 176,4.

metalêpsis, replacement 156,20 ff.; 168,6.9.11.14.15; 169,8.23; 170,16.20.26; 171,9.12.26.28; 172,4.5.6; 173,22.

metapherein, to change; to divert 167,25.28; 172,17; 175,31; 179,8

metathesis, replacement 170,6.

onoma, name; word 131,26 ff.; 142, 27;143,17; 175,29 ff. *passim*

organon, tool 125,10; 126,6; 194,9; 206,8.

ousia, substance 135,20; 137,13; 144,19; 159,5.10.14.16; 162,21.25; 189,6; 212,2.3.4; 213,15.

pantakhothen, from every side 149,14.

pantôs, in all cases; in general 159,24; 161,10 *passim*

parabainein, to deviate; to transgress 134,4.22.25; 135,26; 136,11; 147,16.24.

paradidonai, to present; to give 147,7; 148,16; 158,9; 175,29; 177,9; 204,26; 206,14; 209,22.

paradosis, presentation; transmission 125,4; 126,11; 127,18.20.29.31; 128,30; 129.5; 130,8; 132,32; 133,30.

paragein, to divert 154.26.

parakharassein, to coin new names 134,13.

parakolouthein, to follow upon 127,22 *passim*

parangelma, precept 135,3 ff.

parangelmatikos, preceptive 135,13 ff.; 138,3;144,30; 146,16.

parexelenkhein, to carry out a side-refutation 172,1.14.

paristasthai, to defend 134,5–6; 149,23.

parônumos, paronymous; paronym 136,16 ff.; 137,7 ff.; 161,11.13.17.18.24; 162,1.2.5–7.13; 197,3.20.

peiranesthai, to conclude 172,20.

perigraphê, outline 126,15.

perilêpsis, outline 181,28.

peritteuein para+ acc. en+dat., to go beyond (term in acc.) and reach out to (term in dat.) 128,12.

phthartikos, corruptive 200,17 ff.

phthora, (process of) corruption 200,16 ff.

piston, credible 126,24.

pistousthai, to secure 171,1; 205,28.

pithanos, persuasive 177,1; 214,2

poiêtikos, productive 147,1 ff.; 153,22; 155,8.10.21.22; 197,10.1214; 200,16 ff.; 206,10.

poiotês/(to) poion, quality 137,13; 166,32; 211.16; 212,7; cf. 143,6.12.

posotês/(to) poson, quantity 135,21.22; 137,13; 189,6.7; 211,16; 213,15 cf. 143,5.12.

pragmateia, investigation 125,5; 125,8.

proballomenon, proposed for debate; submitted 129,23; 133,27; 138,4.

problêma, problem 125,10.12.14.16; 129,16 ff. *passim*

proïstasthai, to defend 133,28; 170,31.

prokeimenon, submitted; given 126,22.24.31 *passim*

(ta) pros ti, relative(s) 138,28.31; 139,11.12; 151,6; 165,15.16; 166,31.32; 191,2; 195,21 ff.

prosdialegomenos, interlocutor 172,2; 179,8.

prosekhês, proximate; appropriate 126,22; 126,26; 138,13.17.

proslambanein, to assume in addition; to take as an additional premise 127,13; 169,27; 171,6

protasis, proposition; premise 125,12.14.15.17 *passim*

proteinomenon, submitted; given 129,16 *passim*

prosthesis, addition 132,1; 209.22 ff.; 214,14.15.17; 215,24 ff.

prothesis, objective 125,4.

ptôsis, inflection 196,27 ff.; 200,2 ff.

Index of Passages

Subject Index

Numbers refer to the pages of this volume.

CPSIA information can be obtained
at www.ICGtesting.com
Printed in the USA
LVHW020139030522
717730LV00004B/323